$\mathscr{S}$ENSATIONAL $\mathscr{S}$AUCES

SENSATIONAL SAUCES

LINDA COLLISTER

Photography by Patrice de Villiers

General Editor Jenni Muir

Reader's Digest

The Reader's Digest Association, Inc.
Pleasantville, New York/Montreal

To Alan

A Reader's Digest Book
Designed and edited by Conran Octopus Limited

Text copyright © Linda Collister 1997
Photography copyright © Patrice de Villiers 1997
Design and layout copyright © Conran Octopus 1997

Library of Congress Cataloging in
Publication Data has been applied for
ISBN 0-7621-0059-1

EDITORIAL DIRECTOR: Suzannah Gough
MANAGING/GENERAL EDITOR: Jenni Muir
IN-HOUSE EDITOR: Helen Ridge
AMERICAN EDITOR: Norma MacMillan
ART EDITOR: Sue Storey
HOME ECONOMIST: Meg Jansz
PHOTOGRAPHIC STYLIST: Hilary Guy
PROOFREADER: Victoria Richards
EDITORIAL ASSISTANT: Tanya Robinson
PRODUCTION: Julian Deeming
INDEX: Laura Hicks

Printed in Hong Kong

CONTENTS

INTRODUCTION 6

THE TECHNIQUES OF SAUCE MAKING 14

QUICK AND SIMPLE SAUCES 28
Pan Sauces • Gravy • Flavored Butter • Marinade

SUMMER SAUCES 42
Vinaigrette • Salad Dressings • Dips

CLASSIC SAUCES 56
Béchamel • Hollandaise • Béarnaise • Beurre Blanc

COOKING SAUCES 72
Casseroles • Braises • Fondues

PASTA SAUCES 86
Tomato Sauce • Pestos • Seafood Sauce • Meat Sauce

TANGY SAUCES 100
Salsa • Chili Sauce • Satay • Dipping Sauce • Chutney

SIDE SAUCES 114
Fruit Sauce • Mustard • Relish • Ketchup

DESSERT SAUCES 124
Fruit Sauce • Cream Sauce • Chocolate Sauce • Syrup

INDEX BY ACCOMPANIMENT 140

GENERAL INDEX 142

$\mathscr{F}$OREWORD

Above: in sauce making, the aim is to make a balanced and well-seasoned sauce that will not overwhelm the food it is to accompany.

The purpose of a sauce is to enhance and embellish, to add interest and moisture, and to complement or contrast with the flavor, color, texture, and even temperature of the dish it accompanies. A sauce is, in fact, the counterpoint to the melody on the plate. The art of sauce making is choosing the right one for the principal ingredient of the dish. The craft is making the sauce so well-balanced, so perfectly seasoned that it matches yet doesn't overwhelm the food it is to partner.

A sauce can be as simple or as complicated as you choose. Gravy, which is made from cooking juices of roasted meat or poultry, is often the first sauce a cook attempts. At its best it should be a glossy, translucent brown, richly flavored but not greasy—and it should move on the plate. No real skill is needed just to spoon off the fat and then whisk up the concentrated juices and sediment in the roasting pan. Taste and add salt and pepper, and you have a perfectly good sauce for a roast.

Taste. This is crucial in preparing sauces. In this book, every recipe tells you to add salt and black pepper to taste. I cannot emphasize enough how essential it is to taste the sauce as you prepare it, and again before and after adding the seasoning ingredients. Keep tasting, stirring, and adding until you are happy with the result. Never add a touch of salt and pepper, let alone chili, and then serve without retasting—that way lies disaster. A meal where the saltcellar and sugar bowl have been confused is not easily forgotten. The more you taste, the more experienced you become, and the finer your sauces will be. It's worth building a collection of seasonings so that you have just the right one when you need it.

Types of Sauces

Baste: a butter- or oil-based mixture used to spoon or brush over meat, fish, or vegetables during roasting, broiling, or grilling to prevent them from drying out and to add flavor.

Butter Sauce: *beurre blanc,* or white butter sauce, is an emulsion of white wine, vinegar, shallots, and butter. For *beurre noisette,* the butter is cooked until light brown.

Coulis: strained purée from fruit, such as berries or tomatoes, usually uncooked and unthickened, and served cold.

Egg Emulsion: rich yet light sauce based on butter and egg yolks, usually made in a double boiler. The best-known hot emulsions are *hollandaise* and *béarnaise. Mayonnaise* is a cold emulsification of oil and egg yolks.

Below (clockwise from left): Tomato Salsa, Sorrel Hollandaise, Gravy, Béchamel Sauce, Pesto Genovese.

Gravy: made from the meat juices left in the pan after cooking. The excess fat is removed and stock or wine added to make a thin gravy. Flour can be mixed into the fat first and browned for a thicker gravy. Cream is sometimes added to make cream gravy.

Ketchup: a sweet-sour preserved sauce with a smooth, thick, pourable consistency.

Marinade: a well-flavored combination of oil and wine or fruit juice, plus herbs or spices, designed to tenderize and flavor food before cooking as well as to prevent it from becoming dry during cooking. Sometimes made with yogurt, marinades can be uncooked or cooked, or dry mixtures of herbs and spices rubbed onto the food.

Mousseline: a light, fluffy sauce that is made by vigorous whisking of the mixture, or by folding in some whipped cream.

Purée: a smooth sauce, similar to a coulis, made from vegetables or fruit cooked until very soft and then pushed through a strainer or puréed in a blender or food processor.

Roux-based Sauce: based on a cooked mixture of butter and flour, which is called a roux. *Béchamel* is made from the roux and flavored milk; for a *velouté* the roux is cooked until it is a light straw color, then stock is whisked in; for a traditional *brown sauce* the roux is slowly cooked to a rich chestnut-brown before the stock is added.

Sabayon: made by whisking egg yolks with sugar and wine. White wine is used for the French sabayon and Marsala for the Italian version, *zabaglione,* which is usually served on its own as a dessert.

Above (clockwise from left): Barbecue Ketchup, Mint Raita, Vinaigrette, Zabaglione, Melba Sauce (which is a raspberry coulis).

Salsa: the word means sauce in Italian and Spanish. In Italy, a salsa is usually an uncooked sauce, typically made from nuts, or from herbs, olive oil, and bread crumbs. A Mexican salsa is a spicy relish made from diced onions, chili, lime juice, cilantro, and tomatoes or sweeter fruits. If cooked further the sugar caramelizes and then sets.

Syrup: sugar dissolved in water or fruit juice to make a thin or thick sauce, which can be flavored with herbs and spices.

Vinaigrette: made from oil and an acidic ingredient such as vinegar or lemon juice, flavored with mustard, seasonings, and, often, herbs. Vinaigrettes can be served cold or warm, with vegetables and salads as well as fish or meat.

MAKING STOCKS

When I was training, it was drummed into me that stock forms the basis of savory cooking (the French word for stock is *fond* or "foundation"). Indeed, it was hard to progress until you had proved you could make good stock. A stock is not used in its own right, but is the basis for sauces and soups. Today you can buy fresh stock, as well as good canned broth, so there is no need to resort to a bouillon cube, but it is still worth making your own stock once in a while and then freezing it in small quantities ready for use.

Stock is made from meat, poultry, or fish bones and lean trimmings, plus vegetables, all simmered, not boiled, in water. Beef and chicken are most commonly used for all-purpose stocks (veal was once *de rigueur* for stocks); lamb, pork, and duck stocks are usually made just for dishes containing those meats. Meat used to be the main ingredient, but these days bones, chopped by the butcher to fit your stockpot, make an excellent though less rich stock.

Whole peppercorns (ground pepper turns bitter during prolonged cooking and makes the stock cloudy) and a bouquet garni provide even more flavor. If you like herbs, make a large, fresh bouquet garni that contains a couple of bay leaves, a good-sized bunch of thyme, plenty of parsley (leaves and lots of stems), and a sprig of tarragon. Salt should not be added at the beginning, because the final stock, if well reduced, could be unpalatable.

Remember that it is important to use good-quality fresh ingredients for making stocks: a stockpot is not a way of clearing out the refrigerator.

Basic Beef or Chicken Stock

This is a pale stock suitable for light sauces, veloutés, soups, and subtly flavored dishes.

MAKES ABOUT 2½ QUARTS (2.5 LITERS)

3¼ pounds (1.5kg) beef bones, chopped, or raw chicken carcasses, or a mixture of chicken wings, backs, and necks, or 1 stewing chicken
2 large onions, halved and spiked with 2 cloves
2 large carrots, quartered
2 stalks celery, sliced
1 large bouquet garni
1 teaspoon black peppercorns

Put the beef bones, chicken carcasses or pieces, or whole chicken into the stockpot and cover with cold water. Bring to a boil, then let simmer for 2 to 3 minutes.

Drain the bones, carcasses, or chicken in a colander and rinse under cold running water. Return to the rinsed-out pot, and add the vegetables, bouquet garni, peppercorns, and enough cold water to cover the ingredients—about 3 quarts (3 liters).

Bring the liquid to a boil, skimming it carefully using a slotted spoon, then cover and let simmer gently: 3 hours for beef stock, 1½ hours for chicken stock. Skim from time to time.

Strain the stock to remove the bones and vegetables. If you are using a whole chicken or chicken pieces, the meat can be reserved and used for soups or pies, or served with a sauce made from the reduced stock.

Remove as much fat as possible from the stock. If there is time, chill the stock quickly

Right: straining Basic Chicken Stock to remove the flavorings. You can save the meat from the chicken wings to use in another recipe.

first so that the fat collects on top and is easy to skim off.

The stock can then be boiled vigorously until it has reduced by half. This will give a well-flavored liquid that sets to a jelly as it cools. Cool the stock as quickly as possible. It can be kept in the refrigerator for up to 36 hours or in the freezer for up to 3 months.

Variations: *Brown Beef or Chicken Stock* Roast the meat or poultry bones and vegetables in the oven before making the stock to give the liquid a rich brown color

Making Stocks

and stronger taste. You can add up to 4 ounces (125g) chopped mushroom stems and peelings, and, for a beef stock, 1 or 2 seeded tomatoes. For extra flavor, deglaze the roasting pan with ½ to 1 cup (125 to 250ml) red or white wine or Madeira and enough water to make 1½ cups (350ml), then add this to the pot.

Game Stock
Use the bones and trimmings from duck, grouse, partridge, or pheasant, or make the stock with venison bones. Deglaze the roasting pan with red or white wine, or port.

Lamb Stock
Use lamb bones roasted with the onion and carrot, and add a chopped leek to the pot. For a stronger flavor, deglaze the roasting pan with 1½ cups (350ml) mixed wine and water, then add this to the stock. Simmer for 1½ hours. Skim off the fat before using.

Fish Stock

Fish stock, or *fumet,* must not simmer for more than 20 minutes or it will taste bitter. The vegetables are therefore sweated in butter to extract the maximum flavor before the bones are added. Shellfish adds good flavor, but oily fish is unsuitable as it makes the stock greasy and too strong.

MAKES ABOUT 2 QUARTS (2 LITERS)

1½ tablespoons (20g) unsalted butter
1 large onion or 6 shallots, minced
1 leek, white part only, sliced
2 slices bulb fennel, minced
3¼ pounds (1.5kg) white fish bones and trimmings
1½ cups (350ml) dry white wine, or a mixture of wine and water, or 1½ cups (350ml) water plus 2 slices of lemon
½ teaspoon black peppercorns
1 large bouquet garni

Heat the butter in a stockpot and add the vegetables. Stir well, then cover with a circle of dampened parchment paper and the lid. Cook very gently for about 20 minutes or until the vegetables are really tender but not colored. Stir the vegetables frequently.

Meanwhile, rinse the fish bones and trimmings under cold water and drain well. Chop the bones and any large heads into pieces. When the vegetables are ready, add the bones and trimmings to the pan and stir over low heat for 3 to 4 minutes.

Add the wine and simmer for 5 minutes, then add 2 quarts (2 liters) of cold water to the pot. Bring to a boil, skimming the surface of the stock. Add the peppercorns, bouquet garni, and lemon (if using). Simmer the stock gently, uncovered, for 20 minutes, skimming from time to time.

Strain the stock through a fine-mesh conical strainer. It can then be reduced and used immediately, or cooled and refrigerated for up to 24 hours. It can also be frozen for up to 1 month.

Vegetable Stock

Vary the vegetables here to suit the season and the dish in which the stock will be used. Avoid cabbage, however, as it can dominate the flavor, as well as root vegetables, which will make the stock cloudy.

MAKES ABOUT 1 QUART (1 LITER)

2 medium carrots, thinly sliced
1 parsnip, thinly sliced
2 medium onions, thinly sliced
1 stalk celery, sliced
2 slices bulb fennel
1 small leek, sliced
1 zucchini, sliced, or 3 to 4 green beans
½ teaspoon black peppercorns
1 large bouquet garni
2 cloves garlic, unpeeled
1 cup (250ml) dry white wine

Put the ingredients into a stockpot and add 1½ quarts (1.5 liters) cold water. Bring to a boil. Simmer, uncovered, for 30 minutes, skimming as necessary.

Strain the stock through a fine-mesh conical strainer, then let cool. Store in the refrigerator for up to 36 hours, or freeze for up to 3 months.

Variations: For a darker vegetable stock, add up to 4 ounces (125g) sliced mushrooms or mushroom peelings and a couple of juicy ripe tomatoes, chopped.

Kitchen Bouillon

This is not a recipe you will find in a chef's cookbook. An easy, tasty, opaque broth of indeterminate color, the result is suitable for soups, gravies, and well-flavored everyday sauces. This recipe is an excellent way to recycle the remains of roast meat or a cooked chicken carcass.

bones and carcasses from roasted meat or poultry, chopped
lean raw meat trimmings
2 onions, quartered
2 carrots, quartered
2 stalks celery, sliced
1 leek, white part only, sliced
1 large bouquet garni
1 teaspoon black peppercorns

Put all the ingredients into a stockpot, cover with cold water, and bring to a boil. Skim thoroughly, then let simmer very gently, uncovered, for no more than 1 hour, replenishing the water if necessary.

Strain the stock, discarding the solids, then skim off the fat. The bouillon can then be reduced as necessary. Cool the bouillon as quickly as possible, then store in the refrigerator for up to 36 hours or in the freezer for up to 3 months.

Asian Chicken Stock

You can use this, my favorite stock, for stir-fries and curries as well as soups.

MAKES ABOUT 2½ QUARTS (2.5 LITERS)

2¼ pounds (1kg) chicken wings
2 medium onions, sliced
1 carrot, quartered
1 stalk celery, chopped
1 teaspoon black peppercorns
1½-inch (3.5-cm) piece fresh ginger, unpeeled, thickly sliced
few parsley or cilantro stems, lightly crushed

Put all the ingredients into a stockpot with enough cold water to cover—2½ to 3 quarts (2.5 to 3 liters). Bring to a boil, skimming well. Cover and simmer gently (do not let it boil) for 1 hour, skimming occasionally.

Strain the stock through a fine-mesh conical strainer. Reserve the chicken wings so that you can use their meat in the final dish, but discard the other bits and pieces. Remove as much fat as possible from the stock, then reduce it if necessary. The stock can be cooled and then stored in the refrigerator for up to 2 days or in the freezer for up to 3 months.

Variation: You can include 1 or 2 drumsticks with the chicken wings if you like, but do not use drumsticks exclusively.

Dashi

Dashi is a richly flavored stock for Japanese soups and noodle dishes. It is made from kombu seaweed and shavings of dried bonito tuna, which can usually be found in Asian markets and health food stores.

MAKES 1 QUART (1 LITER)

1 ounce (30g) dried kombu seaweed
1 ounce (30g) dried bonito flakes
FOR DASHI BROTH:
6 tablespoons Japanese soy sauce
¼ cup (60ml) mirin

Put the kombu into a stockpot (there is no need to rinse the seaweed) and add 1 quart (1 liter) cold water. Heat very slowly, stirring often, until the mixture just comes to a boil.

Remove the pot from the heat and lift out the kombu with a slotted spoon. Add the bonito flakes to the stock and stir well, then return the pot to the heat. Bring the liquid to a full rolling boil.

Remove the pot from the heat again and let the stock stand for about 5 minutes. Skim the surface to remove any scum, then strain the liquid through a conical strainer lined with a piece of cheesecloth, a clean linen dish towel, or a paper coffee filter. Let the stock cool. (The kombu and bonito flakes can be used to make a second batch of stock, which will be more concentrated.)

The stock can be diluted to suit the dish. Store in the refrigerator for up to 24 hours, or freeze for up to 1 month.

To make dashi broth, add the soy sauce and mirin just before using the stock.

Left: Dashi can be used to make a healthful bowl of Teriyaki Salmon and Japanese Noodles (see page 98) as well as other Japanese dishes.

 OTHER INGREDIENTS

On the whole, I like to cook with as many organic (and free-range) foods as possible. They not only have, in most cases, much more flavor than intensively produced food, but also more vitamins and minerals. And they are produced with more concern for the welfare of animals and the land.

Butter: fresh (check the sell date) unsalted butter is best for cooking. Salted butter is often very salty, which can alter the flavor balance of a sauce. It also has a less creamy, more greasy flavor than unsalted butter, and it burns more easily. Butter freezes well, so take advantage of any price reductions in the supermarket.

Chocolate: the quality and depth of taste is determined, not by price, but by the quantity and quality of the cocoa solids, or chocolate liquor, used in production. Unsweetened, or baking, chocolate, bittersweet, semisweet, and sweet chocolates are the best for cooking. Avoid anything labeled "artificial chocolate" or "chocolate-flavored."

Cream: cream for whipping should be fresh and well chilled. If overwhipped, it will turn grainy and then separate. Cream can also separate if it is added to acidic ingredients or mixtures, such as a fresh tomato sauce, or if overheated. Crème fraîche has a distinctive nutty, slightly sour flavor and rich texture. It is less likely to separate on heating, but it is not suitable for whipping.

Eggs: choose free-range, if possible, and check the date on the carton for freshness. *Caution*: Remember that raw or undercooked eggs should not be served to the very young, the elderly, pregnant women, and anyone frail or vulnerable to any possible infection that might occur.

Flour: use white all-purpose flour rather than whole-wheat for making sauces. Cornstarch is used in Chinese dishes. Potato flour, or *fécule*, and arrowroot are often used to thicken sauces at the end of cooking.

Herbs: fresh herbs are always used in this book unless otherwise specified. Wash and dry them well before use.

Lemons: always use unwaxed fruit if you want the rind or zest for a recipe, and be sure to scrub them with hot soapy water and then rinse well. The same applies to oranges and other citrus fruit.

Mustard: it is good to have a selection of mustards in the kitchen, for cooking and serving as a condiment. Mustard turns a sauce very bitter if allowed to boil for any length of time, so it is best to add it at the end of cooking, off the heat.

Nuts: their high fat content makes nuts quickly go stale and rancid when exposed to the air, so use the freshest possible and store opened packages in the freezer.

Oils: avoid blended salad or vegetable oils. The best quality, most interesting oils for flavoring are made from the first (low temperature) pressing of a single fruit, grain, or nut. The flavor of olive oil ranges from sweet and delicate through fruity to the powerfully robust, so select an oil suitable for the finished dish. Peanut oil is mild and excellent for frying as it has a high smoke point. Nut oils tend to be expensive and are unsuitable for cooking at high temperatures, but can be excellent on their own or combined with a mild oil for salads. For Asian cooking, choose a sesame oil made from toasted sesame seeds.

Salt and Black Pepper: these seasonings should always be added to taste, unless specific quantities are given in the recipe.

Soy Sauce: choose naturally brewed soy sauce from Japan: the flavor is very different from non-brewed soy made by chemically hydrolyzing vegetable proteins and adding caramel, salt, and sugar. Large bottles of Japanese soy sauce tend to be cheaper at Asian markets.

Tomatoes: choose ripe, well-flavored tomatoes; otherwise, look out for good-quality canned plum tomatoes (after draining, a 14-ounce/400-g can will yield 1 cup tomatoes). Some tomato paste can be very salty, so add it before seasoning. Sun-dried tomato paste has a richer flavor.

Vegetables: for all the recipes in this book, it is assumed that you will thoroughly wash, dry, and trim all vegetables before use. Where vegetables such as carrots, onions, and potatoes are commonly peeled, you should do so unless directed not to do so in the recipe. It is assumed that you will not peel eggplant, zucchini, or sweet peppers, unless otherwise directed.

Vinegars: white and red wine vinegars are the ones most often used in vinaigrettes and other salad dressings. Cider vinegar and tarragon vinegar (white wine vinegar flavored with the herb) are interesting alternatives. Raspberry vinegar makes a distinctive dressing and can be used for deglazing. Balsamic and sherry vinegars are expensive, but useful in the kitchen. Malt vinegar is far too pungent to be used in cooking except for preserving and as a condiment for fish and chips. Japanese and Chinese rice vinegars tend to be mild and slightly sweet.

QUIPMENT

You do not need much in the way of specialized equipment for making sauces, but you will need a good small to medium-size saucepan with sloping sides. The classic pan for making sauces is copper lined with tin, silver, or stainless steel. Copper is a good conductor of heat, and using this sort of pan helps to avoid scorching a sauce as it cooks. The clever design of these pans ensures that the whisk can reach every part, and that the pan does not wobble around on the stove as the sauce is whisked, or topple over when the whisk is leaning against the side. These pans need to be used carefully, as metal implements can scratch the lining.

The next best choice, and probably the most practical for home cooks, would be a heavy-based, well-balanced, good-quality stainless steel pan, again with sloping sides. Many cookware shops and large department stores now stock a range of semi-professional pans with heavy-gauge "sandwich" bases of stainless steel and copper, aluminum, or an alloy. Avoid toughened glass pans, to which sauces may stick.

A small to medium-size straight-sided pan is useful for making sugar syrup and for keeping sauces warm in a water-bath.

A deep roasting pan makes a good water-bath. It should be filled one-third full with warm water and set over low heat.

A large stockpot is always useful and not just for making stock: it can also be used for poaching chickens, cooking pasta, or making soup.

A colander with a long handle and sturdy legs, a conical strainer with small holes, a fine-mesh conical strainer or *chinois*, and a fine-mesh drum sieve or *tamis*, for making smooth, glossy sauces, are all very useful. Stainless steel is the best material for all of these strainers and sieves.

A stainless steel or wire whisk with a large, thick handle is vital. Choose a size appropriate to the size of your pan. Flat coiled wire sauce whisks are also very good, and inexpensive. Avoid using a large balloon whisk, which is better for whipping cream and egg whites. A rotary beater is not a good choice here either.

Several wooden spoons, with long handles and shallow bowls, are good for stirring creamy sauces and vegetable mixtures where you do not need a foamy or frothy texture; however, I think a whisk is more efficient at dispersing lumps. A flat wooden spatula is a good buy: it does not conduct heat, so can be used for stir-frying and slow-cooked dishes. A flexible plastic spatula is handy for scraping out pans.

A small stainless steel ladle with a long handle can be used with a *chinois* for straining or puréeing sauces. A large metal ladle, again with a long handle, can be used for transferring liquids from pan to food processor and back again.

A food processor with a large bowl or a large, powerful blender will make light work of puréeing sauces, and both can be used for making hollandaise and mayonnaise very speedily. These machines can also be used for pestos and nut sauces.

An old-fashioned mortar and pestle is also useful for crushing spices, and for making pestos and other thick sauces. Choose a heavy, fairly large mortar with a non-metal inner surface.

Right (left to right): straight-sided stainless steel saucepan, balloon whisk, large metal ladle, flat coiled wire whisk, tin-lined copper saucepan, measuring spoons, conical strainer with small holes, fine-mesh conical strainer, and a blender.

ℰQUIPMENT

Thickening Sauces

Making sauces well requires skill, of course, but experience and judgment are important, too. The correct thickness for a sauce depends on how it is to be used or what it is to accompany. There are several ways to adjust the consistency to your liking.

BUTTER

Adding ice-cold butter to a sauce just before serving gives the sauce a fine, glossy quality and a richer, creamier flavor as well as making it slightly thicker. It can also make a slightly harsh sauce mellower in flavor.

It is important to use unsalted butter: salted butter will give an undesirable salty, slightly greasy finish to the sauce. The butter should be chilled and firm. Cut it into small cubes.

Bring the sauce to a boil, then remove from the heat and gradually whisk in the pieces of butter so they quickly melt and thicken the sauce. Once a sauce has been thickened with butter it should be served as soon as possible, without reheating.

BEURRE MANIÉ

This is one of the quickest, easiest ways to thicken a sauce. Also known as kneaded butter, it is primarily used for hearty stews and casseroles if they are too thin at the end of cooking. The beurre manié is added just before serving, though a sauce thickened this way can be kept warm or even reheated.

Mash equal quantities of very soft unsalted butter and all-purpose flour together with a fork or metal spatula to give a smooth paste. Whisk or stir small pieces of this paste into the boiling sauce—it works instantly, so you can keep adding the paste until the sauce has the right consistency. Let the sauce boil gently for a couple of minutes in order to cook out the taste of the flour.

CORNSTARCH

This is another simple, quick way to thicken a sauce, and is commonly used in Chinese cooking and for making low-fat sauces.

In a small bowl, mix 1 tablespoon of cornstarch with an equal quantity of cold water, stock, or other cold liquid to make a smooth, pourable paste (this process is sometimes known as slaking). Pour the paste into the boiling sauce while stirring or whisking vigorously—as the sauce boils it will thicken and become slightly opaque.

If necessary, add more of the cornstarch mixture to get the right consistency. The finished sauce should coat the back of a spoon; too much cornstarch will give a jelly-like finish. Gently boil the sauce for 1 minute to cook the cornstarch. A sauce thickened in this way can be kept hot or reheated, and will not become thin if re-boiled.

ARROWROOT AND POTATO FLOUR (FÉCULE)

These are also added at the end of cooking. They have an advantage over cornstarch in that they give a fine, glossy, translucent finish to the sauce. However, sauces thickened this way cannot be cooked further: the sauce will instantly thicken on boiling, but will become thin again if it is simmered for more than 1 minute.

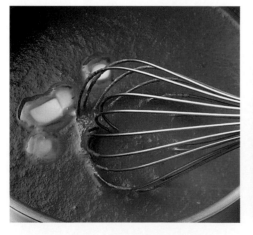

Butter: *take the boiling sauce off the heat and gradually whisk in the cubes of chilled butter so they melt and thicken the sauce.*

Beurre Manié: *add small pieces of the flour and butter paste to the sauce, stirring well after each addition, until it thickens.*

Cornstarch: *pour the mixture of cornstarch and water into the boiling sauce while whisking, then cook the sauce for 1 minute.*

$\mathscr{T}$HICKENING $\mathscr{S}$AUCES

Mix 1 tablespoon of arrowroot or potato flour with an equal quantity of cold water or stock to make a smooth, pourable paste, then whisk it into the boiling sauce. As soon as the sauce thickens, remove it from the heat and serve immediately.

EGG YOLKS AND CREAM

Added at the end of cooking, this mixture will enrich and thicken a sauce, giving it a rich, creamy taste and a velvety-smooth texture. Velouté sauces are often finished in this way, but egg yolks and cream can also be used to enrich béchamel sauces and soups. Remember, the egg yolks will curdle if the mixture is boiled, and the sauce cannot be reheated.

Lightly whisk the egg yolks with an equal quantity of cream (or half-and-half) in a heatproof bowl until just combined. Bring the sauce to a boil, then remove it from the heat. Add some of the hot sauce to the egg mixture, stirring constantly (this gently heats the egg mixture so it is less likely to curdle when it meets the very hot sauce). Stir this mixture into the sauce off the heat, then stir over low heat until the sauce thickens enough to lightly coat the back of a spoon.

Do not overheat the sauce or let it boil, as it will curdle. Serve immediately.

REDUCTION

A thin, runny sauce, or one that is lacking in flavor, can be carefully boiled over medium-high heat (do not let it scorch around the edges) until enough of the liquid has evaporated to make it thicker and more concentrated in flavor. Gravy and stock-based sauces are often thickened this way, to intensify the flavor and give a mellow result; it is best to reduce them before you add any other thickening agent in order to avoid the sauce sticking to the bottom of the pan or scorching. Take care that the sauce does not boil too hard or it will become cloudy and taste bitter.

As the stock or sauce reduces, skim off any froth on the surface using a small ladle or slotted spoon. Check the consistency from time to time by pouring a little of the sauce over the back of a spoon—it can be as thin as milk, like light or heavy cream, or a rich, thick, sticky sauce known as *demiglace*. Sauces such as these are always seasoned after they have been reduced or the flavor may be too intense.

Quick cream sauces can also be made using this method. The cream is brought to a boil in a pan with flavorings such as wine, herbs, and cooking juices, and simmered until thick. Cream can also be boiled until it has reduced by about a third, then added to a hot sauce to thicken it. Choose heavy or whipping cream; crème fraîche tends to curdle when used in this way.

PURÉES

A gravy or casserole that is slightly too thin can be thickened by mashing a cooked potato and stirring it into the sauce before serving. A casserole containing beans or lentils can be thickened by puréeing a cup or so of the mixture, then stirring it into the pot.

Bread crumbs can be stirred in to thicken hearty casseroles and soups, but the sauce then needs to be cooked for 10 minutes or so, stirring frequently, before serving.

Some sauces are thickened simply by puréeing the ingredients in a blender or food processor, or by pushing them through a strainer. This method is often used for sauces made from raw or cooked fruit or from cooked vegetables, and is an excellent way of producing velvety-textured low-fat sauces.

Arrowroot or Potato Flour: *whisk the paste of water and arrowroot or potato flour into the boiling sauce, then remove it from the heat.*

Egg Yolks and Cream: *combine the yolks and cream in a bowl and add a little of the sauce. Stir this mixture into the pan off the heat.*

Reduction: *boil the sauce for several minutes or until enough liquid has evaporated to give a slightly thickened consistency.*

ROUX BASES

A roux is a cooked mixture of butter and flour. Unlike other methods of thickening a sauce, it is used at the very beginning of the recipe, as the base of the sauce. The darker the roux, the more color the final sauce will have. Once the roux has been cooked to the desired color, the pan is removed from the heat and the liquid is gradually whisked into the roux. The sauce is then simmered until it reaches the correct consistency. You will need 2 tablespoons (30g) of butter and 2 tablespoons all-purpose flour for each 1 cup (250ml) liquid to make a sauce with a medium coating consistency. Some cooks prefer to clarify the butter first; however, fresh unsalted butter gives a perfectly good result.

DOS AND DON'TS
- *Use a heavy-based saucepan to prevent the roux from sticking to the bottom of the pan and scorching.*
- *Cook the roux over very low heat so that it bubbles gently.*
- *Do not let the roux scorch or turn dark brown, or the sauce will taste unpleasant.*
- *To avoid lumps in the finished sauce, spread the roux out over the bottom of the saucepan so that it cooks evenly.*
- *If lumps do form in the sauce, pour it through a fine strainer into a clean pan.*

1 A white roux, which can be used for béchamel and velouté sauces, is cooked for just 1 to 2 minutes over low heat so the mixture remains pale in color. The resulting sauce made from milk or a pale stock will also be light in color. The cooled roux can be stored, covered, in the refrigerator for up to 3 days, if desired.

2 If the roux is cooked for 3 to 5 minutes, the flour in the mixture will start to turn a golden color. This is known as a blond or straw-colored roux and is also used for béchamel and velouté sauces. The extra time has the advantage of cooking out the raw taste of the flour.

3 Bacon or ham and vegetables, as well as butter and flour, are included in a brown roux, which is cooked very gently for 10 to 20 minutes or until the flour turns a rich brown color. Some cooks prefer to cook the roux in the oven, which can take as long as 45 minutes. Brown roux is the basis of classic French brown sauce, as well as many Creole recipes such as gumbo.

$\mathscr{S}$AUCE $\mathscr{C}$ONSISTENCY

The consistency you want a sauce to achieve depends on its final use. A thin, delicate, pourable sauce is best for fish or vegetables, as it will not overwhelm them. It can also be used as the basis of soups or other sauces. A sauce of a medium coating consistency will nap the surface of more robust ingredients, and is used in gratins and pasta dishes. The thickest sauces are almost solid and are used as the base for soufflés and for binding together the ingredients for crêpe fillings and croquettes. If a sauce is too thick, work in a little extra milk or stock, then taste and adjust the seasoning. Sauces thicken slightly on reheating, so make them thinner than usual if you are preparing them in advance.

1 A sauce has reached a thin, pourable consistency when it lightly coats the back of a spoon and, when you draw your finger across the spoon, the trail left in the sauce slowly runs back together. This is the best consistency for sauces that are intended to moisten food, and is ideal for flooding the serving plate for a grand and very special presentation.

2 When the sauce is a medium, coating consistency, it will cling to the back of the spoon and a clear trail will be left when you draw your finger across it. This type of sauce will similarly cling to the food, covering the top and oozing down the sides.

3 A sauce of a thick, binding consistency is made with a higher proportion of butter and flour to liquid. The finished sauce will only drop from the spoon when the handle is tapped on the side of the pan. This is the consistency required for soufflé bases and to hold solid ingredients together when making croquettes and similar dishes.

MAKING TOMATO SAUCE

A good tomato sauce, such as this fine, smooth version, is highly versatile and healthful. Use it to dress pasta such as cannelloni, ravioli, or spaghetti, add it to casseroles and stews, or serve it alongside grilled meats. To make a tomato soup, add vegetable stock, milk, or cream until the mixture is of the right consistency.

Tomato Sauce

MAKES 1 QUART (1 LITER)

2 tablespoons olive oil
1 large onion, chopped
2 cloves garlic, minced
1 stalk celery, chopped
1 medium carrot, thinly sliced
2¼ pounds (1kg) tomatoes, chopped
salt and black pepper

EQUIPMENT
• Large heavy saucepan or frying pan with lid
• Wooden spoon
• Conical strainer, food processor, or blender

1 Heat the oil in a heavy saucepan and add the chopped onion. Cover the pan and cook very gently for about 15 minutes or until the onions are soft and golden.

DOS AND DON'TS
• Use ripe, well-flavored tomatoes to avoid a watery-tasting, thin sauce.
• Stir frequently to prevent the sauce from sticking to the bottom of the pan.

2 Stir in the garlic, celery, and carrot. Cover the pan again and continue cooking the vegetables for 5 more minutes. Add the chopped tomatoes and seasoning and cook gently for a further 20 minutes.

3 Strain the sauce through a conical strainer, pressing down on the solids to extract as much liquid as possible. Alternatively, process the mixture until smooth in a food processor or blender, then strain if desired. Taste and adjust the seasoning. The cooled sauce can be stored in the refrigerator for up to 5 days.

MAKING MAYONNAISE

Mayonnaise is a cold, thick emulsion of egg yolks and oil, nicely acidified and flavored with salt, pepper, and mustard. The oil can be a delicate vegetable one, such as safflower or sunflower, light olive oil, or the richest extra virgin olive oil, depending on how the mayonnaise is to be used: a combination of oils often works best.

Mayonnaise

MAKES ABOUT 1 CUP (250ML)

**1 extra large egg yolk, at room temperature
(see caution about eggs on page 11)**
1 teaspoon Dijon mustard, or to taste
**juice of ½ lemon or 2 tablespoons white wine
vinegar**
salt and black pepper
¾ cup (175ml) vegetable or olive oil

EQUIPMENT
• **Small bowl**
• **Damp cloth**
• **Whisk**

1 Put the egg yolk, mustard, half the lemon juice or vinegar, and a little salt and pepper into a small bowl. Stand the bowl on a damp cloth to prevent it from wobbling while you whisk the ingredients until creamy.

DOS AND DON'TS
• *Add the oil very slowly. If the mixture starts to separate, stir in 1 tablespoon warm water.*
• *If the mixture curdles, place a fresh yolk in another bowl and slowly whisk in the curdled mixture. Adjust the seasoning before serving.*

2 Very slowly whisk in the oil, drop by drop at first and then, as the mayonnaise starts to thicken, in a thin, steady stream. Whisk the mixture constantly.

3 When all the oil has been incorporated, taste the mayonnaise and stir in more of the lemon juice or vinegar and more seasoning as required. Stir gently before use. Mayonnaise can be kept, covered, in the refrigerator for up to 2 days.

Blender Mayonnaise: To make mayonnaise in a food processor, blender, or electric mixer, put the egg yolk, mustard, lemon juice or vinegar, salt, and pepper into the bowl and process briefly just until they are mixed.

Then, with the machine running, gradually pour in the oil through the opening in the lid (or wherever appropriate) in a thin, steady stream until you have a thick, emulsified mixture. Taste the mayonnaise and adjust the flavorings as necessary.

Making Béchamel Sauce

Béchamel sauce is infinitely adaptable and versatile. It can be used plain or as a base for innumerable other flavored sauces. When made to a thin consistency it can be used in soups; a medium thickness is best for coating pasta, vegetables, fish, and eggs; and thick béchamel is ideal for binding ingredients together to make fish cakes and croquettes. The milk should be well infused with the flavors of onion, bay leaf, parsley, mace, and peppercorns. The sauce should be whisked constantly as it comes to a boil, to eliminate lumps and give a silky texture, then cooked for 20 minutes so that the flour no longer tastes raw. Béchamel can be kept hot in a water-bath if necessary, and freezes well.

Béchamel Sauce

MAKES 2 CUPS (500ML) MEDIUM-THICKNESS
SAUCE

2 cups (500ml) whole milk
¼ teaspoon black peppercorns
1 bay leaf
2 slices onion
1 blade mace
2 parsley stems, crushed
3 tablespoons (45g) unsalted butter
3 tablespoons all-purpose flour
salt and white pepper
freshly grated nutmeg

EQUIPMENT
• **Heavy saucepan with lid**
• **Strainer**
• **Wire whisk**
• **Wooden spoon (optional)**

1 Heat the milk with the peppercorns, bay leaf, onion, mace, and parsley stems in a medium-size, heavy-based saucepan. As the milk comes up to boiling point, cover the pan, remove it from the heat, and let stand for 20 minutes to allow the flavors to infuse (leave it for up to 1 hour if possible). Strain the milk and discard the flavorings. Rinse out the saucepan.

2 Gently melt the butter in the saucepan. Stir in the flour using a wooden spoon or wire whisk to make a smooth paste. Cook gently, stirring, over very low heat so that the roux bubbles as it cooks.

Making Béchamel Sauce

3 Remove the pan from the heat and, using a wire whisk, gradually whisk in the infused milk until smoothly mixed.

4 Set the pan over medium heat and whisk rapidly as the mixture comes to a boil. It should thicken but remain smooth.

5 Reduce the heat so the sauce barely simmers, then let it cook very gently for 20 minutes, stirring frequently.

6 The correct consistency is reached when the sauce coats the back of a spoon and a clear trail is left when you draw a finger through the sauce. When it is ready, give it a final whisk, then season with salt, pepper, and nutmeg.

7 To keep the sauce warm in a water-bath, press a circle of dampened parchment paper onto the surface of the sauce, or dot the surface with butter, then cover the pan with a lid. The cooled sauce can be stored in the refrigerator for up to 3 days or frozen for up to 1 month.

DO AND DON'TS
• *For the best flavor use good ingredients: whole milk and butter are preferable to skim milk and margarine.*
• *Take care that the sauce doesn't stick to the bottom of the pan; milk easily scorches, which would make the sauce taste unpleasant.*
• *If there are any lumps, whisk the sauce vigorously, press it through a strainer, or process it in a blender or food processor.*

Variations: *Simple White Sauce*
Follow the recipe for Medium-Thickness Béchamel as given, but do not infuse the milk with the flavorings.

Thin Béchamel
Follow the recipe for Medium-Thickness Béchamel, but use 2 tablespoons (30g) butter and 2 tablespoons all-purpose flour. The correct consistency is reached when the sauce is the thickness of light cream: it will only lightly cover the back of a spoon and you will not be able to draw a clear trail through the sauce.

Thick Béchamel
Follow the recipe for Medium-Thickness Béchamel, but use 3 tablespoons (45g) butter and ¼ cup all-purpose flour. The correct consistency is reached when the sauce is semi-solid and drops off the spoon only when the spoon is tapped on the rim of the saucepan.

Cream Sauce
Adding crème fraîche or light or heavy cream to the recipe for Medium-Thickness Béchamel instantly changes the taste and texture, making the sauce velvety smooth and rich. Whisk 4 to 5 tablespoons of cream into the heated béchamel and simmer gently, whisking until the sauce reaches the correct consistency. Taste and adjust the seasoning if necessary. Use cream sauce to coat steamed vegetables, simply poached fish, and plain poultry dishes.

Making Hollandaise Sauce

Hollandaise sauce is one of the lightest and yet richest sauces you can make. A smooth emulsification of egg yolks and butter sharpened with lemon juice, it has to be made with care and attention, or it may curdle. A non-aluminum pan is essential to prevent discoloration of the sauce. Using clarified unsalted butter gives the smoothest result as well as the best creamy flavor, and freshly squeezed lemon juice is a must. Hollandaise is served warm to accompany fish, vegetables, or egg dishes, and can be flavored to suit the dish it is to accompany; fresh herbs, mustard, and orange juice are popular additions. The finished sauce cannot be reheated, but it can be kept warm for a short time before serving.

Hollandaise Sauce

MAKES 1¼ CUPS (300ML)

1 cup (250g) unsalted butter
3 large egg yolks (see caution about eggs on
    page 11)
2 tablespoons water
juice of ½ lemon
salt and white pepper

EQUIPMENT
• Small saucepan
• Small, heavy, non-aluminum saucepan
• Small spoon
• Measuring cup
• Whisk

1 To clarify the butter, very gently melt the butter in a small saucepan. Skim the froth from the surface using a small spoon, then carefully tip the melted butter into a clean pan or measuring cup, leaving the milky sediment behind. Set aside the clarified butter until it is lukewarm. Discard the sediment.

2 Put the egg yolks and water in a small, heavy-based, non-aluminum saucepan and whisk them, off the heat, until frothy.

Making Hollandaise Sauce

• *Keep the heat very low. If the mixture of yolks and water gets too hot, the eggs will scramble and you will have to start again.*
• *Add the butter very slowly and make sure that it is lukewarm, otherwise the sauce will split or separate.*
• *There is no need to throw a curdled sauce away: it can often be saved by vigorously whisking in an ice cube. If that fails, start again with 2 egg yolks and 2 tablespoons of water whisked to a mousse, then gradually whisk in the curdled mixture.*

3 Set the pan over very low heat and whisk constantly for 5 minutes or until the mixture is very thick and mousse-like.

4 Remove from the heat and, whisking constantly, pour in the clarified butter in a slow, steady stream to make a thick sauce.

Variations: For a really light sauce, use 2 yolks for each 1 cup (250g) of butter (this can be a bit difficult to make as the mixture easily splits). Use 4 egg yolks to make a richer, thicker hollandaise.

Sauce Mousseline
Fold ¼ cup (60ml) of crème fraîche or lightly whipped cream into the hollandaise, then taste and adjust the seasonings as necessary. Use to accompany vegetables, chicken, and delicate white fish.

Sauce Moutarde
Make the hollandaise, then stir in 1 tablespoon of Dijon mustard and season to taste. Add more mustard for a really piquant sauce. This goes well with crab and stronger flavored fish, as well as with grilled chops or boneless chicken breasts.

5 Whisk the lemon juice, salt, and pepper into the thickened sauce, and serve as soon as possible. You can keep the sauce warm for 15 minutes or so by covering it and keeping it in a water-bath. Do not use a microwave oven to reheat hollandaise.

Blender Hollandaise: Put the egg yolks (at room temperature) into the bowl of a food processor or blender with the water, lemon juice, salt, and pepper and process briefly until just combined. Heat the clarified butter, but do not let it boil. While the motor is running, pour the butter through the opening in the lid in a thin, steady stream. When the sauce is creamy and thick, adjust the seasoning to taste and serve.

Making Crème Anglaise

Otherwise known as egg custard, this vanilla-flavored dessert sauce is best made from egg yolks and rich, creamy milk—use a combination of whole milk and light cream, or half-and-half. Crème Anglaise can be served warm, at room temperature, or chilled, with a variety of sweet dishes, but it particularly complements fruit desserts and baked puddings. If you prefer, the sauce can be flavored as necessary with a variety of interesting ingredients, including melted chocolate, coffee, cardamom, and nutmeg. To make ice cream, simply chill the finished custard, then combine it with an equal quantity of whipped cream before freezing the mixture in an ice cream machine.

Crème Anglaise

MAKES ABOUT 1 CUP (250ML)

1 vanilla bean
⅔ cup (150ml) very creamy milk
3 extra large egg yolks
2½ tablespoons sugar

EQUIPMENT
• Heavy saucepan with lid
• Small pointed knife
• Wooden spoon
• Damp cloth
• Large bowl
• Conical strainer

1 Split the vanilla bean in half lengthwise, then put it into a heavy-based saucepan with the milk. Heat until scalding hot, then remove the pan from the heat, cover, and let the milk infuse for 15 minutes.

2 Remove the vanilla, but scrape the tiny black seeds from inside the bean back into the milk with the point of a small knife; the milk should look speckled.

DOS AND DON'TS
• *The sauce must be well flavored with vanilla, otherwise it will taste insipid.*
• *Take care not to overheat the egg mixture, or the eggs will scramble and the custard will be ruined.*

Making Crème Anglaise

3 With a wooden spoon, beat the egg yolks and sugar together in a large bowl until the mixture is thick and pale.

4 Slowly pour the hot milk onto the yolk mixture, stirring constantly. Stand the bowl on a damp cloth to keep it stable.

Variations: *Chocolate Custard*
Add 2 ounces (60g) dark chocolate, very finely chopped, to the milk when you remove the vanilla bean. Stir until melted (you may need to warm the mixture).

Espresso Custard
Replace the vanilla bean with 1½ tablespoons of very finely ground espresso coffee.

Cardamom Custard
Replace the vanilla bean with 5 lightly crushed green cardamom pods.

Apricot or Peach Custard
In a food processor, purée the flesh of 4 ripe apricots or 1 peach, then pour in the custard and process until thoroughly combined.

5 Rinse out the milk pan, then pour the mixture back into it. Cook over very low heat, stirring constantly with a wooden spoon, until the custard thickens enough to coat the back of the spoon. This process may take 5 minutes, but do not be tempted to hurry it; if the custard boils, it will curdle and cannot be used.

6 Using a fine-mesh conical strainer, strain the thickened custard into a bowl to give a completely smooth sauce. Serve it warm, if you like, or let it cool.

7 If you want to keep the sauce, sprinkle the surface with a little sugar to prevent a skin from forming. Let it cool, then cover and chill. Use the custard within 2 days.

Making Caramel Sauce

The secret to making caramel sauce—shiny, lustrous, and the color of rich amber—is patience. Watch it carefully and test regularly, as demonstrated here: the simple sugar and water mixture can darken more quickly than expected and, unfortunately, there is no way to save a burned caramel. You will find the result is worth a little trouble, however. The intermittent stages of sugar syrup are as versatile as the finished caramel sauce, and can be used for fruit salads and pouring over cakes. When completed, the caramel sauce can be served warm, at room temperature, or chilled, with ice creams, creamy desserts such as parfaits, mousses, and Bavarian creams, or fresh fruit such as sliced oranges.

Caramel Sauce

MAKES 1¼ CUPS (300ML)

1¼ cups (250g) sugar
1¼ cups (300ml) water

EQUIPMENT
- Medium-size saucepan
- Wooden spoon
- Natural bristle pastry brush
- Candy thermometer (optional)
- Metal spoon
- Bowl of ice water
- White plate
- Oven mitt or dish towel

1 Put the sugar and half of the water into a medium-size heavy saucepan. Set over low heat and stir frequently with a wooden spoon until the sugar dissolves. Do not let the mixture boil at this stage. From time to time, brush down the sides of the pan with a pastry brush dipped in hot water to dissolve any sugar crystals stuck to the side of the pan, as these could cause crystallization. As soon as all the grains of sugar have dissolved, stop stirring and remove the wooden spoon.

2 Bring the syrup to a boil (you can put in a candy thermometer at this stage). Depending on the heat and size of the pan, the syrup will reach thread stage (230°F/110°C) in about 30 seconds. To test this stage without a thermometer, let some syrup fall from a metal spoon: it should fall in a thin, soft thread. Left at this stage, the syrup can be used for poaching fruit and, when cooled, can be kept in the refrigerator for up to 2 months.

MAKING CARAMEL SAUCE

3 Boil the syrup for a further 2 minutes to reach soft ball stage (238°F/113°C). To test without a thermometer, drop about half a teaspoonful of the syrup into a bowl of ice water. You should then be able to roll the syrup into a soft, pliable ball with your fingers. At this stage the syrup can be used to make fondant paste.

Continue boiling the syrup for a further 3 to 4 minutes to achieve hard crack stage (295°F/146°C). The syrup will now be pale gold. It will set hard if a little is dropped in ice water and will snap in two with a crack. At this stage it can be used for decorating cakes when a strong, distinct taste is not needed. Otherwise, continue boiling the syrup to produce a caramel.

DOS AND DON'TS
• *Caution: hot caramel causes bad burns if it touches the skin.*
• *Do not use a tin-lined copper saucepan or a nonstick pan, as the melting point of the lining may be below that of the caramel.*
• *Use a natural bristle brush rather than a nylon brush, as the syrup will be very hot.*
• *Have a large bowl filled with ice water at the ready. If the caramel is cooking too fast, stop it turning darker by immersing the base of the pan in the cold water.*
• *For accuracy, use a candy thermometer. To prevent it from cracking, put it into the syrup as soon as the sugar has dissolved. Cool the thermometer before washing it.*
• *If you don't have a thermometer, drop the syrup on a white plate to check the color.*

4 At 320°F (160°C) the caramel will be a pale amber color (above right) and has a mild flavor. It can be used for pouring over meringue cakes or croquembouche and for spun sugar. Medium caramel (340°F/170°C) is a darker amber color (above left) with a deep, rich taste. This is the stage required for caramel sauce or for caramel custard, where the caramel is poured into the bottom of a cooking mold.

5 To finish making the caramel sauce, remove the pan from the heat as soon as the syrup reaches 340°F (170°C)—the caramel could easily overcook and burn. Let it cool for a few seconds, or until it stops bubbling. Cover your hand with an oven mitt or dish towel and pour in the remaining water—take care as the caramel will boil up and splutter furiously.

6 Cook gently until the caramel dissolves. For a thicker sauce, boil until syrupy. The sauce, once cold, can be kept in the refrigerator for up to 1 week.

Variations: *Creamy Caramel Sauce*
Replace the second addition of water with ⅔ cup (150ml) of heavy cream.

Coffee Caramel Sauce
Replace the second addition of water with black coffee.

QUICK AND SIMPLE

The recipes featured in this chapter are the speediest, easiest ways to add interest to simply cooked meat, fish, and vegetables. No real effort or special skills are needed, just some imaginative ingredients to create fresh, delicious, lively food that can be cooked in very little time.

The simplest way to make a sauce is by deglazing the pan in which the meat, chicken, or fish has been cooked, using a little homemade stock, wine, or even vegetable cooking water. The result is an instant jus, or unthickened gravy.

Some softened butter mashed with plenty of well-flavored ingredients can be kept in the refrigerator to add to steamed vegetables, grilled meat or fish, or even drained hot pasta. Again, the result is instant flavor and interest with very little effort.

Grilling is enjoyed year-round, both outdoors and in, with covered kettle grills and on cast-iron grill pans, so in this chapter I have included some simple recipes for marinades, spice rubs, flavored oils, and barbecue bastes.

Use these ideas to make quick meals as enjoyable as any well-planned, highly organized dinner party.

Left (clockwise from right): Lime-Chili Oil, Tomato and Onion Baste, Pistachio Butter, and Whole-grain Mustard Butter.

Rib-Eye Steak

This is one of the simplest of all sauces for beef, but it is important that you use a good-quality jellied stock or canned consommé.

SERVES 4

3 tablespoons (45g) butter
4 beef rib-eye steaks
½ cup (125ml) well-reduced stock or canned beef consommé
½ cup (125ml) dry red wine

Heat the butter in a large, heavy skillet and, when it is sizzling, add the steak. Cook for 3 to 5 minutes on each side. When done to your liking, remove the steaks to a plate and keep warm.

Add the stock and wine to the skillet to deglaze it: Bring the liquid to a boil, stirring constantly to scrape up the caramelized cooking juices and incorporate them into the sauce. Simmer the sauce vigorously until it has reduced to a pouring consistency, then pour it over the steaks and serve.

Variation: Fry a shallot in the butter before adding the stock and red wine.

Deglazing a pan: pour in the liquid and stir vigorously, scraping the caramelized meat juices from the bottom of the pan and simmering until they dissolve to make a slightly thickened sauce.

Brandied Ginger Steak

SERVES 2

1 to 2 teaspoons ground ginger
2 filet mignons
black pepper
1 teaspoon salt
2 tablespoons (25g) butter
2 tablespoons brandy
1 tablespoon lemon juice
½ teaspoon Worcestershire sauce
1 tablespoon minced parsley

Rub the ginger evenly into both sides of each steak and sprinkle them with black pepper. Let stand for 10 minutes.

Sprinkle the salt evenly over the bottom of a large skillet and heat gently until the salt is lightly browned. Add the steaks to the skillet and cook them for 3 minutes over medium-high heat. Turn the steaks, then add the butter to the skillet and continue cooking for 3 to 5 minutes or until the steaks are done to your liking.

Add the brandy, lemon juice, and Worcestershire sauce to the skillet and stir well, scraping up any sediment and moistening both sides of the steaks with the pan juices. When the sauce is hot, serve, sprinkled with the parsley.

Deviled Steak

SERVES 2

2 filet mignons
black pepper
10 tablespoons (150g) butter
1 clove garlic, minced
2 tablespoons Worcestershire sauce
2 tablespoons minced parsley

Lightly season both sides of each steak with black pepper. Melt the butter in a large skillet and, when it is sizzling, add the steaks. Cook for 2 to 3 minutes. While the

first side is cooking, rub the minced garlic into the top of each steak. Turn the steaks over and continue cooking on the other side.

Deglaze the pan with the Worcestershire sauce and swirl the steaks around in it. When the meat is done to your liking, sprinkle it with the chopped parsley and serve.

Pepper Steaks with Cream and Mushrooms

SERVES 4

2 tablespoons mixed peppercorns, crushed
4 filet mignons
1 tablespoon olive oil
2 tablespoons (25g) butter
1 clove garlic, minced
3 cups sliced mushrooms
2 tablespoons brandy
⅔ cup (150ml) light cream
salt

Press the crushed peppercorns into the steaks. Heat the oil and butter in a large skillet, add the steaks, and cook them over medium-high heat until done to your liking. Remove the steaks and keep warm.

Add the garlic and mushrooms to the skillet and cook them briefly in the cooking juices. Deglaze the pan with the brandy and simmer it for 1 minute, then add the cream and cook the sauce over low heat until it thickens. Season to taste with salt, and pour the sauce over the steaks.

Veal Piccata

SERVES 2

2 tablespoons (25g) butter
2 veal scallops
juice of 1 lemon or ⅓ cup (80ml) Marsala
salt and black pepper

𝒫 A N 𝒮 A U C E S

In a heavy skillet, heat the butter until sizzling and add the veal scallops. Cook them for 2 to 3 minutes on each side. Remove from the pan and keep warm.

Add the lemon juice or Marsala to the skillet and bring to a boil, stirring to incorporate the caramelized cooking juices. When the sauce has reduced by about a third, season to taste and pour it over the veal. Serve immediately.

Pork Tenderloin with Cognac

This is a useful recipe for a quick company dinner made with the minimum of effort.

SERVES 4

2 small pork tenderloins, about 1½ pounds (750g) in total
½ teaspoon coarsely ground black pepper
¼ cup (60g) unsalted butter
2 medium shallots, minced
2 small cloves garlic, minced
¼ cup (60ml) Cognac
¼ cup (60ml) vegetable or chicken stock
salt

Cut the pork tenderloins into rounds about ¾-inch (2-cm) thick, then toss them in the black pepper until evenly coated. Heat the butter in a large, heavy skillet. Add the pork and cook over medium heat for 3 to 4 minutes or until it is browned on each side and cooked through—the meat should not be at all pink. Transfer the pork to a warmed serving dish and keep it hot.

Add the shallots and garlic to the skillet and fry, stirring constantly, for 2 to 3 minutes or until soft and golden. Add the Cognac and stock and stir vigorously over medium heat to scrape up and dissolve the cooking juices on the bottom of the pan. Simmer the sauce for a few seconds, then taste and add salt as necessary. Spoon over the pork and serve.

Lamb with Marsala, Tomato, and Olive Sauce

SERVES 4

2 tablespoons olive oil
4 lamb chops or leg steaks
1 small shallot, minced
1 clove garlic, minced
¼ cup (60ml) Marsala
2 plum tomatoes, peeled, seeded, and sliced
1 heaping tablespoon chopped black olives
black pepper

Heat the oil in a large, heavy skillet, add the lamb, and cook until done to your liking. Remove to a plate and keep warm.

Add the shallot and garlic to the skillet and stir over low heat until softened. Pour in the Marsala and stir well to incorporate the caramelized cooking juices.

Bring the mixture to a boil, then add the tomatoes and simmer for 2 minutes. Remove the pan from the heat and stir in the olives and black pepper to taste. Stir any juices that have collected from the meat into the sauce and serve immediately.

Variations: Beef or pork steaks and chops can be used instead of lamb.

Below: Pork Tenderloin with Cognac makes a fast but classy dinner party dish, here stylishly presented with wild rice and sugar snap peas.

Sole Meunière

In French, a *meunière* is a miller's wife, and this very easy dish involves coating the fish in flour before cooking it in butter. Once on the plate, the fish is doused in lemon juice, and minced parsley and the nut-brown pan juices are added. If you are cooking for more than two, you may have to fry the fish in batches or use two pans, which is why I am giving the quantities per person. You need to work quickly at the end, so have all the ingredients ready.

SERVES 1

½ tablespoon all-purpose flour
salt and black pepper
1 small whole Dover sole or 2 small sole fillets, cleaned, skinned, and trimmed
3 tablespoons (40g) butter, clarified
juice of ½ lemon
½ tablespoon minced parsley
lemon wedge, for garnish

Spread the flour out on a large plate and season it well with salt and pepper. Coat the fish on both sides with the flour, making sure it is generously coated, then shake to remove any excess flour.

Heat the butter in a large, heavy skillet and, when it is starting to turn a light golden brown in color, add the fish (if you are cooking fillets, place them in the pan skin-side up). Cook a whole fish for 4 to 5 minutes on each side, depending on the size and thickness, and sole fillets for 2 to 2½ minutes on each side.

Remove the cooked fish to a warm serving plate. Quickly pour the lemon juice over the fish, then sprinkle it with the minced parsley and pour the hot pan juices over—the butter should be a nice nut-brown color. Add the lemon wedge to the plate to garnish and serve immediately.

Variations: Fish such as trout and flounder can be used instead of true sole.

Cod in Oats with Mild Mustard Sauce

Above: Sole Meunière is a French classic, in which lemon juice and freshly minced parsley add piquancy to a buttery sauce for panfried fish.

SERVES 4

1½ cups (120g) rolled oats
2 tablespoons all-purpose flour
salt and black pepper
4 cod fillets, about 7 ounces (200g) each, skinned
1 egg, beaten

1 tablespoon vegetable oil
2 tablespoons (25g) unsalted butter
¼ cup (60ml) light cream
1 tablespoon whole-grain mustard
1 tablespoon lemon juice

Grind the oats in a food processor until a medium-fine flour (not to a fine powder). Season the all-purpose flour with salt and pepper. Roll the fish fillets in the seasoned flour and dust off the excess, then dip them in the egg to coat evenly. Place in the ground oats and press well onto both sides. Chill for 15 minutes or until ready to cook.

Heat the oil and butter in a large, heavy skillet. Cook the fish for 3 to 4 minutes on each side or until browned and cooked. Drain on paper towels and keep warm.

Pour off all but 2 tablespoons of fat from the skillet. Stir in the cream, mustard, lemon juice, salt, and black pepper. Heat the sauce through, but do not let it boil or it will turn bitter. Taste and adjust the seasoning as necessary, then serve.

Variations: Use halibut instead of cod, or replace the fish with skinless boneless chicken breast halves or turkey scallops.

Salmon with Roasted Garlic and Cilantro

SERVES 4

1 whole bulb garlic
2 tablespoons olive oil
4 salmon steaks
3 tablespoons dry red wine
2 tablespoons minced cilantro
salt and black pepper

Preheat the oven to 375°F. Separate the garlic cloves, but leave them unpeeled. Put them in a baking dish and roast in the hot oven for 15 minutes or until soft and golden.

Meanwhile, heat the oil in a large, heavy skillet and cook the salmon to your liking. Remove from the skillet and keep warm.

Lower the heat and squeeze the garlic cloves from their skins into the skillet. Stir gently to break up the garlic, then add the

wine and simmer for 2 to 3 minutes, stirring constantly, to make a thick sauce.

Stir in the cilantro, then taste and season as necessary. Add any juices from the fish to the sauce and serve immediately.

Variations: This dish can be made with roast lamb or beef, panfried meats, and well-flavored fish such as cod and halibut.

Chicken with Green Peppercorn Sauce

SERVES 2

3 tablespoons (40g) unsalted butter
2 skinless boneless chicken breast halves
1 tablespoon lemon juice
2 tablespoons canned green peppercorns, drained and rinsed
2 egg yolks, beaten
½ cup (125ml) crème fraîche
1 teaspoon Dijon mustard
salt and black pepper

Melt the butter in a large, heavy skillet. Add the chicken and cook it for 4 minutes on each side or until thoroughly cooked. Remove from the pan and keep warm.

Add the lemon juice and peppercorns to the pan and cook for 1 minute. Stir in the remaining ingredients and cook the sauce over low heat until it thickens. Adjust the seasonings as necessary and serve.

Chestnut Cream Chicken

SERVES 2

1 tablespoon olive oil
2 skinless boneless chicken breast halves
¼ cup (60ml) heavy cream
1 tablespoon unsweetened chestnut purée
salt and black pepper

Heat the oil in a heavy skillet and cook the chicken breasts over medium-high heat for 4 minutes on each side or until thoroughly cooked. Remove the chicken from the pan and keep warm.

Add the cream and the chestnut purée to the skillet and stir vigorously to break down the purée and incorporate the caramelized cooking juices from the chicken into the sauce. When the sauce is smooth, let it simmer gently for 1 minute. Taste and season as necessary with salt and plenty of pepper. If the sauce is too thick, stir in more cream. Serve the sauce with the chicken.

Variations: This dish can also be made with turkey scallops or with pork chops, which also suit the sweet flavor of the sauce.

Chorizo with Onions and Sherry Vinegar

SERVES 2

4 chorizo sausage links, about 12 ounces in total
2 medium onions, sliced
2 to 3 tablespoons sherry vinegar

Place the chorizo in a small to medium-size skillet over low heat and cook them slowly until the sausages exude enough fat to fry the onions. Add the onions to the skillet and continue cooking, stirring occasionally, until the onions are softened and beginning to caramelize. Turn the sausages regularly so that they brown evenly.

Remove the chorizo and onions to serving plates. Add the vinegar to the skillet. Raise the heat and bring the liquid to a vigorous boil, stirring constantly to incorporate the caramelized pan juices. Pour the sauce over the chorizo and onions and serve.

Variation: Stir 2 tablespoons heavy cream into the sauce at the last minute, if desired.

Traditional Gravy

The best gravy is made simply from the meat juices left behind in the roasting pan after the roasted meat or poultry has been transferred to a carving board. Old-fashioned gravy is thickened with flour so that the gravy lightly coats the back of a spoon. The more modern thin, flourless gravy is made just from the meat juices deglazed with a little stock or wine. In either case, the gravy must have a good flavor, neither watery and weak, nor so strong that it overwhelms the taste of the meat. This recipe is suitable for any roasted meat or bird—beef, lamb, pork, venison, chicken, turkey, and pheasant and other game birds.

SERVES 4 TO 6

2 tablespoons all-purpose flour
2 cups (500ml) stock
salt and black pepper

Transfer the cooked meat or bird to a carving board or warmed serving plate, cover loosely with aluminum foil, and let rest for 15 minutes before carving so the meat juices can settle.

Carefully remove the excess fat from the roasting pan, but retain all the meat juices. Leave a couple of spoonfuls of fat in the pan to make the gravy. Put the roasting pan on top of the stove and stir in the flour, blending it well into the fat and meat juices. Cook for 2 to 3 minutes over medium heat, stirring constantly to scrape up and mix in the meat juices, until the flour is golden.

Stir in the stock and bring to a boil, stirring constantly to make a smooth thickened gravy. Simmer for 2 to 3 minutes, then taste and season with salt and pepper.

Strain the gravy into a warmed gravy boat and serve piping hot. If it is not to be used immediately, cool the gravy quickly and then refrigerate or freeze. It can be kept in the refrigerator for up to 2 days, or in the freezer for up to 1 month.

Variations: *Flavored Gravies*
For roast chicken and turkey, add 1 to 2 tablespoons good-quality cranberry jelly along with the stock, or, after straining, add 1 tablespoon minced thyme.

For pork, add 1 to 2 teaspoons minced sage leaves with the stock. Alternatively, add the zest of 1 lemon along with the stock, then add 1 tablespoon minced cilantro after straining. If necessary, add a squeeze of lemon juice with the seasoning.

Unthickened Gravy
Omit the flour. After discarding all the fat, add the stock to the roasting pan and deglaze over medium-high heat, stirring to dislodge and dissolve all the caramelized meat juices. Finish the sauce as given.

Rosemary Gravy

SERVES 4 TO 6

1 pound (500g) lamb bones and trimmings
1 handful rosemary sprigs
1 medium onion, quartered
2 carrots, thickly sliced
½ teaspoon black peppercorns
2 tablespoons dry red wine
1 tablespoon red-currant jelly
1 tablespoon arrowroot or potato flour
salt and black pepper

Preheat the oven to 400°F. Put the lamb bones in a roasting pan and roast for 30 minutes or until browned.

Transfer the bones to a stockpot and add the meat trimmings, rosemary, vegetables, peppercorns, and 7 cups (1.7 liters) cold water. Bring to a boil. Thoroughly skim the stock, then let simmer gently for 2 hours.

Cool the stock, then strain it and discard the flavorings. Chill overnight and, next day, remove all the fat from the surface.

Pour the stock into a medium-size saucepan and boil until it has reduced to

⅔ cup (150ml). At this point, the stock can be cooled and stored in the refrigerator for up to 2 days or frozen for up to 1 month.

Once the meat has been roasted, remove from the roasting pan and keep it warm while you make the gravy. Discard all the fat from the pan, leaving the meat juices, then add the wine and stir to deglaze over medium heat. Add the stock and red-currant jelly and simmer for 2 to 3 minutes, stirring.

Mix the arrowroot or potato flour with 1 tablespoon water, then pour it into the bubbling sauce, stirring constantly. The gravy should thicken instantly. Remove it from the heat, then taste and season as necessary. Add any juices that have oozed from the meat while it has been resting, stir, and then strain the gravy.

Serving Suggestion
Serve this delicious gravy with roast lamb.

Onion Gravy

SERVES 4 TO 6

1 tablespoon vegetable oil
2 tablespoons (25g) unsalted butter
1 pound (500g) onions, thinly sliced
½ teaspoon fresh or dried thyme leaves or
**   chopped sage**
1 clove garlic, minced (optional)
1 tablespoon all-purpose flour
1½ cups (350ml) stock
salt and black pepper

Heat the oil and butter in a large, heavy skillet. Add the onions, herb, and garlic (if using) and stir well so that the onions are thoroughly coated with the fat. Cover with the lid or lay a disk of dampened parchment paper on the onions, then cook them over very low heat for about 25 minutes or until soft and tender, stirring occasionally.

Remove the lid, raise the heat under the skillet, and continue cooking the onions,

*G*RAVY

Old-Fashioned Liver and Bacon

SERVES 4

1 pound (500g) calf's liver
3 tablespoons all-purpose flour seasoned with
   salt and black pepper
3 tablespoons vegetable oil
1 pound (500g) onions, thinly sliced
8 ounces (250g) Canadian bacon, sliced
1½ cups (350ml) beef stock
1 tablespoon lemon juice
salt and black pepper

Trim the liver, removing any membranes and cutting out any ducts with kitchen scissors. Cut the liver into wide strips and toss in the seasoned flour to coat. Shake off any excess, and set the liver and remaining flour aside separately.

Heat 2 tablespoons of the oil in a large, heavy skillet. Add the onions and cook over low heat for about 20 minutes or until soft and slightly golden. Raise the heat and fry the onions, stirring, until they are golden brown. Drain the onions and keep them warm. Meanwhile, broil the Canadian bacon and keep it warm.

Heat the remaining oil in the skillet and quickly fry the strips of liver over medium-high heat, turning once, until it is cooked to your liking; do not overcook the liver or it will become hard. Remove the liver from the skillet and keep it warm.

Remove the skillet from the heat and sprinkle in the reserved flour. Gradually stir in 1¼ cups (300ml) of the stock, followed by the lemon juice and seasoning. Bring to a boil, stirring constantly, then simmer for 2 to 3 minutes. The gravy should be thick enough to coat the back of a spoon. Taste and adjust the seasoning, adding the remaining stock if the gravy is too thick.

Spoon the onions onto a warmed plate, arrange the liver and bacon on top, and serve with the gravy alongside.

Above: succulent sausages are topped with rich Onion Gravy and accompanied by creamy mashed potatoes to make a warming meal.

stirring frequently, until they are a rich chestnut-brown but not burned. Stir in the flour and cook, stirring constantly, until it is light brown in color (if the flour is too pale the sauce will look unappetizing; if it becomes dark the sauce will taste bitter).

Stir in the stock and bring to a boil, stirring, until you have a smoothly thickened gravy. Simmer gently for about 10 minutes,

stirring frequently, to cook the flour and let the onions melt into the stock. Season to taste with salt and black pepper, and serve the gravy piping hot.

Variations: For a stronger flavor, replace ½ cup (125ml) of the stock with an equal quantity of dry red or white wine, or beer.

Serving Suggestions
Serve with grilled sausages, sautéed calf's liver, steak, or roast beef. You can also make this into a simple onion soup by adding extra stock to the gravy.

35

Maître d'Hôtel Butter (Parsley Butter)

SERVES 4 TO 6

juice of ½ lemon
1½ tablespoons minced parsley
¼ teaspoon sea salt
½ cup (125g) unsalted butter, softened
black pepper

In a small bowl, beat the lemon juice, parsley, and sea salt into the butter until well combined. Add black pepper to taste.

Place the butter on a piece of wax paper or aluminum foil, and use the paper or foil to shape the butter into a cylinder about 1¼ inches (3cm) across. When wrapped, chill until firm. Store in the refrigerator for up to 1 week or freeze for up to 1 month.

Serving Suggestions
This classic butter is traditionally served with grilled meat and fish or vegetable dishes.

Anchovy Butter

SERVES 4 TO 6

8 anchovy fillets, finely chopped
½ cup (125g) unsalted butter, softened
squeeze lemon juice
pinch cayenne pepper
black pepper

Pound the anchovies to a paste in a mortar. Thoroughly blend the anchovy with the softened butter, then work in the remaining ingredients to taste. Shape and store as for the Maître d'Hôtel Butter, left.

Variations: *Smoked Salmon Butter*
Replace the anchovies with 2 ounces (60g) of pounded smoked salmon.

Pistachio Butter
For an attractive topping for fish, chicken, or rice, omit the lemon juice and cayenne pepper and replace the anchovies with 1 tablespoon of pounded pistachio nuts.

Serving Suggestions
Serve with fish, pasta, and potatoes. I use anchovy butter to make the roux when preparing a béchamel sauce for fish pies.

Four-Pepper Butter

SERVES 4 TO 6

1 teaspoon minced hot chili pepper
½ teaspoon paprika
¼ teaspoon black pepper
¼ teaspoon crushed sea salt
⅛ teaspoon cayenne pepper
½ cup (125g) unsalted butter, softened

In a small bowl, beat the minced chili, paprika, black pepper, sea salt, and cayenne pepper into the butter until thoroughly combined. Shape and store as for the Maître d'Hôtel Butter, left.

Variation: *Ginger and Lemon Grass Butter*
Add 1 teaspoon minced fresh lemon grass, 1 teaspoon minced fresh ginger, and ¼ teaspoon finely grated lime zest to the butter instead of using the salt and four varieties of pepper.

Serving Suggestions
Grilled meats and fish, pasta, rice, or vegetable dishes go well with this butter.

Left (from left to right): Four-Pepper, Pistachio, Whole-grain Mustard, and Smoked Salmon butters are as delicious as they are colorful.

Horseradish Butter

SERVES 4 TO 6

1 tablespoon finely grated fresh horseradish
¼ teaspoon crushed sea salt
½ cup (125g) unsalted butter, softened
black pepper

Beat the horseradish and salt into the butter, and add black pepper to taste. Shape and store as for the Maître d'Hôtel Butter, left.

Variation: *Whole-grain Mustard Butter*
Replace the horseradish with 4 teaspoons whole-grain mustard.

Serving Suggestions
Use with steaks, cold beef sandwiches, hot smoked fish, and broiled trout.

Aromatic Oil

Peanut oil is specified for this recipe, as it works best at high cooking temperatures.

MAKES ½ CUP (125ML)

1 large sprig thyme
1 large sprig rosemary
2 small dried hot chili peppers
½ cup (125ml) peanut oil
4 cloves garlic, peeled
½ teaspoon sea salt
¼ teaspoon black pepper

Lightly crush the herb sprigs and chilies. Put all the ingredients into a large jar with a tight-fitting lid and shake well to combine. Let the oil infuse at room temperature for 30 minutes before using. Use immediately.

Serving Suggestions
Brush sparingly on vegetables to be roasted, broiled, or grilled. This very handy oil can also be used for meat and fish, or as a quick salad dressing.

Lime-Chili Oil

MAKES ½ CUP (125ML)

1 strip of lime zest
½ cup (125ml) olive oil
1 fresh hot chili pepper, such as serrano
3 to 4 basil leaves
1 teaspoon mixed peppercorns

Combine all the ingredients in a bowl and stir them together. Let the oil infuse at room temperature for 30 minutes before using. Use immediately.

Above: fresh herb sprigs, chili, and garlic are marinated in peanut oil to give an Aromatic Oil for basting roasted and grilled fresh vegetables.

Variation: For a subtle Thai flavor, add a stem of lemon grass, lightly crushed with a rolling pin. Crush the peppercorns, too.

Serving Suggestions
You will find this zesty mixture a very good basting oil for fresh seafood, especially grilled steaks of meaty fish such as salmon, swordfish, or tuna.

Simple Soy Baste

FOR 2 TO 6 SERVINGS

2 tablespoons soy sauce
2 tablespoons (25g) unsalted butter, melted

Mix together the soy sauce and melted unsalted butter. Brush on the food before grilling or broiling.

Serving Suggestions
What treatment could be simpler for meat, fish, and vegetables?

Tikka Marinade

FOR 4 SERVINGS OF MEAT OR POULTRY

3 cloves garlic, chopped
1 medium red onion, chopped
juice of 1 lemon
3 tablespoons plain whole-milk yogurt
½-inch (1-cm) piece fresh ginger, minced
1 heaping tablespoon blanched almonds
1 teaspoon ground coriander
½ teaspoon ground cumin
½ teaspoon garam masala
½ teaspoon sea salt

Place all the ingredients for the marinade in the bowl of a food processor and process to make a thick, almost smooth paste, scraping down the side of the bowl frequently. Pour the marinade over your choice of meat and mix thoroughly. Cover and let marinate for 30 minutes at room temperature, or for up to 12 hours in the refrigerator.

Variation: For a hotter effect, replace the garam masala with cayenne pepper.

Serving Suggestions
My preference is to use chicken thighs for grilling, as they stay moist and juicy during cooking, and they have the best flavor. Boneless chicken breasts, turkey, or leg of

lamb can also be used. Cut the meat into large cubes before marinating. When ready to cook, loosely thread the cubes of meat onto metal skewers—if the pieces are pushed too tightly together they will not cook evenly. Grill or broil until cooked through, turning the skewers frequently. Serve the meat hot or cold, with warm naan or pita bread and a tossed salad.

Red Spicy Marinade

By adjusting the amount of hot red pepper sauce, this marinade for grilled and roasted meat can be mildly flavored or hot and fiery.

FOR 4 SERVINGS OF MEAT OR POULTRY

juice of 1 lemon
1 tablespoon sweet paprika
1 tablespoon ground coriander
1 tablespoon olive oil
¼ teaspoon garam masala
4 drops hot red pepper sauce, or more to taste
3 cloves garlic, minced
¼ teaspoon freshly ground black pepper
¼ teaspoon sea salt

Mix all the ingredients to make a thick paste, then smear it all over the meat, into each and every crevice. Cover tightly and let marinate, on a non-metal plate, at room temperature for 30 minutes, or in the refrigerator for up to 12 hours.

Variation: Dot with butter before cooking for a richer taste.

Serving Suggestions
Use this for boneless chicken thighs, with the skin left on (the dark meat remains moist when grilled). You could also use meaty pork sirloin chops. Grill or broil the marinated pieces of chicken or pork. Alternatively, cook in a greased baking dish in a hot oven, basting occasionally with the marinade.

Apricot Marinade with Yogurt Sauce

The idea for this unusual recipe comes from South Africa, where the spicy flavors are a favorite with barbecued meats.

FOR 4 SERVINGS OF MEAT OR POULTRY

1 tablespoon olive oil
1 small onion, chopped
2 bay leaves
2 cloves garlic, minced
⅓ cup (100g) apricot jam
juice of 1 lemon
¼ cup (60ml) dry sherry
2 tablespoons brown sugar
1 teaspoon dried chili pepper flakes
½ teaspoon ground cinnamon
½ teaspoon ground coriander
½ teaspoon ground cumin
½ teaspoon turmeric
FOR THE SAUCE:
4 slices bacon
⅓ cup (75ml) thick strained plain yogurt

Heat the oil in a skillet, add the onion and bay leaves, and cook over low heat, stirring frequently, for 5 minutes. Add the garlic to the skillet and continue cooking gently for 5 minutes or until the onion is softened but not browned.

Add the jam, lemon juice, sherry, sugar, and spices to the skillet. Bring to a boil and simmer for 5 minutes, stirring occasionally. Transfer the mixture to a large bowl and let it cool before adding your choice of meat. Let marinate for 30 minutes at room temperature, or cover and marinate for up to 24 hours in the refrigerator.

Meanwhile, broil or fry the bacon until very crisp, then drain and cool. Crumble the bacon into a small bowl and set it aside.

When ready to cook the meat, remove it from the marinade, allowing the excess to drip back into the bowl. Transfer the marinade to a small saucepan. Bring it to a

Marinade and Baste

boil and simmer for 2 to 3 minutes or until thick. Remove from the heat and stir in the yogurt and bacon. Serve with the meat.

Serving Suggestions
This marinade is suitable for chicken, lamb, or pork to be broiled or grilled. Marinate them as whole portions or, to make kebabs, cut into cubes before marinating.

Tomato and Onion Baste

FOR 6 TO 8 SERVINGS OF MEAT OR POULTRY

¼ cup (60ml) ketchup
⅓ cup (50g) minced onion
2 tablespoons Worcestershire sauce
2 tablespoons cider vinegar
½ teaspoon English mustard powder
3 to 4 drops hot red pepper sauce, or to taste

In a medium bowl, stir all the ingredients together. Let the mixture stand at room temperature for 30 minutes before use.

The sauce can be kept, covered, in the refrigerator for up to 3 weeks.

Serving Suggestions
Use as a baste for chicken, lamb, and pork.

Five-Spice Marinade

FOR 4 SERVINGS OF MEAT OR POULTRY

2 tablespoons rice wine
2 tablespoons honey
2 tablespoons soy sauce
1 tablespoon five-spice powder
1 teaspoon Asian sesame oil
2 cloves garlic, minced
¾-inch (2-cm) piece fresh ginger, minced

Combine all the ingredients in a large bowl, then add your choice of meat or poultry and turn until thoroughly coated in the mixture. Cover and let marinate at room temperature for 30 minutes, or cover and marinate in the refrigerator for up to 6 hours.

When you are ready to cook the meat, remove it from the marinade, allowing any excess to drip back into the bowl. Bring the leftover marinade to a boil in a small saucepan, then brush the hot marinade onto the meat as it cooks.

Serving Suggestions
I particularly like this marinade with pork country-style ribs, which are large, meaty, and nicely veined with fat. This recipe can also be used for skinless chicken breasts, steaks, and kebabs. The meat can be cooked over charcoal, under the broiler, or on a ridged cast-iron grill pan.

Left: brushing the hot Five-Spice Marinade onto country-style ribs during cooking will give a tasty coating to the meat and keep it moist.

Marinade and Baste

Spicy Lemon Marinade

This marinade works well with both lamb and chicken to be roasted, giving a crisp, fragrantly spicy exterior while helping to keep the meat moist during cooking.

FOR 1 ROAST OF MEAT OR WHOLE CHICKEN

1 lemon
1 tablespoon olive oil
1½ teaspoons salt
½ teaspoon freshly ground black pepper
½ teaspoon ground cumin
½ teaspoon garam masala

Grate the zest from the lemon and then squeeze the juice. Put them in a small bowl and stir in the other ingredients.

Below: roast chicken is enhanced with the flavors of lemon, oil, and Indian spices by marinating and then basting with Spicy Lemon Marinade.

Brush the marinade over a leg or shoulder of lamb, or a whole chicken, then leave for 30 minutes at room temperature, or up to 2 hours in the refrigerator, before roasting. The marinade can also be used to baste the meat during cooking: bring it to a boil first.

Saffron Marinade

Saffron works particularly well with fish.

FOR 4 SERVINGS OF FISH

½ teaspoon saffron threads
¼ cup (60ml) boiling water
¼ cup (60ml) dry white wine
¼ cup (60ml) olive oil
sea salt and black pepper

Crumble the saffron into a small heatproof bowl and pour the boiling water over. Cover

and let soak for 10 minutes (or overnight, if possible). Add the wine, oil, and seasonings and mix well. Brush this marinade over both sides of fish fillets until they are evenly coated. Keep any leftover marinade to baste the fish halfway through baking.

Let the fish marinate for 20 minutes at room temperature (unless the weather is hot), or up to 12 hours in the refrigerator, well covered, then bake in a hot oven until the fish is opaque.

Serving Suggestions
Almost any fish fillets can be used with this marinade: thick skinless cod or haddock, flounder, lemon sole, chunky pieces of monkfish, snapper, or halibut. Serve the fish with small potatoes baked in an earthenware pot with unpeeled garlic cloves, whole shallots, and sprigs of thyme.

Lime Marinade

This is a sweet citrus-flavored marinade for chicken or fish.

FOR 4 SERVINGS OF CHICKEN OR FISH

grated zest and juice of 2 large limes
½ teaspoon sea salt, or to taste
freshly ground black pepper
4 teaspoons light brown sugar (preferably raw Demerara or Turbinado sugar)
4 teaspoons olive oil

Mix all the ingredients together in a non-metal shallow dish. Add the chicken or fish and coat it thoroughly with the mixture. Cover and let marinate for 10 to 20 minutes at room temperature, or cover and marinate for up to 12 hours in the refrigerator.

When ready to cook, lift the chicken or fish out of the marinade and broil, or grill over hot coals. Use the leftover marinade to baste the chicken or fish halfway through the cooking time.

Marinade and Baste

Variation: Add 1 teaspoon minced cilantro to the marinade.

Serving Suggestions
This is excellent for thick steaks of fresh tuna, as well as salmon, halibut, and cod, or skinned and boned chicken pieces.

Rosemary Marinade

This robust marinade doubles as a simple sauce. Use freshly squeezed fruit juices, pungent fresh rosemary, and a good white wine for the best result.

FOR 4 SERVINGS OF FISH

1 small red onion, minced
½ cup (125ml) lemon juice
½ cup (125ml) orange juice
½ cup (125ml) dry white wine
¼ cup (60ml) soy sauce
1 heaping tablespoon minced rosemary
1 large clove garlic, minced
1 strip lemon zest
¼ teaspoon coarsely ground black pepper

Put all the ingredients into a non-aluminum saucepan and slowly bring to a boil. Remove the pan from the heat and let the mixture cool completely before use.

When ready, pour the cooled marinade over fish steaks and turn them in the mixture until thoroughly coated. Cover the dish and let marinate for 30 minutes. If you wish to leave the fish in the marinade for longer, you can refrigerate it for up to 4 hours.

To make a sauce from the marinade, return it to the saucepan and boil rapidly until it has reduced to a syrupy sauce. Keep the sauce warm until needed, then serve it alongside the fish.

Serving Suggestions
This marinade works best with firm-fleshed, well-flavored steaks of fish such as halibut,

salmon, shark, swordfish, or tuna, but it is also excellent with small whole fish like sardines and mackerel (slash them several times on each side before marinating). You may need to brush the fish, broiler pan, or grill with oil before cooking to prevent the fish from sticking.

Herb Marinade

This is an excellent French-style marinade for beef, featuring chopped fresh green herbs, red wine vinegar, and garlic.

FOR 4 STEAKS

6 tablespoons olive oil
6 tablespoons red wine vinegar
¼ cup (15g) minced mixed herbs, such as basil, oregano, parsley, and thyme
4 large cloves garlic, minced
freshly ground black pepper

Above: Rosemary Marinade is used to flavor kebabs made from tender cubes of fresh halibut. Once grilled, the kebabs are drizzled with a sauce made from the reduced marinade.

Combine all the ingredients in a shallow non-metal dish and stir well to mix. Add your choice of meat and turn to coat it thoroughly in the marinade. Cover the dish and let the meat marinate for up to 30 minutes at room temperature, or, preferably, up to 2 days in the refrigerator.

When ready to cook, remove the meat from the marinade, reserving any liquid left in the dish to use as a baste halfway through the cooking.

Serving Suggestions
Use for steaks that are to be grilled, broiled, or panfried, or for beef to be roasted. For maximum flavor, let the meat marinate for as long as possible.

Summer Sauces

Warm weather food should take advantage of the wealth of gorgeous produce in the market—it is hard to resist snatching up the first bundle of asparagus, or tiny purple globe artichokes, or fava beans the size of a small fingernail. This is the time to make vibrant vegetables the focus of the meal, and relegate meat and fish to the sidelines.

Salad dressings and vinaigrettes should add flavor and moisture without overwhelming the principal ingredients of the dish. Choose a delicate dressing of extra virgin olive oil, white wine vinegar, and seasoning for mild, tender green leaves; cold cooked tiny leeks can support a more robust mixture including a little garlic and plenty of herbs. Crunchy, hearty leaves or potatoes benefit from a thicker, more intensely flavored dressing.

Dips and spreads, made ahead and then chilled, are ideal for outdoor eating and picnics. Add a bowl of colorful sliced vegetables, some really interesting breads, a couple of cheeses, perhaps a pâté, and you have lunch. For cooler evenings, when appetites are flagging, warm salads are a good compromise between a hot meal and a snack.

Left (from left to right): Tartar Sauce, Cottage Cheese and Walnut Dip, dressing for Crispy Duck Salad, Lemon Vinaigrette.

Basic Vinaigrette

This is the easiest, quickest dressing you can make, yet it really makes a salad come alive. Vinaigrette is infinitely variable, so you can add herbs, spices, and other flavorings to suit your meal. The usual proportions of vinaigrette are one part vinegar to three parts oil, but I find this to be too sharp, and prefer the mellower flavor that comes with using more oil.

MAKES ⅔ CUP (150ML)

½ cup (125ml) olive or vegetable oil
2 tablespoons vinegar
2 teaspoons Dijon mustard
salt and black pepper

Put all the ingredients into a jar with a tight-fitting lid, cover, and then shake well. Taste and adjust the flavor balance as needed: if the dressing is too oily, add a teaspoon more vinegar and a little extra seasoning; if it is too sharp, add another teaspoon or two of oil and a large pinch of salt.

The vinaigrette can be kept, covered, in the refrigerator for up to 1 week. Bring it back to room temperature and shake well before using.

Variation: For an herb vinaigrette, add 2 tablespoons minced herbs just before using the dressing.

Lime or Lemon Vinaigrette

A pinch of sugar enhances the citrus flavor.

MAKES ¾ CUP (175ML)

1 lime or lemon
½ teaspoon sugar
salt and black pepper
¼ cup (60ml) olive oil
¼ cup (60ml) sunflower oil

Finely grate the zest from the lime or lemon, then squeeze the juice from the fruit. Combine the grated zest with 2 tablespoons of the juice in a mixing bowl. Add the sugar and a little salt and pepper, then whisk in the two oils. Taste and add more seasoning and lime juice, if needed. The dressing should taste quite sharp.

Below: the sweet-sour flavor of a zesty citrus vinaigrette makes a lively dressing for Avocado, Papaya, and Watercress Salad.

Avocado, Papaya, and Watercress Salad

This salad is a real taste of the tropics, combining a tangy Lime Vinaigrette with the rich flavors of exotic papaya and avocado.

SERVES 4

1 large bunch watercress
2 avocados
2 papayas
Lime Vinaigrette (see left)

𝒱INAIGRETTE

Rinse the watercress and trim off the coarse stems. Halve, pit, and peel the avocados, then slice them crosswise. Halve the papayas and remove the black seeds. Peel the skin off with a sharp knife, and slice the flesh crosswise.

Arrange the slices of papaya and avocado and the sprigs of watercress on four plates or combine them gently in a bowl. Pour the dressing over the top and serve immediately.

Variation: Fresh, ripe mangoes can be substituted for the papayas.

Lime and Walnut Dressing

Walnuts are one of the most versatile nuts, suitable for a wide range of sweet and savory dishes; however, they do turn rancid quickly. You can keep walnuts at their best by storing them in the freezer.

MAKES ¾ CUP (175ML)

½ cup (50g) walnut pieces
1 lime
2 tablespoons walnut oil
2 tablespoons olive oil
1 teaspoon Dijon mustard
salt and black pepper

Finely chop the walnuts, and squeeze the juice from the lime. Place all the ingredients in a small bowl and whisk together until thoroughly combined. Season to taste with salt and black pepper.

Serving Suggestions
Toss this dressing with crisp green salad leaves and your choice of chicken or seafood. Fillets or pieces of grilled mackerel or lightly poached trout are a particularly good match with the walnuts and lime. For a slightly different flavor, try toasting the walnuts in a skillet before chopping them.

Lime Pickle Dressing

Choose your favorite brand of lime pickle (available in Indian markets) for this simple but unusual combination.

MAKES JUST UNDER ½ CUP (100ML)

1 tablespoon lime pickle
juice of ½ lime
¼ cup (60ml) olive oil
salt and black pepper

If the lime pickle is chunky, chop it finely. Place it in a small bowl and add the lime juice and olive oil. Whisk until thoroughly combined, then season to taste with salt and black pepper.

Serving Suggestions
An excellent accompaniment to roast duck, this dressing can also be served with poached or grilled chicken and turkey. It makes an interesting Indian-style salad when tossed with freshly grated carrot.

Lemon and Cumin Dressing

This unusual and richly flavored dressing takes inspiration from the cooking of Middle Eastern countries in its use of ground cumin and coriander, and lemon juice.

MAKES ½ CUP (125ML)

juice of 1 lemon
2 garlic cloves, minced
½ teaspoon ground cumin
½ teaspoon ground coriander
¼ cup (60ml) olive oil

Combine the lemon juice and minced garlic in a small bowl. Add the ground cumin and coriander and stir to make a paste. Gradually whisk in the olive oil until the mixture is smooth.

Serving Suggestions
Serve spooned over grilled or broiled shellfish such as shrimp and squid, or stirred into rice salads.

Poppyseed Dressing

MAKES JUST UNDER ½ CUP (100ML)

1 tablespoon lemon juice
1 teaspoon honey
⅓ cup (80ml) peanut oil
1 tablespoon poppyseeds
salt and black pepper

Stir the lemon juice into the honey. Add the oil, whisking to make a smooth, thickened vinaigrette. Stir in the poppyseeds, then taste and add salt and pepper as needed. If the taste of the poppyseeds is too strong, add a little more honey.

Serving Suggestions
Serve with a romaine salad and with well-flavored vegetables.

Orange and Sesame Dressing

MAKES GENEROUS ½ CUP (130ML)

¼ cup (60ml) peanut oil
3 tablespoons orange juice
2 tablespoons toasted sesame seeds
salt and black pepper

Put all the ingredients into a jar with a tight-fitting lid, cover, and shake well. Taste and adjust the seasonings as needed. Chill the dressing thoroughly before use.

Serving Suggestion
The fresh orange flavor of this dressing works particularly well with grated carrots.

COOKED SALAD DRESSING

Crispy Duck Salad

A really fast, well-flavored, and substantial warm salad that makes a main dish for two or a first course for four.

SERVES 2 TO 4

2 boneless duck breast halves, about ¾ pound (350g) total
1 tablespoon vegetable oil
1 small head romaine or iceberg lettuce
½ head radicchio
1 small bulb fennel, cut into thin wedges
1 small bunch watercress
FOR THE MARINADE AND DRESSING:
1 tablespoon soy sauce
2 tablespoons orange juice
1 teaspoon Asian sesame oil
½ teaspoon ground toasted Szechuan peppercorns

Wipe the duck breasts and prick the skin well with a fork. Mix together the soy sauce, orange juice, sesame oil, and Szechuan peppercorns in a shallow dish. Add the duck breasts and let marinate, uncovered, for 20 minutes at room temperature. Meanwhile, preheat the oven to 425°F.

Remove the duck from the marinade, reserving the liquid, and pat it dry with paper towels. In a skillet that can be used in the oven as well as on top of the stove, or in a small roasting pan, heat the vegetable oil. Put the duck breasts in the pan, skin-side down, and cook for 3 to 4 minutes or until browned. Turn the breasts over, then put the pan in the oven. Cook for 20 minutes or until the juices run clear when the meat is pierced with a skewer.

Meanwhile, separate the romaine and raddicchio leaves and put them into a large salad bowl with the fennel wedges and trimmed watercress.

When the duck is cooked, remove to a carving board and let rest for 5 minutes.

Put the roasting pan over medium heat and add the reserved marinade to the

cooking juices. Bring the mixture to a boil, scraping and stirring with a spoon to dissolve all the caramelized juices in the bottom of the pan. When the sauce is well blended, taste and add a little more orange juice as necessary—the dressing should be highly flavored.

Cut the duck breasts, on the diagonal, into thin slices and place them on top of the salad. Spoon the hot dressing over, toss the salad quickly, and serve immediately.

Variations: Change the mix of salad greens as you desire, including Belgian endive or Napa cabbage, if they are available.

Above: soy sauce, fresh orange juice, and the caramelized cooking juices of tender duck breasts make a warm dressing for Crispy Duck Salad.

Lemon-Chili Dressing

MAKES ⅔ CUP (150ML)

5 tablespoons olive oil
1 fresh hot red chili peppper, seeded and minced
1 shallot, minced
2 cloves garlic, minced
juice of 1 lemon
salt and black pepper

Cooked Salad Dressing

Heat the olive oil in a small, heavy saucepan, add the chili and shallot, and cook until soft, stirring occasionally. Add the garlic to the pan and cook gently without letting it burn.

Remove the pan from the heat and whisk in the lemon juice. Season to taste with salt and black pepper, and serve immediately.

Serving Suggestions
This dressing is delicious with a salad of freshly cooked shrimp. You could also stir it into cooked pasta or grilled mushrooms.

Lemon, Anchovy, and Cilantro Dressing

If your anchovies have been preserved in brine and not oil, rinse them in a little water or milk before using to remove some of the salty flavor, then pat dry.

MAKES ½ CUP (125ML)

¼ cup (60ml) extra virgin olive oil
4 to 5 anchovy fillets, drained
2 tablespoons minced cilantro
2 tablespoons lemon juice
black pepper

In a small, heavy saucepan, gently heat the olive oil. Chop the anchovies to a thick paste, then add to the oil and cook over very low heat, stirring frequently, for about 10 minutes or until thick and saucelike.

Let the anchovy mixture cool slightly, then stir in the cilantro and lemon juice. Taste and season as necessary with plenty of black pepper. The dressing can be stored in a jar in the refrigerator for up to 4 days.

Serving Suggestions
Serve with robust green vegetables such as artichokes, green beans, or broccoli. A good combination is green beans, new potatoes, and strips of red sweet peppers tossed in the dressing.

Sauce Vierge

SERVES 6

3 tablespoons olive oil
2 tablespoons water
1 tablespoon sherry vinegar
1 clove garlic
8 coriander seeds, crushed
1½ cups (225g) tomatoes, peeled, seeded, and diced
2 tablespoons minced chervil
1 tablespoon minced parsley
1 tablespoon minced tarragon
salt and black pepper

Place the olive oil, water, vinegar, garlic, and coriander seeds in a small saucepan and heat gently for 5 minutes so the flavors can infuse. Strain the mixture and discard the flavorings. Add the tomato and all the herbs, then season with salt and pepper.

Serving Suggestions
Serve with poached or grilled fish or chicken, or with ham, salads, or soft cheese.

Caesar Salad

For this classic salad, the ingredients for the dressing are added separately to the romaine leaves and then tossed together.

SERVES 4 TO 6

1 large head romaine
4 large cloves garlic, sliced
¼ cup (60ml) extra virgin olive oil
3 thick slices white bread, crusts removed
5 tablespoons olive oil or vegetable oil
7 anchovy fillets, drained
3 tablespoons milk
1 extra large egg (see caution about eggs on page 11)
juice of 1 large lemon
½ cup (60g) freshly grated Parmesan cheese
black pepper

Put the washed and dried romaine leaves into a large plastic bag and chill for at least 2 hours to crisp the leaves.

Place 2 of the sliced garlic cloves in a small bowl with the extra virgin olive oil. Cover and let infuse for 2 hours.

Dice the bread. Heat the remaining garlic very gently with the olive or vegetable oil in a skillet. Discard the garlic when it is golden brown, then raise the heat. Add the diced bread and fry until crisp and golden. Drain the croutons on paper towels.

Meanwhile, soak the anchovy fillets in the milk for about 15 minutes. Drain and mince.

When ready to serve, tear up the romaine and place it in a large salad bowl. Discard the garlic from the extra virgin oil, then pour the oil over the lettuce. Toss gently. Put the egg into a pan of boiling water and cook it for 1 minute, then break the egg into the salad bowl. Toss the salad. Pour the lemon juice over and toss again, then add the anchovies and Parmesan and toss well. Add pepper to taste and scatter on the croutons.

Serving Suggestions
Serve this as a main course salad, with added grilled chicken or shrimp, if desired, or as a first course.

Adding the egg: break it directly onto the Caesar Salad, then toss until it coats the leaves, forming the basis of the thick, creamy dressing.

Green Mayonnaise

MAKES 1½ CUPS (350ML)

1½ cups (150g) young spinach leaves
1 cup (250ml) Mayonnaise (see page 19)
3 tablespoons crème fraîche
1 clove garlic, or to taste, minced
salt and black pepper
freshly grated nutmeg

Cook the spinach with 2 to 3 tablespoons of water for 2 minutes or until floppy. Drain thoroughly, then squeeze out as much water as possible. Chop the spinach finely, then let it cool completely.

Combine the spinach with the mayonnaise, crème fraîche, and garlic in a bowl and stir to mix. Or, for a really smooth and bright-colored dressing, blend the ingredients together in a food processor. Taste and add salt, pepper, and nutmeg as needed.

Variation: *Green Goddess Dressing*
Add 1 teaspoon minced anchovy fillets and another clove of garlic to the mixture. Serve with avocados, cold cooked vegetables, and chilled cooked seafood.

Serving Suggestions
To make a delicious potato salad, toss the Green Mayonnaise with 1½ pounds (750g) boiled new potatoes, halved or quartered and let cool. Cover and chill the salad for 2 hours before serving.

Watercress Mayonnaise

MAKES 1 CUP (250ML)

1 bunch watercress
1 cup (250ml) Mayonnaise (see page 19)

Twist and remove the leaves from the bunch of watercress; discard the watercress stems. Mince the watercress leaves and stir them into the mayonnaise.

Variations: For a lower fat dressing, replace some or all of the mayonnaise with skim-milk ricotta cheese or Quark cheese. The watercress can be replaced with a large bunch of cilantro (the stems, leaves, and white roots can all be minced). Add the grated zest and juice of 1 small lime for a really tangy mayonnaise.

Serving Suggestions
Serve with cold poached salmon and other seafood.

Creamy Salad Dressing

MAKES 1 CUP (250ML)

½ cup (125ml) Mayonnaise (see page 19)
7 tablespoons (100ml) whole milk
3 tablespoons snipped chives
2 to 3 drops hot red pepper sauce
white wine vinegar, to taste
salt and black pepper

Place the mayonnaise in a bowl and whisk in the milk until the mixture is the consistency of light cream. Whisk the chives and the hot red pepper sauce into the mixture. Add a little vinegar to taste, then season.

Use the dressing immediately or store it, covered, in the refrigerator for up to 4 days.

Serving Suggestions
This dressing goes best with robust salad greens such as romaine and spinach.

Chantilly Mayonnaise

MAKES 1 CUP (250ML)

⅓ cup (80ml) heavy cream, chilled and
** whipped, or ⅓ cup (80ml) crème fraîche,**
** well chilled**
1 cup (250ml) Mayonnaise (see page 19)
salt and black pepper

Fold the cream into the mayonnaise, then taste and adjust the seasoning as needed. Use immediately for the best texture.

Serving Suggestions
The version with whipped cream makes a light, mild dressing for delicate vegetables such as asparagus. Using crème fraîche gives a heavier dressing for cold shellfish.

Thousand Island Dressing

MAKES 1¼ CUPS (300ML)

1 tablespoon sun-dried tomato paste
1 cup (250ml) Mayonnaise (see page 19), not
** highly seasoned**
1 extra large egg, hard-cooked and chopped
3 heaping tablespoons green olives, chopped
1 tablespoon snipped chives
1 tablespoon lemon juice
black pepper

Stir the tomato paste into the mayonnaise. When combined, stir in the other ingredients. Taste and add more pepper or lemon juice as needed. Serve the dressing immediately, or cover and store in the refrigerator for up to 1 day. Stir well before using.

Serving Suggestions
Serve with crunchy salads and seafood.

Aïoli

This rich garlic mayonnaise is not for the faint of heart. Be sure to use fresh garlic.

MAKES 1¼ CUPS (300ML)

1 cup (250ml) Mayonnaise (see page 19), made
** with a high proportion of olive oil**
1 tablespoon minced garlic

Mayonnaise Dressing

¼ teaspoon sea salt
freshly ground black pepper

Chill the mayonnaise well. Pound the garlic with the salt until smooth using a mortar and pestle. Stir into the mayonnaise. Add black pepper to taste. Use immediately or cover very tightly and keep in the refrigerator for up to 24 hours.

Variation: Peel and roughly chop 1 whole head of garlic. Put it into a food processor with ¼ teaspoon sea salt, a little black pepper, and 1 extra large egg yolk (see caution about eggs on page 11). Process to a purée. Gradually pour in 1 cup (250ml) olive oil in a thin stream. Add the juice of 1 large lemon, then taste and adjust the seasonings as needed.

Serving Suggestions
Serve with fish soup, such as *bourride*, hard-cooked eggs, and cooked or raw vegetables.

Tartar Sauce

MAKES 1¼ CUPS (300ML)

1 cup (250ml) Mayonnaise (see page 19)
1 hard-cooked egg, minced
1 tablespoon capers, minced
1 tablespoon minced cornichon
1 tablespoon minced parsley
1 teaspoon minced tarragon
salt and black pepper

Combine all the ingredients in a bowl and stir to mix. Season. Chill for up to 12 hours.

Left: for Coronation Chicken, fresh red chili, green onions, garlic, and cilantro enhance a cold curried sauce for pieces of poached chicken.

Serving Suggestions
Tartar sauce is the classic accompaniment for breaded deep-fried fish and seafood such as calamari (squid) and shrimp.

Coronation Chicken

This delicous cold chicken salad was invented in London in 1953 for a luncheon celebrating the coronation of Queen Elizabeth II. The sauce uses homemade mayonnaise and fresh herbs and spices to give a lively fresh taste and appearance.

SERVES 4 TO 6

1 3½-pound (1.5-kg) chicken, or 4 chicken
  pieces, poached
FOR THE SAUCE:
1 cup (250ml) Mayonnaise (see page 19)
1 large fresh mild red chili pepper, cored,
  seeded, and minced
1 green onion, minced
1 small clove garlic, minced
2 teaspoons lime juice, or to taste
2 teaspoons minced cilantro
large pinch cayenne pepper
1 to 2 tablespoons crème fraîche, to taste

Remove the skin and bones from the chicken, keeping the meat in large pieces wherever possible. Cover and refrigerate until ready to use.

Mix together all the sauce ingredients, then taste and add more lime juice if needed. If the sauce is too strong, add a little more crème fraîche. Cover and chill until needed.

Just before serving, combine the chicken and sauce in a bowl. Store leftovers, covered, in the refrigerator for up to 1 day.

Mayonnaise and Puréed Dressings

Mustard-Dill Dressing

MAKES ½ CUP (125ML)

1 extra large egg yolk (see caution about eggs on page 11)
2 tablespoons mild German or American mustard
1 teaspoon sugar
¼ teaspoon sea salt
black pepper
2 tablespoons vegetable oil
2 tablespoons white wine vinegar
1 tablespoon minced dill

Mix the egg yolk and mustard together in a small bowl, then stir in the sugar, salt, and a little pepper. Gradually stir in the oil, as for mayonnaise, then the vinegar and dill.

Taste the dressing: you may need to add more vinegar, sugar, or pepper to suit your palate. Store, tightly covered, in the refrigerator for up to 24 hours.

Serving Suggestions
This dressing is usually served with thinly sliced gravlax, but it is also good with smoked salmon or used to dress a salad of cold cooked fresh salmon.

Rouille

A rust-colored mayonnaise flavored with hot red chili peppers, rouille is traditionally made using a mortar and pestle, but a food processor will save your weary arm muscles.

MAKES ABOUT ½ CUP (125ML)

5 large cloves garlic, minced
¼ teaspoon sea salt
½ to 1 fresh hot red chili pepper, such as serrano, cored, seeded, and minced
2 extra large egg yolks (see caution about eggs on page 11)
½ cup (125ml) olive oil
1 teaspoon sun-dried tomato paste
black pepper

Put the garlic, salt, and chili in the mortar and crush them to a smooth paste. Mix in the egg yolks, then slowly and gradually work in the olive oil to make a thick sauce. Stir in the tomato paste and a little pepper. Taste and adjust the seasoning as necessary. Serve, or cover tightly and chill for up to 24 hours. Stir well before using.

To make rouille in a food processor, put the garlic, salt, chili, and egg yolks in the bowl of the processor and purée until smooth, scraping down the side from time to time. With the machine running, pour the oil through the opening in the lid in a slow, steady stream. Add the tomato paste and seasoning to taste.

Serving Suggestions
Rouille is commonly served with French *bouillabaisse* and other fish soups.

Guacamole

This avocado sauce, or dip, from Mexico should be thick and full of flavor. Try to use fully ripe, black-skinned Hass avocados.

SERVES 4 TO 6

1 clove garlic, minced
1 small shallot or green onion, minced
½ fresh hot green chili pepper, such as jalapeño, seeded and minced
1 small bunch cilantro, chopped
sea salt and black pepper
2 large ripe avocados, halved
juice of 1 lime
2 medium tomatoes, peeled, seeded, and diced
few drops hot red pepper sauce

Put the garlic, shallot, chili, cilantro, and a pinch of salt in a mortar and crush them to a rough paste. Scoop the flesh from the avocados and add it to the mortar with the lime juice. Work the avocados into the chili paste until roughly crushed.

Stir in the diced tomatoes, then taste and add red pepper sauce, salt, and pepper as needed. Serve, or cover tightly and chill for up to 4 hours. The surface will have turned slightly brown, so stir well before serving.

Serving Suggestions
Use as a sauce with grilled fish or poultry, as part of a fajita platter, or as a dip with raw vegetables and tortilla chips.

Gazpacho Dressing

MAKES ABOUT 1 CUP (250ML)

1 medium red sweet pepper
2 medium tomatoes, peeled and seeded
3-inch (7.5-cm) piece English cucumber, thickly sliced
1 large green onion, thickly sliced
1 to 2 cloves garlic, or to taste, roughly chopped
¼ cup (60ml) olive oil
1 tablespoon red wine vinegar
sea salt and black pepper

Preheat the broiler. Broil the sweet pepper until the skin blackens, turning to char all sides. Cool, then peel and discard the core and seeds. Chop the flesh roughly.

Put the flesh into a food processor or blender with the tomatoes, cucumber, green onion, and garlic and process until smooth. With the motor running, slowly pour in the oil, then add the vinegar. Taste the dressing and adjust the seasoning as needed. Press through a coarse strainer, then cover and chill thoroughly. If the dressing becomes too thick on chilling, stir in an ice cube. It can be kept for up to 1 day in the refrigerator. Stir before serving.

Serving Suggestions
Best icy cold with warm poached salmon or sea trout or with a hot chicken salad. This dressing is also excellent with grilled vegetables and cold rice salads.

Puréed Dressing

Cilantro and Lime Dressing

MAKES ⅔ CUP (150ML)

½ cup (125ml) olive oil
2½ to 3 tablespoons lime juice
2 small green onions, roughly chopped
1 small bunch cilantro
salt and black pepper

Put all the ingredients into a food processor or blender and process until finely chopped. Taste and adjust the seasoning as needed.

The finished dressing can be stored, tightly covered, in the refrigerator for up to 8 hours. Let it come back to room temperature and stir well before using.

Serving Suggestions
This is a sharp, tangy dressing, so serve it with grilled oily fish, especially mackerel and trout, or with chicken. You can also whisk it into the pan juices at the end of cooking. Alternatively, use it to dress a crunchy salad.

Salsa Verde

SERVES 4 TO 6

½ cup (25g) fresh white bread crumbs
1 tablespoon red wine vinegar
1 cup (40g) parsley
⅓ cup (15g) tarragon
1 clove garlic
3 anchovy fillets
⅔ cup (150ml) olive oil
salt and black pepper

Put the bread crumbs into the bowl of a food processor or blender and moisten them with the vinegar. Let the bread crumbs stand while you prepare the other ingredients.

Pluck the parsley and tarragon leaves from their stems, and roughly chop the garlic and anchovies. Add them all to the bowl. Process the mixture just until it is finely chopped. With the machine still running, add the oil in a thin, steady stream.

Taste and season as necessary. Do not overwork the mixture or it will become gluey. Serve the sauce at room temperature. It can be stored, tightly covered, in the refrigerator for up to 24 hours. Stir well before using.

Variation: For a thin, smooth herb dressing, omit the anchovies and bread crumbs.

Serving Suggestions
In Italy, Salsa Verde is made to accompany *bollito misto*, a selection of boiled meats such as beef, chicken, sausage, and veal plus boiled carrots and potatoes. In the south of the country, basil is added and the sauce is tossed with pasta. Salsa Verde is delicious with baked ham and ham terrines.

Below: anchovies and red wine vinegar add pungency to Italy's "green sauce," Salsa Verde.

𝒴OGURT 𝒟RESSING

Mango, Chili, and Yogurt Dressing

MAKES 1 CUP (250ML)

1 medium mango, peeled and chopped
½ cup (125ml) thick plain yogurt
1 teaspoon whole-grain mustard
1 small bunch chives
1 tablespoon minced fresh mild red chili pepper
black pepper

Purée the mango, yogurt, and mustard in a food processor or with a hand-held immersion blender. Snip in the chives and stir in the chili and black pepper to taste. Serve at room temperature or chilled.

Serving Suggestions
Dollop this thick, creamy mixture onto salmon salads, serve it as an unusual cold sauce for asparagus, or use in potato salad.

Yogurt Salad Dressing

When it comes to plain yogurt, most people have a definite preference for one type or another. Choose your favorite for this well-flavored dressing—it does not matter if you use a fat-free yogurt or the whole-milk type. After all, it's your salad.

MAKES ABOUT 1 CUP (250ML)

⅔ cup (150ml) plain yogurt
1 clove garlic, minced
1 bunch watercress
1 tablespoon olive oil
salt and black pepper
few drops hot red pepper sauce

Put the yogurt and garlic into the bowl of a food processor. Hold the bunch of watercress in your hand, like a bunch of flowers, then twist off the leaves. Add them to the bowl with the oil, a little salt, and several twists of black pepper from the mill.

Above: watercress adds its peppery flavor and attractive green color to Yogurt Salad Dressing. Here it is drizzled over lightly steamed then cooled new potatoes to make a hearty salad.

Process until the dressing is fairly smooth. Taste and adjust the seasoning, adding a few drops of hot pepper sauce. Cover the dressing and chill until ready to use. It can be kept in the refrigerator for up to 24 hours. Stir well before using.

Variations: Reduce the quantity of yogurt to ½ cup (125ml) to make a dip. If you like, crème fraîche can be used instead of yogurt.

Serving Suggestions
This is not a dressing for delicate leaves, but is good on crisp, crunchy salads made from romaine and iceberg lettuce. You can use it on sliced ripe tomatoes or as a dressing for potato salad. It is also good with salmon.

Roasted Eggplant and Yogurt Dressing

MAKES 1 CUP (250ML)

1 medium eggplant
½ cup (125ml) thick plain yogurt
1 clove garlic, minced
2 to 3 tablespoons minced parsley
salt and black pepper

Roast the eggplant until the skin is charred, preferably over charcoal, otherwise in a very hot oven. Allow to cool slightly, then peel and discard the skin. Put the eggplant flesh into a food processor with the remaining ingredients and process until smooth. Adjust the seasoning. Serve at room temperature.

Serving Suggestions
Serve with grilled or broiled chicken or use as a dip for flat breads and crudités.

BUTTERMILK AND CHEESE DRESSINGS

Buttermilk Dressing

Buttermilk makes a lovely creamy salad dressing (and good pancakes, too).

MAKES 1¼ CUPS (300ML)

1 cup (250ml) buttermilk, or ¼ cup (60ml) crème fraîche mixed with ¾ cup (175ml) milk
1 tablespoon cider vinegar, sherry vinegar, or wine vinegar
1 clove garlic, minced
1 tablespoon minced fresh mild red chili pepper
¼ cup minced herbs such as basil, cilantro, oregano, and parsley
salt and black pepper

In a small bowl, stir the buttermilk or the mixture of crème fraîche and milk with the remaining ingredients. Taste and season as necessary with salt and black pepper. Chill for 30 minutes before serving.

Serving Suggestions
This thick dressing is good for crunchy salad greens tossed with cooked fresh or canned fish such as salmon and tuna. It can also be used in hearty salads featuring black beans, kidney beans, chicken, or tomatoes.

Blue Cheese Dressing

This thick, creamy, gray-blue dressing is usually made with Roquefort cheese, but you can substitute any other blue cheese. The crumbled cheese is mixed with a vinaigrette made with a light vegetable oil. Honey mustard softens and mellows the flavor.

MAKES ¾ CUP (175ML)

½ cup (75g) crumbled Roquefort cheese
¼ cup (60ml) vegetable oil
1 tablespoon white wine vinegar
1 to 2 teaspoons honey mustard
black pepper

Put the cheese into a small bowl and whisk in the other ingredients to make a creamy dressing—it need not be entirely smooth. Taste and add plenty of black pepper: you will not need to add salt if the cheese is very tangy. Use immediately or keep, tightly covered, in the refrigerator for up to 24 hours. Stir well before using.

Serving Suggestions
Pour over robust salad greens, or use as a dressing for pasta salads or small pieces of cold poached chicken.

Below: Roquefort, white wine vinegar, and sweet honey-flavored mustard are combined to make a rich, creamy Blue Cheese Dressing.

White Bean and Rosemary Dip

SERVES 6 TO 8

1½ cups (250g) dried white beans
1 large sprig rosemary, plus 1½ tablespoons
    minced rosemary leaves
1 onion, peeled but left whole
7 tablespoons extra virgin olive oil
4 cloves garlic, or to taste, minced
juice of 1 lemon, or to taste
salt and coarsely ground black pepper

Soak the beans overnight in enough cold water to cover them. Drain the beans and rinse them thoroughly.

In a large saucepan, cover the beans well with fresh cold water. Bring to a boil, skimming off the scum, then boil the beans rapidly for 10 minutes. Add the large sprig of rosemary and the onion. Cover and simmer for 45 minutes or until the beans are very tender. Drain the beans, reserving the cooking liquid. Discard the rosemary sprig and onion.

In a medium-size saucepan, gently warm 5 tablespoons of the olive oil with the garlic and 1 tablespoon of the minced rosemary leaves. Add the drained white beans and cook them, stirring frequently, over low heat for about 5 minutes.

Mash the cooked bean mixture to a rough paste using a potato masher. Stir in lemon juice to taste, then season with salt and pepper. Beat in just enough of the reserved cooking liquid to make a thick dip.

Drizzle the remaining 2 tablespoons of olive oil over the dip and garnish with the remaining minced rosemary before serving.

The dip can be cooled and then stored, covered, for up to 3 days in the refrigerator.

Variation: Replace the minced rosemary with a generous spoonful of basil pesto and, if you like, add some finely chopped roasted eggplant or black olives to the mixture.

Serving Suggestions
Offer this as an informal first course with fresh or roasted vegetables and slices of warmed or toasted Italian bread such as foccacia or ciabatta, flavored with herbs or olives if you like. When cold, the bean mixture can be used in sandwiches or stuffed into pita bread with some green salad to make a healthful lunch.

Above: White Bean and Rosemary Dip, served here with olive-flavored bread, is garnished with a drizzle of extra virgin olive oil, black pepper, and some minced fresh rosemary.

Goat Cheese Dip

Choose a creamy goat cheese, as mild or strongly flavored as you like.

SERVES 4

4 ounces (125g) soft goat cheese
juice of ½ lemon
2 tablespoons extra virgin olive oil
2 tablespoons minced herbs
salt and black pepper

Beat the cheese until creamy, then beat in all the remaining ingredients, adding plenty of pepper (salt may not be necessary if the cheese is salty). Taste and adjust the seasonings as necessary. Cover and chill for up to 4 hours before serving.

Variations: Replace the goat cheese with a creamy cows' milk cheese, such as Boursin Naturel, or ricotta for a low-fat choice. Add ¾ cup (100g) flaked smoked trout fillet (free of skin and bones) and include plenty of dill with the herbs. Process the mixture until it is smooth, then cover and chill for up to 4 hours before serving.

Serving Suggestions
Serve this quick summery dip with raw vegetables, bread sticks, slices of French bread, or chicken kebabs.

Cottage Cheese and Walnut Dip

SERVES 4 TO 6

¾ cup (175g) cottage cheese
1 tablespoon grated Parmesan cheese
2 tablespoons olive oil
1 green onion, chopped
2 tablespoons minced parsley
½ cup (50g) walnuts, chopped
salt and black pepper

Combine all the ingredients in a medium-size bowl and stir until thoroughly mixed. Taste and adjust the seasoning as necessary. If the mixture seems too thick, add a little water or milk.

Variations: Replace the parsley with basil and the cottage cheese with ricotta.

Serving Suggestions
Serve with toasted flat breads or crudités.

Hummus

Hummus made with freshly cooked dried chickpeas tastes far nicer than that made with canned chickpeas, although you do have to plan ahead—the chickpeas need to be soaked for 12 hours, then boiled until really tender. There are no short cuts in terms of time, but the recipe is extremely simple and you can flavor the hummus just as you like: my preference is to have plenty of lemon juice but only a touch of garlic.

SERVES 6 TO 8

½ cup (100g) dried chickpeas (garbanzo beans)
1 small onion, peeled but left whole
4 cloves garlic, or to taste
juice of 1 large lemon, or to taste
2 tablespoons tahini
2 to 3 tablespoons olive oil
salt and black pepper
1 sprig cilantro

Soak the chickpeas overnight in plenty of cold water. Next day, drain the chickpeas, rinse them with cold water, and put them into a medium-size saucepan with plenty of fresh cold water to cover. Do not add salt, as this will toughen the chickpeas.

Bring to a boil and boil rapidly for 10 minutes. Skim if necessary, then add the onion and 2 whole peeled cloves of garlic.

Simmer gently for 1¼ to 1½ hours or until the chickpeas are really tender, replenishing as necessary with hot water to keep the chickpeas well covered during cooking.

Drain the chickpeas, reserving the cooking liquid but discarding the onion and garlic. Tip the drained chickpeas into a food processor and add 1 or 2 cloves of garlic, the lemon juice, tahini, 1 tablespoon of olive oil, and 2 tablespoons of the reserved cooking liquid. Process the mixture until smooth. Taste and add salt and pepper, plus more lemon juice, garlic, and tahini as desired. The hummus should be the consistency of whipped cream; if it is too thick, add a little more of the reserved cooking liquid.

Tip the hummus into a serving bowl and smooth the surface. Spoon the remaining 1 or 2 tablespoons of olive oil over the top (this also prevents the dip from becoming crusty) and garnish with cilantro.

The hummus, minus the cilantro, can be stored, tightly covered, in the refrigerator for up to 2 days. Stir well before serving. The flavor is much improved if the hummus is made 12 to 24 hours in advance.

Variations: Add ½ teaspoon of ground coriander or cumin with the tahini. Or stir in 1 tablespoon of minced cilantro, or ½ fresh red (medium-hot or mild) chili pepper, cored, seeded, and minced, just before serving. For a slightly textured hummus, remove a heaping tablespoon of the cooked chickpeas before processing, chop them roughly by hand or mash with a fork, then stir them into the dip before serving.

Serving Suggestions
Serve as a dip with warm pita bread or with crunchy raw vegetables. Hummus makes a great sandwich spread, too, layered with chopped fresh dates and cilantro leaves. Alternatively, thin down the hummus with some more of the cooking liquid to make a runny dressing for cold cooked vegetables or raw vegetable salads.

CLASSIC SAUCES

These are the cook's showpieces. Here, experience and technique, attention to detail, and careful seasoning are the deciding factors between success and failure.

Feather-light butter sauces and the gloriously rich emulsions of egg yolk and melted butter are less difficult than you may think. With the freshest possible eggs and creamy, unsalted butter, a touch of lemon juice, and seasoning, you can have a sauce to make the heart, as well as a perfectly poached fish, sing.

The grandest restaurants take great pride in their glossy, refined, and reduced brown sauces. These are based on carefully made stock, strained or clarified, then reduced to produce a dark, well-flavored, slightly syrupy sauce. The trick is to avoid both a watery result and an over-concentrated, gelatinous finish. A sauce should, after all, enhance, and not overwhelm.

They may sound like a lot of trouble, but, once mastered, these sauces can turn a simple piece of grilled meat, poultry, or fish into an elegant dinner party dish.

Left (from left to right): Sauce Meurette, Sorrel Sauce, Saffron Hollandaise.

Parsley Sauce

The intense flavor of this sauce comes from the crushed parsley stems added to the milk infusion, as well as plenty of chopped leaves added just before serving. If possible, use really fresh organic parsley.

MAKES 2¼ CUPS (550ML)

2 cups (500ml) whole milk
1 onion, peeled and spiked with 2 whole cloves
½ teaspoon black peppercorns
1 bay leaf
1 cup (45g) parsley
2 tablespoons (25g) unsalted butter
3 tablespoons all-purpose flour
3 tablespoons heavy cream
salt and white pepper

Put the milk, onion, peppercorns, and bay leaf into a medium-sized saucepan. Pick the parsley leaves from the stems and reserve; crush the stems and add them to the milk. Heat the milk slowly until scalding hot but not boiling, then cover the pan, remove it from the heat, and let the milk infuse for 30 minutes to 1 hour. Meanwhile, mince the parsley leaves.

Strain the milk and discard the flavorings. Rinse out the pan and in it melt the butter. Stir in the flour and cook over low heat for 1 minute, stirring constantly. Remove the pan from the heat and gradually add the flavored milk, whisking constantly.

Set the pan over medium heat and whisk the mixture briskly until thick. Lower the heat so the sauce barely simmers, then let it cook gently for 20 minutes, stirring often. Whisk in the minced parsley and cream, then season the sauce to taste with salt and white pepper. Serve immediately.

Serving Suggestions
Delicious with poached or steamed white fish, such as cod, haddock, or flounder, and with steamed vegetables, such as Swiss chard, cauliflower, or summer squash.

Cheese Sauce

In this *Sauce Mornay*, cheese and egg yolk thicken the thin béchamel considerably.

MAKES 2¼ CUPS (550ML)

2 cups (500ml) Thin Béchamel Sauce (see page 21)
½ cup (60g) grated cheese, such as aged Cheddar, Emmental, or Gruyère
2 tablespoons heavy cream
1 extra large egg yolk
salt and black pepper

Bring the sauce to a boil, then remove it from the heat and stir in the grated cheese until it has melted completely. Mix the cream with the egg yolk, stir into the sauce, and season to taste. Do not bring the sauce back to a boil or the cheese may turn stringy and the egg may start to scramble.

Variation: When making macaroni and cheese, add 1 teaspoon of Dijon mustard to the sauce for a more robust flavor.

Serving Suggestions
Use in gratins, to coat steamed broccoli or cauliflower, or mixed with fish and hard-cooked eggs to make a fish pie.

Onion Sauce

MAKES 2¼ CUPS (550ML)

2 tablespoons (25g) unsalted butter
3 medium onions, thinly sliced
1 bay leaf
2 cups (500ml) Thick Béchamel Sauce (see page 21), kept warm
2 tablespoons crème fraîche or heavy cream
salt and black pepper

Heat the butter in a skillet, add the onions and bay leaf, and stir well. Press a circle of dampened parchment paper on top of the onions, then cover the pan with a lid and cook very gently for about 25 minutes, stirring occasionally, until the onions are meltingly soft but not browned.

Add the onions to the béchamel sauce and cook gently for 5 minutes, stirring constantly. Purée the sauce in a blender or food processor or push it through a fine-mesh strainer. Reheat the sauce. Stir in the crème fraîche, then adjust the seasoning.

Serving Suggestions
This sauce is good with pork chops and poached or steamed vegetables.

Mushroom Sauce

Small, white button mushrooms will give this sauce a delicate flavor and appearance. For a stronger taste and darker color, choose crimini or wild mushrooms.

MAKES 2¼ CUPS (550ML)

1 tablespoon (15g) butter
1 small shallot, minced
1 cup (75g) thinly sliced mushrooms
2 tablespoons water
squeeze lemon juice
2 cups (500ml) Medium Béchamel Sauce (see page 20), kept warm
2 tablespoons crème fraîche or heavy cream
salt and black pepper

Heat the butter in a heavy pan and cook the shallot very gently for a few minutes until softened. Add the mushrooms, water, and lemon juice and stir well. Cover the surface with a circle of dampened parchment paper, then the pan lid, and cook for 5 minutes or until the mushrooms are tender.

Stir the mushroom mixture and any cooking liquid into the béchamel sauce. Heat gently, stirring frequently, until the sauce is the correct consistency. Stir in the crème fraîche, then adjust the seasoning.

$\mathscr{B}$ÉCHAMEL $\mathscr{S}$AUCE

Variation: Add 1½ to 2 tablespoons minced herbs, such as parsley or tarragon, and a few drops of Worcestershire sauce. For even more flavor, add 1 tablespoon of dry white vermouth to the mushrooms as they cook.

Serving Suggestions
Serve with chicken, fish, and vegetables.

Sorrel Sauce

MAKES 2¼ CUPS (550ML)

1½ tablespoons (20g) unsalted butter
1½ cups (150g) young sorrel leaves, stems removed
1 cup (250ml) Medium Béchamel Sauce (see page 20), kept warm
3 tablespoons heavy cream
salt and black pepper
pinch grated nutmeg

Heat the butter in a non-aluminum pan, add the sorrel, and cook gently for 5 to 7 minutes, stirring frequently, until very soft. Drain well, then roughly chop the leaves.

Stir the sorrel into the sauce along with the cream and reheat gently. Simmer for 2 minutes, then taste and add salt, pepper, and nutmeg as needed. If the sauce is too sharp, whisk in an extra 1½ tablespoons (20g) of butter at the end.

Serving Suggestions
Serve with fish, such as salmon, trout, or cod, or spooned over vegetables.

Tomato Sauce

MAKES 2¼ CUPS (550ML)

½ cup (125ml) tomato purée
2 cups (500ml) Medium Béchamel Sauce (see page 20), kept warm
2 to 3 tablespoons heavy cream

Put the tomato purée in a small non-aluminum saucepan and boil vigorously until the volume has reduced to ¼ cup (60ml).

Whisk the reduced purée into the sauce, then reheat. Add the cream and simmer for 5 minutes. Taste and season as necessary.

Variation: For a well-flavored shrimp sauce add ½ teaspoon anchovy paste and 1 cup (125g) peeled cooked small shrimp to the sauce just before serving.

Serving Suggestions
This pale pink, creamy sauce is delicious with pasta, a variety of steamed vegetables, warm hard-cooked eggs, and poultry.

Below: fresh young beans and Italian bacon add color and texture to Fava Bean and Pancetta Sauce. Serve with steamed Belgian endive.

Fava Bean and Pancetta Sauce

MAKES 2¼ CUPS (550ML)

4 ounces (125g) pancetta or bacon, diced
2 cups (500ml) Medium Béchamel Sauce (see page 20), kept warm
1 cup (150g) shelled fresh fava beans, cooked and skinned
black pepper

Put the pancetta or bacon in a cold skillet and heat gently to render the fat. Fry until lightly browned, then drain on paper towels. Add to the sauce with the beans. Gently reheat and season to taste with pepper.

Serving Suggestions
Serve with Belgian endive, leeks, or pasta.

Velouté Sauce

The word *velouté* translates as velvety, and this sauce should be super-smooth and rich.

MAKES 1¾ CUPS (400ML)

2 cups (500ml) stock or reduced poaching liquid
2 tablespoons (25g) unsalted butter
3 tablespoons all-purpose flour
squeeze lemon juice
salt and black pepper

Heat the stock if necessary. Melt the butter in a medium-size heavy saucepan and stir in the flour to make a roux. Cook gently, stirring constantly, for about 3 minutes or until it turns a golden straw color.

Remove the pan from the heat and cool for a minute, then whisk in the stock. Return the pan to the heat and whisk as the sauce comes to a boil and thickens. Reduce the heat and simmer very gently, uncovered, for 30 minutes, skimming occasionally.

At the end of the cooking time the sauce should coat the back of a spoon. If it is too thin, reduce by boiling gently. Taste and add lemon juice, salt, and pepper as necessary. For a super-glossy, smooth sauce, pass it through a fine-mesh conical strainer.

Variations: Add 2 tablespoons of dry sherry to the finished sauce. Alternatively, add ¼ cup (60ml) of crème fraîche, bring back to a boil, whisking, and then season.

Sauce Aurore
Add ½ cup (125ml) of tomato purée after the sauce has simmered for 20 minutes. Continue simmering for 15 more minutes, then whisk in 2 tablespoons (25g) chilled unsalted butter cut in small dice. Add 1½ tablespoons of minced chervil or basil just before serving, if you like.

Serving Suggestions
Velouté Sauce is best served with poultry and steamed vegetables.

Saffron Sauce

The stock used for the velouté base can be made from fish bones and trimmings, or from shellfish shells and heads.

MAKES 2 CUPS (500ML)

1 heaped teaspoon saffron threads
2 cups (500ml) Velouté Sauce (see left)
2 tablespoons (25g) unsalted butter,
**   chilled and diced**

Preheat the oven to 350°F. Toast the saffron for 10 minutes in the oven, then crumble it into a small bowl. Bring the sauce to a boil. Remove ¼ cup (60ml) of the simmering sauce, pour over the saffron, and let soak for 20 to 30 minutes.

Strain the reduced sauce into a clean pan, stir in the saffron mixture, and simmer for 10 minutes. Season to taste, then remove the pan from the heat and whisk in the butter. Serve immediately.

Serving Suggestions
Serve Saffron Sauce with fish and shellfish.

Sauce Allemande

MAKES 2¼ CUPS (550ML)

2 cups (500ml) Velouté Sauce (see left)
1 cup (60g) mushroom stems or sliced button
**   mushrooms**
1 shallot, minced
1 extra large egg yolk
squeeze lemon juice
salt and black pepper
2 tablespoons (25g) unsalted butter, chilled and
**   diced**

Prepare the velouté sauce up to the simmering stage. Add the mushrooms and shallot and simmer for 30 minutes, stirring occasionally. When cooked, the sauce should just coat the back of a spoon.

Strain the sauce through a fine-mesh conical strainer and return it to the rinsed-out pan. In a small heatproof bowl, whisk a ladle or two of the sauce with the egg yolk, then whisk this mixture into the hot sauce. Gently reheat the sauce, stirring constantly, so it thickens slightly; do not let it boil.

Remove the pan from the heat and season to taste with lemon juice, salt, and pepper. Whisk in the butter, then serve.

Variations: *Sauce Poulette*
Whisk in 1½ tablespoons minced parsley and the juice of ½ lemon, or more to taste. Serve with rich poultry and variety meat dishes.

Sauce Suprême
Omit the shallot and egg yolk. When the sauce has reached coating consistency, stir in ¼ cup (60ml) of crème fraîche or heavy cream. Serve with poached chicken.

Serving Suggestions
Sauce Allemande is excellent served with vegetables and makes chicken a real treat, especially if you use the stems and trimmings from fresh chanterelles.

Texan Meat Pie

Almost any kind of meat can be used in this pie: beef, lamb, pork, turkey, or venison. Lean cuts cook quickly, but allow longer for the better-flavored, cheaper stew meat.

SERVES 4 TO 6

FOR THE VELOUTÉ SAUCE:

3 tablespoons (45g) unsalted butter
¼ cup (35g) all-purpose flour
2 teaspoons ground coriander
2 teaspoons ground cumin
1 to 2 teaspoons ground dried chili peppers, to
**   taste**
2½ cups (600ml) beef stock
1 teaspoon dried oregano

Velouté Sauce

simmer the sauce, uncovered, over very low heat for 20 minutes, stirring occasionally.

While the velouté sauce is cooking, heat the oil in a heavy skillet and add the diced meat in batches, frying quickly to sear and brown it on all sides. As the meat is browned, remove it from the pan with a slotted spoon and add it to the simmering velouté sauce.

When all the meat is cooked, add the onion and garlic to the skillet and stir them over low heat for 4 to 5 minutes or until softened. Add them to the sauce with some salt and pepper. Partially cover the saucepan and simmer gently until the meat is really tender: this can take up to 2 hours, depending on the quality of the meat. (If you want to use a casserole, the sauce can be cooked in the oven at 325°F.)

When the meat is cooked, add the beans and continue cooking, uncovered, for about 15 minutes or until the chili is slightly thickened. Taste and adjust the seasoning. Transfer the chili to a baking dish and let it cool completely.

Cook the potatoes in boiling salted water until just tender. Drain thoroughly, then mash until smooth. Beat in the butter and just enough milk to make a smooth, spreadable mixture. Season to taste with salt and pepper.

Spread the potato mixture in an even layer on top of the chili. At this point the dish can be left until cold, then covered and stored in the refrigerator for up to 3 days, or frozen for up to 1 month (defrost the pie overnight in the refrigerator).

To finish the pie, preheat the oven to 350°F and bake for about 30 minutes or until the chili is bubbling and piping hot throughout. Serve the pie with a bowl of chilled fresh tomato salsa (see page 102) for extra piquancy.

Variations: The chili can be served with rice instead of adding the potato topping. If you prefer a really hot chili, increase the amount of ground dried chili pepper to taste.

FOR THE CHILI:
2 tablespoons olive oil
1½ pounds (750g) lean chuck steak, finely diced
1 medium onion, minced
3 cloves garlic, minced
salt and black pepper
2½ cups (400g) cooked pinto beans
FOR THE TOPPING:
1½ pounds (750g) potatoes, peeled and diced
3 tablespoons (45g) unsalted butter, diced
⅓ cup (75ml) hot milk
salt and black pepper

Melt the butter for the velouté sauce in a medium-size heavy saucepan. Remove it

Above: classic Velouté Sauce is given a spicy kick with ground dried chili, coriander, and cumin, then used to make Texan Meat Pie.

from the heat and stir in the flour. Return the pan to low heat and stir until the roux becomes the color of dark straw. Add the coriander, cumin, and ground chili pepper and cook, stirring constantly, for 1 minute.

Remove the pan from the heat and let the roux cool for 1 minute, then slowly whisk in the stock. Return the pan to the heat and bring the sauce to a boil, whisking constantly until smooth and thick. Add the oregano. Reduce the heat and gently

Hollandaise Sauce

Spinach Tarts with Hollandaise

This is an elegant yet easy first course or brunch dish that is infinitely adaptable. The individual tarts and their filling of spinach and anchovy can be prepared in advance, then assembled just before serving. For this recipe you will need six 4½-inch (12-cm) tart pans with removable bottoms.

SERVES 6

FOR THE PASTRY:
2 cups (300g) all-purpose flour
⅔ cup (150g) unsalted butter, chilled and diced
¼ teaspoon salt
⅛ teaspoon black pepper
2 large egg yolks
2 to 3 teaspoons ice water

FOR THE FILLING:
1 pound (500g) baby spinach leaves
8 to 10 anchovy fillets, drained and chopped
black pepper

FOR THE GLAZE:
1¼ cups (300ml) Hollandaise Sauce, made with
⅛ teaspoon cayenne pepper (see page 22)

To make the pastry, put the flour, butter, salt, and pepper into a food processor and process until the mixture resembles fine crumbs. With the machine running, add the egg yolks and water through the opening in the lid. Mix just until the dough comes together. Remove the dough from the bowl, wrap, and chill for 20 minutes or until firm.

Roll out the dough on a floured work surface. Cut out 6 rounds, each 5½ inches (14cm) in diameter, using a saucer as a guide. Use the rounds of dough to line the tart pans. Chill them for 15 minutes. Meanwhile, heat the oven to 400°F.

Right: a rich cayenne-spiked sauce provides a creamy topping for these simple yet elegant Spinach Tarts with Hollandaise.

Line each tart shell with a round of parchment paper and fill them with dried beans. Arrange the pans on a baking sheet and bake for 12 minutes or until the pastry is lightly golden and only just firm. Carefully remove the paper and beans from the tart shells. Lower the oven temperature to 350°F and bake for a further 5 to 7 minutes or until the pastry is completely cooked, light golden, and crisp.

Cool the shells for 1 minute or until they are firm enough to unmold, then remove from the pans. Let cool on a wire rack.

To make the filling, steam the spinach until wilted, then remove it from the heat and let cool. Squeeze out the excess water from the cooked spinach, chop it roughly, and mix with the anchovies and plenty of black pepper.

When ready to finish the tarts, arrange the pastry shells on a baking sheet and divide the spinach filling among them. Gently warm the tarts in a low oven while you are making the sauce. Preheat the broiler.

Make the hollandaise sauce, adding the cayenne pepper along with the seasoning: be sure not to add too much salt, as the anchovies will be salty enough. Spoon the sauce over the filling in each tart, then quickly put them under the broiler, close to the heat, to brown the tops. Serve hot.

Hollandaise Sauce

Variations: The spinach and anchovy filling can be replaced by steamed asparagus spears or broccoli florets, cut to fit into the tart shells. Or, mix the roughly chopped cooked spinach with crisply cooked bacon and fill the tart shells, then top with either seared, sliced scallops or halved hard-cooked quail eggs.

Saffron Hollandaise

A brilliant yellow, aromatic version of hollandaise sauce, this has a wonderfully intense flavor.

MAKES 1¼ CUPS (300ML)

1 heaping teaspoon saffron threads
2 tablespoons warm water
3 large egg yolks
1 cup (225g) clarified unsalted butter, warmed
juice of ½ lemon
salt and white pepper

Preheat the oven to 350°F. Toast the saffron in the oven for 10 to 12 minutes. Put the toasted saffron into a small bowl with the warm water and let soak overnight or for at least 4 hours.

Put the egg yolks and saffron mixture into a small, heavy, non-aluminum saucepan and whisk them, off the heat, until frothy. Set the pan over very low heat and whisk for about 5 minutes or until you have a very thick mousse-like mixture.

Remove the saucepan from the heat and, whisking continuously, pour in the warm clarified butter in a slow, steady stream until you have a thickened sauce. Whisk in the lemon juice, salt, and pepper. Serve the sauce as soon as possible.

Serving Suggestions
Crab, lobster, scallops, shrimp, poached salmon, and trout are all lovely with this brightly colored sauce.

Sauce Maltaise

Sauce Maltaise is traditionally made with blood oranges, which, though small, contain a fair amount of tart red juice.

MAKES 1¼ CUPS (300ML)

2 small blood oranges
1¼ cups (300ml) Hollandaise Sauce (see page 22), kept warm

Grate the zest from one orange and set it aside, then squeeze the juice from both oranges. Put the juice into a small pan and heat until it is lukewarm. Whisk the juice and zest into the warm hollandaise and serve.

Serving Suggestions
This is a good sauce to serve with richer fish such as salmon, sea trout, red snapper, large shrimp, and monkfish, or with green vegetables such as lightly steamed asparagus and broccoli.

Hollandaise with Tomato and Basil

Choose tomatoes with plenty of flavor as well as a good color for this sauce.

MAKES ABOUT 1¼ CUPS (300ML)

2 ripe tomatoes, peeled, quartered, and seeded
1 bunch basil
1¼ cups (300ml) Hollandaise Sauce (see page 22), kept warm

Cut each tomato quarter into 2 or 3 strips. Pluck the basil leaves from their stems and roughly shred the leaves. Stir the tomatoes and basil into the warm hollandaise sauce and serve immediately.

Serving Suggestions
This is a good accompaniment to simply steamed white fish or globe artichokes.

Sorrel Hollandaise

MAKES ABOUT 1¼ CUPS (300ML)

1 heaping cup (125g) young sorrel leaves
1½ tablespoons (20g) unsalted butter
1¼ cups (300ml) Hollandaise Sauce (see page 22), kept warm

Remove the stems and center ribs from the sorrel. Heat the butter in a medium-size non-aluminum saucepan, add the leaves, and stir well. Cook for 5 minutes or until very soft. Drain in a colander, then chop to give a thick purée. Stir into the warm hollandaise, adjust the seasoning, and serve.

Serving Suggestions
This is a pretty green-colored sauce for poached monkfish, salmon, or turbot.

Almond and Herb Sauce

MAKES 1 CUP (250ML)

3 extra large egg yolks (see caution about eggs on page 11)
1 tablespoon minced parsley
1 tablespoon minced blanched almonds (not ground almonds)
1 teaspoon grated lemon zest
1 clove garlic, minced
salt and black pepper
¾ cup (175g) clarified unsalted butter, warmed

Mix the yolks, parsley, almonds, lemon zest, garlic, and a little seasoning in a heatproof bowl (or top of a double boiler). Set the bowl in a water-bath to warm the ingredients, then remove from the heat. Pour the butter onto the yolk mixture in a thin stream, whisking constantly. Adjust the seasoning, then serve. This sauce can be kept warm or reheated.

Serving Suggestions
An unusual, modern sauce, this is delicious with roast lamb or lamb chops.

Sauce Béarnaise

Béarnaise is thicker and more substantial than hollandaise, but nevertheless should have the texture of lightly whipped cream.

MAKES 1½ CUPS (350ML)

⅓ **cup (15g) tarragon, leaves minced and stems crushed**
3 tablespoons tarragon vinegar
2 shallots, minced
1 blade mace
1 teaspoon black peppercorns, crushed
4 large egg yolks
2 tablespoons cold water
1 cup (225g) clarified unsalted butter, warmed
1 tablespoon minced chervil
squeeze of lemon juice
pinch cayenne pepper
salt and white pepper

Put the tarragon stems into a small, heavy saucepan with the vinegar, shallots, mace, and peppercorns. Boil the mixture until it has reduced to 1 tablespoon. Let cool.

Strain the reduction into a clean pan. Add the yolks and water and whisk the mixture off the heat until it is frothy. Set the pan over very low heat and whisk constantly for 5 minutes or until very thick and mousse-like.

Remove the pan from the heat and slowly whisk in the warm clarified butter. Whisk in the minced tarragon and chervil, then season the sauce to taste with lemon juice, cayenne, salt, and white pepper. Serve at once.

Variations: *Sauce Choron*
Replace the lemon juice with 1½ tablespoons of tomato purée.

Sauce Paloise
Replace the tarragon with mint.

Sauce Ravigote
Stir 2 teaspoons each of snipped chives and minced parsley plus 1 teaspoon minced

capers into the sauce. Add extra lemon juice to make it nicely sharp.

Serving Suggestions
Serve with grilled steaks or roast beef.

Beurre Blanc

This classic French sauce must not become too hot, or the butter will melt and separate instead of emulsifying into a creamy sauce.

MAKES 1 CUP (250ML)

⅓ **cup (40g) minced shallots**
2 tablespoons white wine vinegar
2 tablespoons dry white wine
2 tablespoons cold water
14 tablespoons (200g) unsalted butter, chilled and diced
squeeze of lemon juice
salt and black pepper

Put the shallots, vinegar, and wine into a small, heavy saucepan and simmer until the liquid has reduced to 1 tablespoon. Whisk in the water, then gradually whisk in the butter, moving the pan on and off the heat, until the sauce is creamy and thick. Season to taste with lemon juice, salt, and pepper. Serve.

Variations: For a smoother sauce, strain through a fine-mesh conical strainer.

Beurre Blanc à la Crème
Replace the water with 2 tablespoons of crème fraîche or heavy cream.

Sauce Beurre Rouge
Replace the vinegar and the wine with ¼ cup (60ml) of dry red wine and add 2 tablespoons heavy cream instead of water.

Serving Suggestions
Beurre blanc is the perfect sauce for any steamed or poached fish or vegetables.

Sauce Vin Blanc

Here chicken, fish, or vegetable stock is added to flavor the sauce with the main ingredient of the dish with which the sauce is to be served.

MAKES 1 CUP (250ML)

½ **cup (125ml) dry white wine**
½ **cup (125ml) chicken, fish, or vegetable stock**
⅓ **cup (40g) minced shallots**
2 tablespoons crème fraîche or heavy cream
14 tablespoons (200g) unsalted butter, chilled and diced
squeeze of lemon juice
salt and black pepper

Put the wine, stock, and shallots into a small, heavy-based saucepan and boil gently until the liquid has reduced by two-thirds. Add the crème fraîche and simmer until the mixture has reduced by half.

Gradually whisk in the butter, moving the pan on and off the heat so the mixture is hot but not boiling. Taste and season with lemon juice, salt, and pepper. Serve immediately.

Serving Suggestions
Serve with chicken, fish, or vegetables.

Salmon with Champagne Beurre Blanc

SERVES 4

½ **cup (60g) minced shallots**
½ **cup (125ml) champagne**
½ **cup (125ml) fish stock or water**
1 small bouquet garni
4 salmon fillets or steaks
14 tablespoons (200g) unsalted butter, chilled and diced
¼ **cup (50g) salmon caviar**
salt and black pepper
squeeze lemon juice, or extra champagne

ℬeurre ℬlanc

Put the shallots, champagne, stock or water, and bouquet garni into a non-aluminum sauté pan or other shallow pan. Cover and simmer gently for 5 minutes. Add the salmon and bring the liquid back to a boil. Cover again and simmer for 8 to 10 minutes or until the fish is just cooked. Remove the fish, drain it thoroughly, and keep it warm.

Gently boil the cooking liquid until it has reduced to 2 tablespoons of syrupy concentrate. Strain the liquid through a fine-mesh conical strainer into a small, heavy-based saucepan, then reheat it.

Over low heat, whisk in the butter a few pieces at a time, moving the pan on and off the heat so the sauce is hot but not boiling and the texture is glossy. Very gently stir in the salmon caviar, then taste the sauce and add salt, pepper, and lemon juice or some extra champagne, as needed. Spoon the sauce over the fish and serve.

Beurre Blanc with Herbs

MAKES ⅔ CUP (150ML)

¼ cup (60ml) white wine vinegar
¼ cup (25g) minced shallots
2 tablespoons dry white wine
1 bunch herbs (see Serving Suggestions below), leaves minced and stems crushed
2 tablespoons crème fraîche or heavy cream
7 tablespoons (100g) unsalted butter, chilled and diced
salt and white pepper

Put the vinegar, shallots, wine, and the stems of the herbs into a small, heavy saucepan. Simmer until reduced by two-thirds. Add the crème fraîche and simmer until the mixture has reduced by half.

Strain the reduction, pressing lightly on the shallots and stems in the strainer. Return the reduction to the pan and reheat.

Above: tarragon-flavored Beurre Blanc with Herbs is a good match for salmon, here presented on layers of spinach and potatoes.

Gradually whisk in the butter, moving the pan on and off the heat so the mixture is hot but not boiling. Remove the sauce from the heat and season to taste with salt and pepper. Whisk in 1 tablespoon of minced herbs and serve immediately.

Serving Suggestions
A beurre blanc flavored with tarragon is lovely with rich seafood, such as salmon and scallops. Choose basil for monkfish and chicken; parsley for cod; chervil for delicate fish like sole and flounder. A sauce flavored with cilantro (with or without a little grated fresh ginger) is good with crab, salmon, and large shrimp.

CREAM SAUCE

Crab Sauce

Adding whole-grain mustard to this butter sauce finished with cream prevents it from tasting too rich. Use freshly cooked crab meat wherever possible for the best flavor.

MAKES 1½ CUPS (350ML)

4 tablespoons (60g) unsalted butter
1 small shallot, minced
1 cup (250ml) dry white wine
½ cup (125ml) heavy cream, plus an extra
¼ cup (60ml) heavy cream, whipped
1 cup (125g) white crab meat
¾ teaspoon whole-grain mustard
salt and white pepper

Below: fresh is best for this distinctive Crab Sauce flavored with shallot, wine, and mustard. Its rich and unctuous texture comes from a combination of heavy cream and whipped cream.

Melt 1 tablespoon of the butter in a medium-size saucepan and cook the shallot over low heat for 3 to 4 minutes or until it is soft but not colored. Add the wine, bring to a boil, and simmer until it has reduced by half.

Add the ½ cup (125ml) cream, bring the mixture back to a boil, and cook gently until the sauce just coats the back of a spoon. Add the crab and cook, stirring, until the sauce just comes to a boil.

Remove the pan from the heat and stir in the remaining butter. When it is thoroughly combined, fold in the whipped cream and mustard. Taste the sauce and add salt and pepper as necessary. Serve immediately.

Serving Suggestions
Other types of seafood are excellent with this sauce. Try it spooned over steamed or poached fish steaks, shrimp, or scallops, or with steaks or pasta.

Shallot and Sauternes Sauce

Using sweet white wine in this sauce gives a delicious flavor: the result would simply not be as succulent if a dry wine were used. Sauternes is pricey, but there are many good, inexpensive muscatel wines available.

MAKES 1½ CUPS (350ML)

4 shallots, minced
2 tablespoons minced mushroom
1 tablespoon minced carrot
1 tablespoon minced celery
2 tablespoons (25g) butter
1 cup (250ml) sweet white wine, such as
Sauternes or muscatel
1 cup (250ml) chicken or fish stock
⅔ cup (150ml) heavy cream
salt and black pepper

CREAM SAUCE

Put the minced shallots, mushroom, carrot, and celery into a medium-size saucepan with the butter. Cover the pan and cook the vegetables over low heat until they are thoroughly softened but not brown.

Raise the heat under the pan, add the sweet wine and stock, and bring the mixture to a boil. Boil vigorously until the volume of the liquid has reduced by half.

Lower the heat under the pan a little, add the cream, and simmer the sauce for 2 minutes or until it is thick. Season to taste with salt and pepper and serve.

Variation: For a richer, smoother sauce, press the mixture through a fine strainer to create a purée, then return the sauce to the heat and add 6 tablespoons (75g) diced chilled butter, whisking until it is glossy.

Serving Suggestions

Serve the sauce with poached, grilled, or roasted chicken or fish, varying your choice of stock to suit the meat.

Leek and Chive Sauce

The flavor of this very easy sauce seems to appeal to everyone.

MAKES JUST UNDER 1 CUP (250ML)

3 tablespoons (45g) unsalted butter
2 leeks, minced
2 shallots, minced
6 tablespoons dry white wine
1 cup (250ml) heavy cream
1 small bunch chives
salt and black pepper

Melt the butter in a small saucepan and add the leeks and shallots. Cook them gently for 5 minutes or until soft but not colored.

Raise the heat a little, add the white wine, bring to a boil, and simmer until the volume of liquid has reduced by half. Pour in the cream, bring the mixture to a boil again, and simmer gently until the sauce has reduced to a coating consistency.

Snip the chives into the sauce, stir briefly to combine, and then taste and season as necessary with salt and pepper.

Serving Suggestions

A luxurious sauce, this adds sophistication to hot poached salmon or chicken. You could also serve it with a colorful mixture of steamed vegetables, or as an alternative to hollandaise when making Eggs Benedict.

Whisky Cream Sauce

The traditional reduction of wine is replaced by whisky in this unusual but simple sauce.

MAKES 1 CUP (250ML)

3 tablespoons (45g) unsalted butter
2 shallots, minced
6 tablespoons Scotch whisky
2 tablespoons prepared white horseradish
1 cup (250ml) heavy cream
1 small bunch dill, minced
salt and black pepper

Melt the butter in a small saucepan, add the shallots, and cook them gently over low heat until they are soft but not colored. Add the whisky, raise the heat a little, and simmer until the volume of liquid has reduced by half. Stir in the horseradish and the cream and simmer gently until the sauce has reduced to a coating consistency.

Add the minced dill, stir, and then season the sauce to taste with salt and pepper.

Serving Suggestions

Serve this slightly sweet cream sauce with hot smoked or fresh salmon, chicken, or lamb. For a Scottish theme, serve alongside roast venison and mashed rutabaga, plus some crisp-steamed green beans or broccoli.

Curry Cream Sauce

MAKES 1 CUP (250ML)

3 tablespoons (45g) butter
1 shallot, chopped
1 small carrot, chopped
1 stalk celery, chopped
1 clove garlic, minced
¼ teaspoon cayenne pepper
¼ teaspoon ground coriander
¼ teaspoon ground cumin
¼ teaspoon ground ginger
¼ teaspoon turmeric
seeds of 1 cardamom pod
salt and black pepper
1¼ cups (300ml) chicken or vegetable stock
⅔ cup (150ml) heavy cream

Heat the butter in a small saucepan, add the chopped shallot, carrot, celery, and garlic, and cook them gently for 5 minutes or until the vegetables have softened slightly. Stir in the spices, including a pinch of black pepper, and continue cooking over low heat for a further 5 minutes.

Pour the stock into the saucepan, raise the heat to medium-high, and simmer the mixture until it has reduced in volume by half. Stir in the cream, lower the heat, and cook the sauce for 10 more minutes, stirring frequently.

Strain the sauce, pressing down on the vegetables in the strainer to extract as much juice as possible, then taste and season as required with some salt and extra black pepper. Reheat if necessary before serving.

Serving Suggestions

Serve with chicken, egg, fish, and rice dishes. Spoon the sauce over a mixture of hard-cooked eggs, smoked haddock, and rice to make a kedgeree, or use to coat hard-cooked or poached eggs, served with toast and salad. The sauce can also be used to bind canned salmon or tuna: top the mixture with bread crumbs and grated cheese, then broil to brown the top.

Brown Sauce

A glossy, concentrated sauce, this was traditionally thickened with a roux cooked to a nut-brown color, then dark brown stock was added and the sauce simmered for many hours. These days, most chefs prefer to use arrowroot, or potato flour (*fécule*), as a thickener after the stock has been reduced. If you are using this recipe as the basis for another sauce, use potato flour, not arrowroot, and omit the seasoning.

MAKES 1¼ CUPS (300ML)

1¼ cups (300ml) Brown Beef Stock (see page 8)
1 tablespoon potato flour *(fécule)* or arrowroot
2 tablespoons Madeira or cold water
salt and black pepper

Reheat the stock if necessary, bringing it to a simmer; it should already have been reduced to a good flavor and well skimmed. Mix the potato flour or arrowroot with the Madeira until smooth, then whisk this mixture into the simmering stock. It will thicken instantly and should just coat the back of a spoon. As soon as the sauce boils, remove from the heat and season to taste.

Brown sauce can be cooled, then stored in the refrigerator for up to 2 days, or frozen for up to 1 month.

Sauce Chasseur

MAKES JUST UNDER 2 CUPS (450ML)

4 tablespoons (60g) unsalted butter, chilled and diced
1 medium shallot, minced
1¼ cups (100g) thinly sliced button mushrooms
⅔ cup (150ml) dry white wine
1¼ cups (300ml) Brown Sauce (see above) or Brown Beef Stock (see page 8)
4 tablespoons tomato purée
salt and black pepper
1 tablespoon minced mixed herbs

Melt 1½ tablespoons (20g) of the butter in a medium-size heavy saucepan. Stir in the shallot and cook gently for 3 to 4 minutes or until it is very soft but not browned. Add the mushrooms and stir well, then cook gently, stirring often, for 5 to 7 minutes or until soft.

Drain the vegetable mixture in a strainer or fine colander, then return it to the rinsed-out pan. Add the wine to the vegetables and boil vigorously until the liquid has reduced in

Above: freshly minced herbs add a final flourish to steak with Sauce Chasseur.

volume to about 4 to 5 tablespoons. Stir in the brown sauce or stock and the tomato purée. Bring the sauce back to a boil and simmer for 1 minute. When it is ready, the sauce should very lightly coat the back of a spoon. Season with salt and black pepper.

*B*rown *S*auce

Remove the pan from the heat and whisk in the remaining butter, 2 pieces at a time. Stir in the herbs and serve immediately. (Once the butter has been added, the sauce will separate if boiled or reheated.)

Variation: Choose crimini mushrooms instead of the white button variety if you are making a sauce for dark meats. Vary your choice of stock and herbs to suit the meat.

Serving Suggestions

Sauce Chasseur made with beef stock can be served with panfried, grilled, or roast beef. When made with chicken stock and flavored with chives, parsley, and tarragon, it is also an ideal sauce for roast or grilled chicken and game birds.

Sauce Bordelaise

This sauce can be made using Brown Sauce or with a really well-flavored homemade beef stock, which will give a different taste and consistency. Ultimately, of course, the quality of any sauce will depend on the quality of the stock used. Choose a value-for-money red wine that you think is worth drinking, rather than something top-notch and expensive or one that resembles paint stripper. The marrow scooped from a beef bone used to be *de rigueur* for classic French Sauce Bordelaise, so I have included some optional instructions.

MAKES 1½ CUPS (350ML)

⅔ cup (150ml) hearty dry red wine
2 medium shallots, minced
¼ teaspoon black peppercorns, crushed
1 bouquet garni
1¼ cups (300ml) Brown Sauce (see page 68)
   or Brown Beef Stock (see page 8)
salt and black pepper
2 tablespoons (25g) unsalted butter, chilled and
   diced

Put the red wine, shallots, and crushed peppercorns in a small, heavy-based saucepan. Bring to a boil and boil vigorously over medium heat until the wine has reduced to about 3 tablespoons.

Add the bouquet garni and the brown sauce or beef stock and simmer gently for 5 minutes. Strain through a fine-mesh conical strainer into a clean pan, pressing lightly on the shallots in the strainer with the back of a ladle to extract all the juices.

When ready to serve, reheat the sauce, then taste and add salt and pepper as required; you may need to add a little extra red wine to lift the flavor. Remove the hot sauce from the heat and gradually whisk in the diced butter to thicken the sauce. Serve immediately; the sauce will separate if reheated or allowed to boil.

Variation: To add bone marrow, ask your butcher to chop a large marrow bone into pieces about 1½ inches (4cm) long. Blanch them in boiling water for 1 minute, then scoop out the marrow and slice it thinly. Put the marrow into a small pan with a little stock or cold water to cover. Bring to a boil, simmer for 1 minute, and drain. Add the marrow to the sauce after the butter.

Serving Suggestions

This is perfect for a rib-eye steak, or indeed any grilled steak or roast beef. Slices of panfried calf's liver, slightly pink in the center, are also good with this sauce.

Sauce Robert

This piquant, opaque sauce, flavored with onions and mustard, has been served with pork for several centuries — probably since the late Middle Ages. Dijon mustard is the best to use, as it is pale and pungent yet does not overwhelm the flavor of the meat. The brilliant-yellow English style of mustard

is too fiery. Once the mustard is added, the sauce should not be allowed to boil or it will turn unpleasantly bitter.

MAKES 1½ CUPS (350ML)

1½ tablespoons (20g) unsalted butter
1 small onion, minced
½ cup (125ml) dry white wine
3 tablespoons white wine vinegar
¼ teaspoon black peppercorns, crushed
1¼ cups (300ml) Brown Sauce
   (see page 68) or Brown Beef Stock (see
   page 8)
2 to 3 teaspoons Dijon mustard
salt and black pepper

Heat the butter in a small, heavy-based saucepan. Add the onion and stir well, then cover with a circle of dampened parchment paper and the pan lid. Cook the onion very gently, stirring frequently, for 20 minutes or until really soft but not colored.

Stir in the wine, vinegar, and peppercorns and boil until the liquid has reduced to 3 tablespoons. Stir in the brown sauce or stock and simmer gently for 5 minutes. Strain the sauce through a fine-mesh conical strainer into a clean pan, pressing lightly on the onion in the strainer to extract all the juices. Reheat the sauce and add the mustard and salt and pepper to taste, whisking well to make a smooth sauce. Serve immediately.

Variation: Add 4 small cornichons, cut into julienne or matchsticks, before serving.

Serving Suggestions

Serve Sauce Robert with the traditional pork, roasted, grilled, or panfried, or try it with a mixed grill, including bacon, lamb chops, sausages, and some tasty mushrooms.

BROWN AND WINE SAUCES

Sauce Bigarade

This is the sauce for duck *à l'orange,* which nobody seems to serve in the classic way anymore. Properly made, it was a *tour de force* and part of a chef's final exams. The bitter orange sauce should be made from bigarade or Seville oranges to complement the richness of the meat. When they are out of season, the sauce needs to be sharpened with lemon juice; it should not be at all sweet. If you are using stock, make sure it is thoroughly skimmed of fat.

MAKES 1½ CUPS (350ML)

1 Seville or bitter orange
1 tablespoon (15g) unsalted butter
1 medium shallot, minced
½ cup (125ml) dry white wine
1¼ cups (300ml) Brown Sauce (see page 68) or chicken or game stock
salt and black pepper
sugar or lemon juice to taste

Pare the zest from the orange, then cut the strips into fine julienne, or needle-like shreds. Blanch the zest for 1 minute in a small pan of boiling water, then drain and set aside.

Squeeze the juice from the orange and

Zesting an orange: use a vegetable peeler to remove the zest in strips. Take only the colored layer of zest, leaving the white pith on the fruit.

discard the seeds. Heat the butter in a small, heavy-based saucepan and gently cook the shallot until soft but not colored.

Add the wine and the orange juice, bring to a boil, and simmer until the mixture has reduced to about ¼ cup (60ml). Add the brown sauce or stock and simmer for 2 minutes, then strain through a fine-mesh strainer into a clean pan, pressing down lightly on the shallots to extract all the flavor.

Reheat the sauce, then taste and season as necessary with salt and pepper. Add a little sugar if the sauce is very bitter, or lemon juice if the sauce lacks acidity. Just before serving, stir in the orange zest.

Serving Suggestions
This sauce can be served with chicken as well as duck, and also goes well with pork.

Sauce Diable

MAKES 1½ CUPS (350ML)

½ cup (125ml) dry white wine
¼ cup (60ml) white wine vinegar
2 medium shallots, minced
½ teaspoon black peppercorns, crushed
1 small bouquet garni
1¼ cups (300ml) Brown Sauce (see page 68) or chicken stock
3 tablespoons tomato purée
salt and black pepper
2 to 3 drops hot red pepper sauce
2 to 3 drops Worcestershire sauce
2 tablespoons (25g) unsalted butter, chilled and diced

Put the wine, vinegar, shallots, peppercorns, and bouquet garni into a small, heavy saucepan and boil the mixture until it has reduced to about ¼ cup (60ml). Stir in the brown sauce or stock and the tomato purée, return to a boil, and simmer for 5 minutes.

Strain the sauce through a fine-mesh strainer into a clean pan. Reheat and season

to taste, adding just enough pepper sauce and Worcestershire sauce to give the sauce a kick. Remove the pan from the heat and gradually whisk in the pieces of butter.

Serve immediately; the sauce will separate if boiled or reheated.

Variation: Add 2 tomatoes, peeled, seeded, and cut into thin strips, plus 1 tablespoon of minced flat-leaf parsley to the sauce after adding the butter.

Serving Suggestions
Sauce Diable can be served with grilled or broiled chicken or turkey.

Tarragon and Sherry Sauce

MAKES ¾ CUP (175ML)

1 tablespoon olive oil
2 medium shallots, minced
½ cup (125ml) chicken stock
½ cup (125ml) Amontillado sherry
1 sprig thyme
½ cup (125ml) heavy cream
salt and black pepper
1½ to 2 tablespoons minced tarragon

Heat the olive oil in a small, heavy-based saucepan and cook the shallots until they are soft but not colored. Add the stock, sherry, and thyme, and simmer until the mixture has reduced by half.

Stir in the cream and season, then simmer until the sauce is thick enough to coat the back of a spoon. Strain into a clean pan. Add the tarragon, and adjust the seasoning. Gently reheat before serving if necessary.

Serving Suggestions
This is an excellent sauce for chicken breasts that have been quickly browned in olive oil and then baked until tender.

Wine Sauce

Quick White Wine Sauce

Because this simple, quick, low-fat sauce contains few ingredients, it is absolutely essential that they are the best quality.

MAKES 1¼ CUPS (300ML)

**⅔ cup (150ml) sweet white wine, such as
   Sauternes or muscatel
2 teaspoons cornstarch
⅔ cup (150ml) chicken stock
1 bouquet garni**

In a small bowl, blend 1 tablespoon of the wine with the cornstarch until you have a smooth, pourable paste. Put the remaining wine, the stock, and the bouquet garni into a small non-aluminum saucepan and heat until the mixture just comes to a boil.

Remove the pan from the heat and whisk in the cornstarch paste. Return to the heat and simmer the sauce for 2 minutes, stirring constantly, until it is smooth and thick. Discard the bouquet garni and serve.

Serving Suggestions
Serve this strongly flavored sauce in small quantities with chicken or white fish.

Sauce Meurette

An oft-quoted rule is that one should not serve red wine sauces with light-colored ingredients, but this is an exception.

MAKES 2½ CUPS (600ML)

**2 tablespoons (25g) butter
1 teaspoon thyme leaves
1 tablespoon minced onion
1 tablespoon minced carrot
1 tablespoon minced celery
3 cups (750ml) red Burgundy wine
2 cups (500ml) stock
1 tablespoon (15g) very soft butter
1 tablespoon all-purpose flour**

Melt the 2 tablespoons (25g) butter in a large, heavy saucepan. Add the thyme and all the vegetables, and cook gently until they are softened but not browned. Pour in the wine and stock. Bring to a boil and simmer until the liquid has reduced by half.

Meanwhile, mash the soft butter with the flour on a small plate to make a beurre manié. Use it to thicken the reduced sauce by gradually whisking small pieces of the paste into the liquid. Serve the sauce hot.

Above: Sauce Meurette is easy to make, yet boasts a complex flavor, achieved by simmering good red wine with vegetables, herbs, and stock.

Serving Suggestions
This rich French sauce is traditionally served with fish or with poached eggs. If you like, the eggs and sauce can be accompanied by fried strips of Canadian bacon and mushrooms to make a brunch dish.

71

COOKING SAUCES

In casseroles, the sauce is an integral part of the dish, used as a cooking medium rather than just to accompany the main ingredient. The sauce infuses the fish, meat, poultry, or vegetables with flavor, and it helps to tenderize and moisten them.

This is vital for casseroles and stews made from less expensive ingredients. When cooked slowly over time, the results can be memorable—for example, the aroma of a well-simmered French beef daube, redolent of red wine and orange, is long remembered. Sauces for lean, tender roasts and pieces of meat and poultry, which are quickly cooked at high temperature, are an important part of the cook's repertoire, too.

Most of these recipes are one-pot dishes—all that is necessary for a comforting, hearty meal. Timing is not vital: another few minutes in the oven will not be a problem. In fact, most of these dishes benefit from reheating.

Left: Seafood Stew.

Beef in Wine and Port

Ask the butcher to wrap the beef in a strip of barding fat, tied with string, to keep the meat moist during cooking.

SERVES 6

1 3-pound (1.3-kg) beef pot roast
3 tablespoons olive oil
2 onions, minced
⅔ cup (150ml) beef or game stock
salt and black pepper
1 tablespoon all-purpose flour
1 tablespoon (15g) unsalted butter, softened
FOR THE MARINADE:
1¼ cups (300ml) full-bodied red wine
⅔ cup (150ml) port
1 large onion, cut in wedges
2 large carrots, thickly sliced
½ teaspoon black peppercorns
1 bouquet garni

Put the beef in a deep china or glass bowl and add all the marinade ingredients. Cover and let marinate for 3 days in the refrigerator, turning the beef every half day.

When you are ready to cook the beef, preheat the oven to 325°F. Lift the beef from the marinade, drain it thoroughly, and pat dry with paper towels. Strain the marinade, reserving the liquid.

Heat the oil in a large ovenproof Dutch oven and cook the onions very gently for about 20 minutes or until very soft. Raise the heat and add the beef, cooking it briskly until it is browned on all sides and the onions are crisp but not burned.

Add the reserved marinade liquid and the stock to the Dutch oven, plus a little salt and pepper. Bring the liquid to a boil. Cover with a tight-fitting lid and cook gently in the oven for about 3 hours, stirring occasionally, until the beef is tender.

When cooked, lift out the pot roast and keep it warm. Bring the sauce to a boil on top of the stove. Mash the flour and butter together, then whisk the paste into the bubbling sauce until it thickens. Taste the sauce and adjust the seasoning as necessary. Thickly slice the beef and serve it with the sauce.

Variation: Replace the beef with venison.

Serving Suggestions
Mashed or steamed potatoes and a green vegetable or salad are best with this dish.

Aromatic Braised Steak

SERVES 6

3 tablespoons all-purpose flour
salt and black pepper
2¼ pounds (1kg) beef chuck or flank steak, thickly sliced
3 tablespoons olive oil
2 stalks celery, minced
2 medium onions, minced
2 medium carrots, minced
2 cloves garlic, minced
6 whole cloves
1 stick cinnamon
1¾ cups (400ml) port
½ cup (125ml) water or vegetable stock

Preheat the oven to 325°F. Season the flour with a little salt and pepper and use to coat the meat lightly, shaking off any excess.

In a large ovenproof Dutch oven, heat the oil over medium-high heat and quickly brown the meat on both sides, a couple of slices at a time. Set the steak aside.

Add the minced vegetables and garlic to the fat left in the Dutch oven, then lower the heat and cook gently, stirring frequently, until golden and softened. Stir in the cloves and cinnamon and cook for 2 to 3 minutes.

Add the port and water or stock, then return the meat to the Dutch oven and bring to a boil. Season with a little salt and plenty of pepper. Cover and cook in the oven for 1½ to 2 hours or until the steak is tender.

Check and stir frequently: if the liquid is simmering too fast, reduce the oven temperature; if the sauce is evaporating too much, add a little more water.

Taste the sauce and adjust the seasoning, then remove the whole spices. Serve hot.

Variation: Replace the beef with venison.

Serving Suggestions
Mashed potatoes or creamed celery root would make a perfect accompaniment.

Beef Carbonnade

SERVES 4

3 tablespoons all-purpose flour
salt and black pepper
1½ pounds (750g) beef chuck or flank steak, cubed
2 tablespoons (25g) butter
1½ cups (225g) chopped onions
1¼ cups (300ml) dark beer
1¼ cups (300ml) beef stock
3 tablespoons minced parsley

Preheat the oven to 300°F. Lightly season the flour with salt and pepper, then toss the meat in it, shaking off any excess. Heat the butter in an ovenproof Dutch oven and brown the cubes of meat all over. Remove from the pan and set aside.

Add the onions to the hot fat and cook, stirring frequently, until translucent. Return the meat to the Dutch oven and add the beer and stock. Cover and cook in the oven for 2½ hours or until the meat is tender.

Before serving, adjust the seasoning to taste and sprinkle with parsley.

Variation: Use venison instead of beef.

Serving Suggestion
Creamy mashed potatoes are the best accompaniment to this Flemish specialty.

Beef Dishes

Boeuf en Daube Provençale

This dish is named after a pot-bellied casserole, or *daubière*, designed for long, slow cooking. The stew tastes best if it is chilled so the excess fat can be removed, and then carefully reheated.

SERVES 6

2¼ pounds (1kg) beef chuck or flank steak, cubed
5 slices bacon, cut in strips
1 tablespoon olive oil (optional)
4 large plum tomatoes, roughly chopped
8 ounces (250g) button mushrooms
¾ cup black olives, pitted and roughly chopped, or 1 2-ounce (50-g) can anchovy fillets, drained and roughly chopped

FOR THE MARINADE:
1 75-cl bottle full-bodied dry red wine (3 cups/750 ml)
2 medium onions, cut in wedges
2 medium carrots, thickly sliced
3 cloves garlic, sliced
8 black peppercorns
1 large bouquet garni
1 tablespoon olive oil
zest of 1 orange, preferably Seville

Place the meat in a large china or glass bowl. Add the marinade ingredients. Mix well, then cover and let the beef marinate in the refrigerator for 12 to 24 hours.

When ready to cook, preheat the oven to 325°F. Remove the meat from the marinade and pat it dry with paper towels. Strain the marinade to separate the liquid from the vegetables; discard the peppercorns. Reserve both liquid and vegetables.

In a large, ovenproof Dutch oven, cook the bacon over medium heat. Remove the bacon with a slotted spoon and set it aside. Brown the meat in batches in the hot bacon fat, adding the oil if needed, then remove the meat and set aside with the bacon.

Add the reserved marinated vegetables and flavorings to the Dutch oven and stir well. Return the beef and bacon. Gently stir in the tomatoes, mushrooms, olives or anchovies, and the marinade liquid.

Bring to a boil, then cover and transfer the pan to the oven. Cook for 3½ hours or until the meat is very tender. Stir the stew occasionally and replenish the liquid with hot water if the stew is looking dry. If the liquid is bubbling vigorously, lower the oven temperature so that it only just simmers.

Above: Mediterranean flavorings of orange and black olives or anchovies make Boeuf en Daube Provençale a very special stew.

When cooked, stir the stew gently, then taste and season as necessary. Discard the orange zest and bouquet garni. The sauce should just coat the back of a spoon.

Serving Suggestions
Serve with spaghetti, noodles, or macaroni.

Irish Stew

SERVES 4

2 pounds (1kg) boneless lamb shoulder, cubed
2 pounds (1kg) potatoes, cubed
2 large onions, sliced
1 tablespoon pearl barley
salt and black pepper
about 1¼ cups (300ml) stock or water
2 tablespoons minced parsley

Preheat the oven to 250°F. In a casserole, layer the meat and potatoes with the onions, sprinkling each layer with a little pearl barley; finish with a layer of potatoes. Season lightly, then add enough stock or water to come halfway up the side of the casserole. Cover and cook in the oven for 3 hours. Serve sprinkled with the parsley.

Serving Suggestion
This is delicious with braised red cabbage.

Gigot Brayaude

SERVES 8

1 4-pound (2-kg) leg of lamb, tied with kitchen
   string
2 onions, sliced
2 carrots, sliced
1 sprig thyme
1 bay leaf
salt and black pepper
2 cups (500ml) cold water
½ cup (125ml) brandy

Preheat the oven to 250°F. Put the lamb in a large casserole with the vegetables, herbs, salt, and pepper. Add the water. Cover and cook in the oven for 5 hours. Turn the meat 3 or 4 times during cooking, and add a little more water if the casserole seems to be drying out. If the liquid starts to simmer, reduce the heat so that it bubbles very gently.

After braising for 5 hours, add the brandy.

Continue cooking for 1 more hour. The meat should be meltingly tender.

Remove the string from the lamb and carve into thick slices. Strain the sauce, discarding the vegetables, then skim off fat.

Serving Suggestion
Accompany with potatoes and carrots.

Lamb and Fava Bean Tagine

This spicy Moroccan stew is traditionally made in an earthenware casserole with a conical lid. The distinctive flavor of preserved lemon (found in ethnic and gourmet food markets) is essential.

SERVES 4

1 pound (500g) boneless lean lamb, cubed
3 garlic cloves, minced
1 large onion, minced
½ teaspoon black pepper
½ teaspoon ground ginger
¼ teaspoon sea salt
large pinch saffron threads, crumbled
1 pound (500g) shelled fresh fava beans
1 preserved lemon, rinsed and quartered
1 bunch cilantro, minced

Put the lamb, garlic, onion, pepper, ginger, salt, and saffron in a tagine or ovenproof Dutch oven and mix well. Add just enough cold water to cover the meat, then bring to a boil. Cover and reduce the heat so that the liquid just simmers. Cook for 1 hour or until the meat is tender, stirring occasionally and adding more water if it becomes dry.

Add the fava beans and lemon and mix in thoroughly. Cover again and cook until the beans are tender: 10 minutes for young beans, 20 minutes for older ones. Stir in the cilantro, then taste and add more pepper if needed. If the sauce is watery, boil to reduce it before adding the cilantro.

𝓛AMB 𝓓ISHES

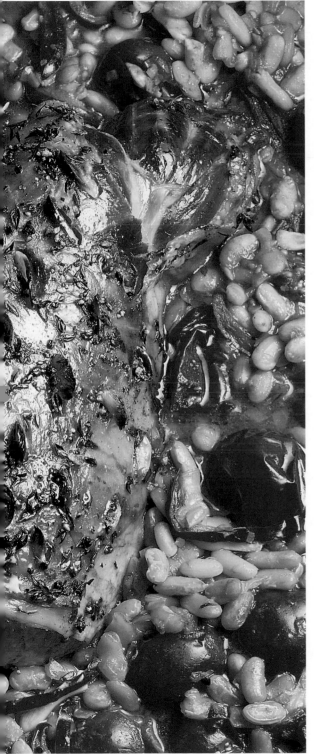

Leg of Lamb with Flageolet Beans

In Brittany, in northwestern France, roast lamb is often served with white beans. For a richer taste, I like to cook green flageolet beans around the meat, in a tomato and sweet pepper sauce. This makes an excellent winter dish for entertaining, as all the preparation can be done in advance and the meat can be left to cook while you chat with your guests.

SERVES 8

FOR THE BEANS:
2¾ cups (500g) dried flageolet or white beans
1 carrot, quartered
1 medium onion, peeled but left whole
2 bay leaves
1 large sprig thyme
FOR THE SAUCE:
3 tablespoons olive oil
2 medium onions, minced
4 to 6 cloves garlic, to taste, finely sliced
1 tablespoon thyme leaves
2 medium red sweet peppers, cored and sliced
1 28-ounce (800-g) can plum tomatoes in purée
salt and black pepper
FOR THE LAMB:
1 5½-pound (2.75-kg) leg of lamb
3 cloves garlic
1 tablespoon olive oil
1 tablespoon thyme leaves
sea salt and coarsely ground black pepper

Soak the beans in plenty of cold water overnight, or for at least 12 hours. Drain and rinse thoroughly.

In a large saucepan, cover the beans with fresh water and bring to a boil. Skim off any scum, then boil hard for 10 minutes. Add the

Left: for Leg of Lamb with Flageolet Beans, tender beans in a sauce of red sweet peppers and tomatoes are cooked with a juicy leg of lamb that is spiked with slivers of garlic and thyme leaves.

vegetables and herbs, but no salt at this stage. Cover and simmer for 45 minutes or until the beans are tender (the exact time will depend on the age of the beans). Drain the cooked beans, saving the liquid but discarding the flavorings.

Meanwhile, prepare the tomato and pepper sauce. Heat the olive oil in a large, heavy saucepan. Add the onions, garlic, and thyme. Cover and cook very gently for about 20 minutes or until the onions are soft and golden. Add the sweet peppers and cook for 5 more minutes. Add the tomatoes with their purée and remove the pan from the heat. (The sauce can be made up to this point 1 day in advance and kept, tightly covered, in the refrigerator.)

To cook the meat, preheat the oven to 425°F. If necessary, trim the lamb to remove all but a thin covering of fat. Slice the garlic into slivers. Make small, deep slits in the meat with a sharp knife and insert the garlic so the lamb is liberally and evenly spiked. Rub with the olive oil, then sprinkle with the thyme leaves and season with salt and pepper. Place the leg of lamb in a large casserole, baking dish, or deep roasting pan and roast, uncovered, for 30 minutes.

Add the drained beans to the tomato and pepper sauce and season to taste. Reheat if necessary. The mixture should be soupy, so, if necessary, add some of the reserved bean cooking liquid.

Reduce the oven temperature to 400°F. Spoon the beans and sauce into the casserole around the lamb and bake, uncovered, for a further 45 minutes, stirring the beans occasionally. If the mixture becomes dry, add more of the reserved bean liquid.

Present the leg of lamb on a large platter, and carve the meat into thick slices. Serve the beans in their sauce in a bowl alongside.

Variations: 2 pounds (1kg) fresh cherry tomatoes can be used instead of canned plum tomatoes.

Pork Chops Braised with Dried Fruits

I first ate this hearty, really warming winter dish one freezing day in northern France, and I have since enjoyed similar versions in Germany and in Lancaster County, Pennsylvania, as part of a large Mennonite meal. (The Pennsylvania Dutch, or Deutsch, originally came from Germany, and have kept their traditional dishes.) Oddly enough, my husband has a student from Tunisia who makes a similar dish with chicken in a tagine, but uses a tablespoon of honey to finish it rather than lemon juice.

SERVES 4

1 tablespoon all-purpose flour
salt and black pepper
4 pork loin chops, about 2 pounds (1kg) in total
1 tablespoon vegetable oil
1¾ cups (400ml) chicken or vegetable stock
½ lemon
¾ cup (100g) dried apricots
½ cup (100g) prunes
1 large tart apple, peeled, cored, and
**   cut into 8 wedges**

Preheat the oven to 350°F. Season the flour with a little salt and pepper and use to coat the chops lightly. Heat the oil in a large ovenproof skillet and brown the chops, 1 or 2 at a time, until they are golden brown on each side. Remove the chops and pour out the fat, leaving the cooking juices and brown sediment behind in the skillet.

Add the stock to the skillet and bring the mixture to a boil, stirring and scraping to dissolve all the sediment and caramelized cooking juices. Using a vegetable peeler, pare the zest from the lemon half and add the zest to the skillet, along with the apricots, prunes, and apple. Bring the mixture to a boil. Add a little seasoning and stir well. Replace the chops, then cover the skillet with the lid and place it in the

oven. Cook until the meat is very tender—about 40 minutes. If the mixture is cooking too fast, turn down the oven temperature to 325°F.

Stir before serving: the apples should have partially broken down to slightly thicken the sauce. Taste, adding salt, pepper, and lemon juice as needed.

Above: plump apricots, prunes, and apple add delicious natural sweetness to Pork Chops Braised with Dried Fruits.

Serving Suggestions
Offer a bowl of plainly cooked couscous or steamed rice alongside this dish.

Pork Dishes

Country Red Wine Casserole

This is a robust, dark, and richly flavored red wine casserole. It is easy and quick to make for such an impressive result. Reducing the wine before adding the other ingredients drives off the harsh alcohol flavors, making the sauce taste as though it has been simmered for several hours.

SERVES 4 TO 6

¼ cup (35g) all-purpose flour
salt and black pepper
1½ pounds (750g) thick pork chops
¼ cup (60ml) olive oil
4 thick slices Canadian bacon, diced
4 ounces (125g) crimini mushrooms
8 ounces (250g) small shallots, peeled
3 cups (750ml) hearty dry red wine
2½ to 3 cups (600 to 750ml) beef stock
4 large cloves garlic, minced
1 large bouquet garni

Mix the flour with enough salt and freshly ground black pepper to season the pork lightly, then use to coat the meat, dusting off any excess.

Heat the oil in a large, heavy saucepan or Dutch oven and fry the chops in batches until well browned on both sides. Remove with a slotted spoon and reserve. When all the chops have been browned and removed, add the Canadian bacon to the pan and cook, stirring frequently, until it is lightly browned. Remove the bacon and reserve it in a bowl.

Add the whole mushrooms and shallots to the pan, with a little more oil if necessary, and cook them for a few minutes until lightly browned, stirring constantly. Lift out the vegetables and add them to the bacon. Add all but 2 tablespoons of the wine to the pan and deglaze over medium-high heat, stirring well to dislodge and dissolve all the caramelized meat juices.

Boil the wine fairly rapidly until it has reduced by half. Stir in 2½ cups (600ml) of the stock and boil the liquid until it has reduced by a third, stirring frequently.

Add the garlic and bouquet garni and stir well. Return the chops to the saucepan. Bring the liquid back to a boil, then cover and let simmer very gently for 1½ hours or until the pork is almost tender. Stir from time to time, adding a little more stock if the sauce is reducing too quickly and leaving the meat exposed.

When the meat is almost cooked, return the reserved bacon to the pan, along with the mushrooms and shallots. Stir well, adding a little more stock if needed. Cover the pan and cook for a further 20 minutes or until the meat is very tender.

Remove the bouquet garni and stir well. The sauce should be dark and syrupy. If it is thin and runny, boil it uncovered for a few minutes until it coats the back of a spoon; if it is well flavored but a little thin, add some beurre manié (see page 14) to the boiling sauce; if it is too thick, add some more stock, then bring back to a boil.

When the sauce has reached the correct consistency, taste it and add salt and pepper as necessary. Add the remaining wine—this livens up the sauce, giving it a fresh taste, and also cuts any excess richness—then serve. The casserole is even better if made a day or so in advance, kept refrigerated, and then thoroughly reheated.

Variations: Replace the pork with cubed beef chuck steak, chunks of venison, or large portions of chicken, pheasant, or grouse on the bone, and select the flavor of the stock to suit the meat you have chosen. The length of time the casserole should be simmered before the bacon and vegetables are added depends on the size and quality of the meat chosen. Chicken pieces need only be simmered for around 40 minutes, whereas tougher game birds and venison will require 1 hour or more.

Serving Suggestion
Serve with buttered noodles and a robust green salad.

Filet de Porc Normande

SERVES 4

2 tablespoons (25g) butter
1 1½-pound (750-g) pork tenderloin
1 medium onion, thinly sliced
1 apple, peeled, cored, and sliced
1 tablespoon all-purpose flour
⅔ cup (150ml) stock
½ cup (125ml) hard cider, or a mixture of apple cider and white wine
2 tablespoons heavy cream
salt and black pepper

Preheat the oven to 350°F. Gently heat the butter in an ovenproof Dutch oven, then add the whole pork tenderloin and brown it all over. Remove it from the pan and set aside. Add the onion to the pan and cook for 2 to 3 minutes, then add the apple and continue cooking until both onion and apple are golden brown.

Add the flour to the pan. Stir in the stock and cider and bring the mixture to a boil. Return the pork tenderloin to the pan, burying it in the sauce. Cover and cook in the oven for 30 to 35 minutes.

When thoroughly cooked, remove the tenderloin from the pan and slice it. Keep it warm while you finish the sauce.

Purée the cooking liquid in a food processor or blender, then return it to the pan and reduce by boiling a little if necessary. Add the cream. Taste and season as needed with salt and pepper. Pour the sauce over the meat and serve.

Serving Suggestions
Serve with steamed green vegetables and, if desired, boiled new potatoes or some very lightly buttered noodles.

Chicken with Chanterelles Sauce

SERVES 4 TO 6

1 4-pound (2-kg) chicken
3 tablespoons (45g) unsalted butter
2 tablespoons vegetable oil
8 ounces (250g) fresh chanterelles, trimmed
4 large shallots, cut into wedges
2 cloves garlic, thinly sliced
1¼ cups (300ml) chicken stock
juice of ½ lemon
½ cup (125ml) crème fraîche
2 egg yolks
salt and black pepper
sprigs flat-leaf parsley for garnish

Preheat the oven to 350°F. Wipe the chicken inside and out with paper towels, and trim off any large lumps of fat at the opening to the body cavity.

Heat half the butter with the oil in an oven-proof Dutch oven and brown the chicken on all sides. Remove it from the pan and set aside. Wipe the pan with paper towels.

Heat half the remaining butter in the pan and quickly cook the mushrooms until they are lightly colored. Remove with a slotted spoon and reserve. Melt the remaining butter in the pan, add the shallots and garlic, and cook, stirring frequently, until golden. Replace the chicken in the pan. Pour in the stock and bring to a boil.

Cover the pan and cook in the oven for 1 hour or until a skewer inserted in the thickest part of the chicken's thigh releases clear juices. After the chicken has been cooking for about 45 minutes, add the mushrooms to the pan.

To finish, remove the chicken and keep it warm. Bring the sauce to a boil and simmer, uncovered, for 5 minutes or until slightly reduced. Stir in the lemon juice.

Mix the crème fraîche and egg yolks together in a small bowl, then stir in a ladle of the cooking liquid. Remove the pan from

Above: the pretty shapes of the mushrooms make Chicken with Chanterelles Sauce a feast for the eyes as well as the tastebuds.

the heat and pour in the egg yolk mixture, stirring, until the sauce thickens. Do not boil it. Taste and add salt, pepper, and more lemon juice as necessary. Carve the chicken, spoon the sauce over, and garnish with sprigs of flat-leaf parsley.

Variations: Add a handful of Canadian bacon strips to the sauce before putting the pan in the oven. If fresh chanterelles are not available, 2 ounces (60g) dried chanterelles, soaked in hot water for 30 minutes, can be used instead.

Serving Suggestions
Serve with potatoes, plain noodles, or rice. The sauce makes a good topping for pasta.

Chicken Dishes

Coq au Vin

A classic French dish like this is always appreciated by guests and family.

SERVES 4 TO 6

1 4-pound (2-kg) chicken
4 ounces (125g) bacon or thick-cut salt pork, diced
4 tablespoons (60g) unsalted butter
2 tablespoons brandy
2½ cups (600ml) dry red wine
2 cups (125g) sliced mushrooms
1 cup (125g) boiling onions, peeled
1 large clove garlic, minced
2½ cups (600ml) chicken stock
2 tablespoons all-purpose flour
salt and black pepper
2 tablespoons minced parsley

Preheat the oven to 300°F. Wipe the chicken inside and out with paper towels, and trim off any large lumps of fat at the opening to the body cavity.

Cook the bacon or salt pork in an ovenproof Dutch oven until the pieces are lightly browned and the fat is translucent. Remove the bacon or salt pork with a slotted spoon. Melt 2 tablespoons (30g) of the butter in the pan, then add the chicken and brown in the bacon fat and butter.

Meanwhile, heat the brandy in a small pan. When the chicken is browned all over, spoon off any excess fat from the Dutch oven. Set the brandy alight, then pour it flaming over the bird. When the flames have subsided, return the bacon or salt pork to the Dutch oven and add the wine, mushrooms, onions, and garlic. Pour in enough stock to come halfway up the sides of the bird.

Cover the pan and cook in the oven for 1 hour or until the chicken is tender and the juices run clear when a skewer is inserted in the thickest part of the thigh. Turn the bird twice during cooking.

When the chicken is cooked, remove it from the oven and carve it into pieces. Lift the onions, bacon, and mushrooms from the pan and place them on a serving platter with the chicken. Keep them warm in the oven while you prepare the sauce.

Bring the cooking juices to a boil and reduce by about a third. Work the remaining 2 tablespoons (30g) of butter and the flour together to make a beurre manié. Gradually whisk small pieces of the paste into the sauce until it thickens. Season to taste with salt and pepper. Pour the sauce over the chicken and vegetables and garnish with the parsley.

Variations: You can substitute a pork or beef roast for the chicken, replacing the chicken stock with beef stock if preferred.

Chicken in Paprika Sauce

SERVES 4

2 tablespoons (25g) unsalted butter
1 tablespoon olive oil
4 boneless chicken breast halves (with skin)
3 stalks celery, thickly sliced
2 shallots, thinly sliced
1 medium carrot, thickly sliced
½ cup (125ml) dry white wine
salt and black pepper
1 bouquet garni
1 cup (250ml) crème fraîche
1 tablespoon paprika

Heat the butter and oil in a large sauté pan, add the chicken breasts, and brown on both sides. Remove to a plate. Lower the heat and add the vegetables to the pan. Cook gently, stirring frequently, for 15 minutes or until softened and lightly colored.

Return the chicken to the pan and pour in the wine. Bring the mixture to a boil. Season lightly and add the bouquet garni. Cover the pan and simmer gently for 25 to 30 minutes or until the chicken is thoroughly cooked.

Lift the chicken from the pan, draining it thoroughly, and keep it warm in a serving dish. Skim the sauce if necessary, then stir in the crème fraîche and paprika. Simmer until the sauce just coats the back of a spoon. Taste and adjust the seasoning with salt and pepper as necessary. Strain the sauce through a fine-mesh strainer over the chicken breasts and serve.

Variations: This lovely dish can also be made with pheasant and guinea fowl.

Serving Suggestion
The paprika sauce is complemented by noodles and a side dish of zucchini.

Chicken with Lemon and Rosemary Sauce

SERVES 4

1½ tablespoons (20g) unsalted butter
1 tablespoon olive oil
4 boneless chicken breast halves (with skin)
juice of 1 lemon
4 cloves garlic, peeled but left whole
2 strips lemon zest
1 large sprig rosemary
salt and black pepper

Heat the butter and oil in a heavy sauté pan. Add the chicken breasts and cook until golden brown on both sides.

Reduce the heat and add the rest of the ingredients. Stir well, then bring the liquid to a simmer. Cover the pan and cook gently for 20 minutes or until the chicken is tender, turning occasionally. Add salt, pepper, or more lemon juice to taste, then remove the lemon zest and serve.

Serving Suggestions
Boiled or steamed new potatoes and green beans or salad are the best accompaniments.

Saffron Fish Casserole

This one-pot recipe makes a fine summer supper. The tiniest ingredient (saffron) makes the most impact; the saffron threads are briefly toasted and then soaked, to give a glorious golden color to the stock. This is poured over thinly sliced potatoes layered with thick fish fillets (choose well-flavored fish such as haddock or orange roughy) and sliced ripe tomatoes.

SERVES 4

1 large pinch saffron threads
1¼ cups (300ml) fish stock
2 tablespoons olive oil
4 shallots, minced
2 cloves garlic, minced
2 teaspoons minced thyme leaves
4 medium-large boiling potatoes, peeled and very thinly sliced
salt and black pepper
4 fish fillets, skinned if desired
4 medium tomatoes, thinly sliced
2 tablespoons (25g) unsalted butter, diced

Preheat the oven to 400°F. Toast the saffron in a small ramekin or other ovenproof dish for 10 to 12 minutes or until it is darker in color but not scorched. Crumble the threads, then mix with ¼ cup (60ml) of the stock. Cover and let the saffron soak for 1 hour (or overnight if possible).

Heat the oil in a medium saucepan and gently cook the shallots, garlic, and thyme for 10 to 12 minutes or until the shallots are very soft and golden.

Thoroughly butter a large earthenware dish that will take the fish fillets in a single layer. Put a layer of sliced potatoes, overlapping slightly, in the bottom of the dish. Season lightly, then scatter half the shallot mixture over. Arrange the fish fillets on top and season lightly again. Cover this with the tomatoes, then the rest of the shallots. Season again, and top with two layers of potatoes, seasoning as you go.

Combine the saffron liquid with the rest of the stock. Carefully pour the mixture into the earthenware dish so that it seeps down between the layers evenly rather than gathering around the sides of the dish. When you have finished, the stock should come about halfway up the side of the dish.

Dot the top with the diced butter. Bake uncovered for 40 to 50 minutes or until the top is golden and crisp and the potatoes are tender (test with a skewer).

Seafood Stew

Choose your favorite fish—sea bass, red snapper, hake, and tilefish are very good. For maximum flavor, add a couple of handfuls each of mussels, clams, and large shrimp in shell. A good selection need not be expensive.

SERVES 4

heaping ½ cup (100g) dried large lima beans
about 3 pounds (1.5kg) fish and shellfish, including shells
3 cups (350g) finely diced potatoes
4 ripe tomatoes, peeled and roughly chopped
1 cup (250ml) fish stock
½ cup (125ml) dry white wine
1 large bouquet garni, including 1 sprig rosemary
3 tablespoons olive oil
3 shallots, minced
2 to 4 cloves garlic, minced
lemon juice (optional)
salt and black pepper

Soak the beans overnight in plenty of cold water. Drain, then put them into a medium-size saucepan with fresh cold water to cover. Bring to a boil, skimming well, then boil for 10 minutes. Reduce the heat and simmer the beans for 25 to 30 minutes or until tender. Drain the beans and set aside.

Preheat the oven to 325°F. Cut the fish into medium-size chunks. Scrub the mussels

and remove any hairy beards; discard any that do not close when tapped sharply. Scrub the clams and discard any that do not close in the same way.

Put the beans, fish and seafood, and all the remaining ingredients into a large ovenproof Dutch oven and stir gently. Bring to a boil, then cover and cook in the oven for 30 to 40 minutes or until the fish and potatoes are tender. Discard any unopened mussels or clams.

Stir gently, then taste the sauce and adjust the seasonings as necessary: you may need a squeeze of lemon juice. The sauce should be soupy, thickened with the potatoes and beans. Discard the bouquet garni and serve as soon as possible.

Variations: Add 1 sliced bulb of fennel to the vegetables. You can replace some of the fresh tomatoes with sun-dried tomatoes packed in oil and use the flavored oil in place of the olive oil. Substitute vermouth for the wine and finish the dish with 2 tablespoons of minced herbs.

Mussels with Cilantro, Chili, and Lemon Grass

My favorite way of cooking mussels, this reminds me of the restaurant where I met my husband. This is its most popular dish.

SERVES 2 TO 4

2 pounds (1kg) mussels
2 tablespoons (25g) unsalted butter
4 medium green onions, minced
2 cloves garlic, minced
1 stem lemon grass, minced
1 small very hot fresh red chili pepper, seeded and minced
⅔ cup (150ml) dry white wine
freshly ground black pepper
1 small bunch cilantro, leaves and stems chopped

ℐ*HELLFISH* 𝒟*ISHES*

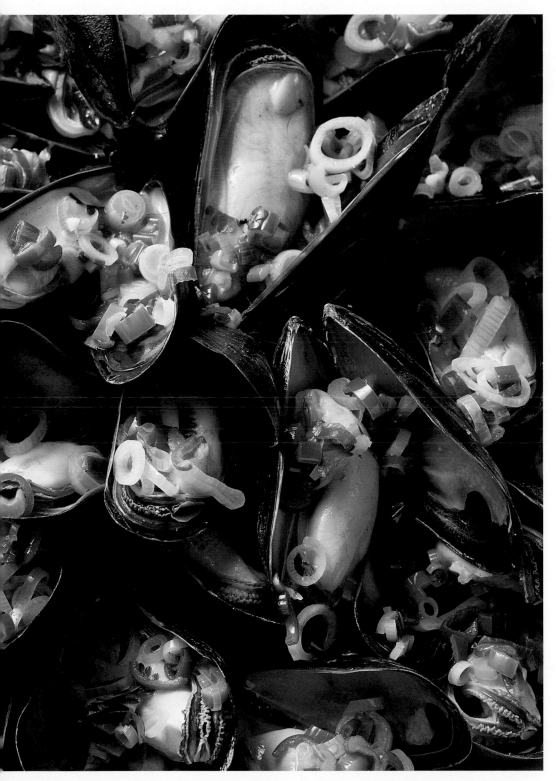

To prepare the mussels, put them into a large bowl or a sink of cold water and stir gently. Leave them for 5 minutes, then lift the mussels out of the water so the grit and sand is left at the bottom. Scrub the mussels under cold running water and scrape off any barnacles and dirt with a small knife. Pull away the hairy black beards. Put the cleaned mussels into another bowl of cold water. Discard any mussels with broken or damaged shells and any open mussels that do not close when tapped.

Melt the butter in a large pan, add the green onions and garlic, and cook very gently for 1 minute or until softened. Add the lemon grass and chili and cook for another minute. Pour in the wine and boil rapidly to reduce the liquid by about a third. Add the mussels to the pan and stir well. Cover with a lid and cook over medium-high heat for about 2 minutes or until the mussels have opened, shaking the pan frequently. Discard any mussels that do not open.

Using a slotted spoon, lift the mussels out of the pan and into warmed serving bowls. Add freshly ground black pepper to taste to the sauce left in the pan, then stir in the chopped cilantro. Spoon the sauce over the mussels and serve immediately.

Serving Suggestions
Serve the mussels as a first course for four people, with plenty of fresh white bread to mop up the sauce. Alternatively, this dish makes a delicious main course for two. You can pick the mussels from their shells using a fork or use an empty shell as a scoop.

Left: the fresh taste of the sea is highlighted in this simple yet beautiful dish of Mussels with Cilantro, Chili, and Lemon Grass.

Cheese Dishes

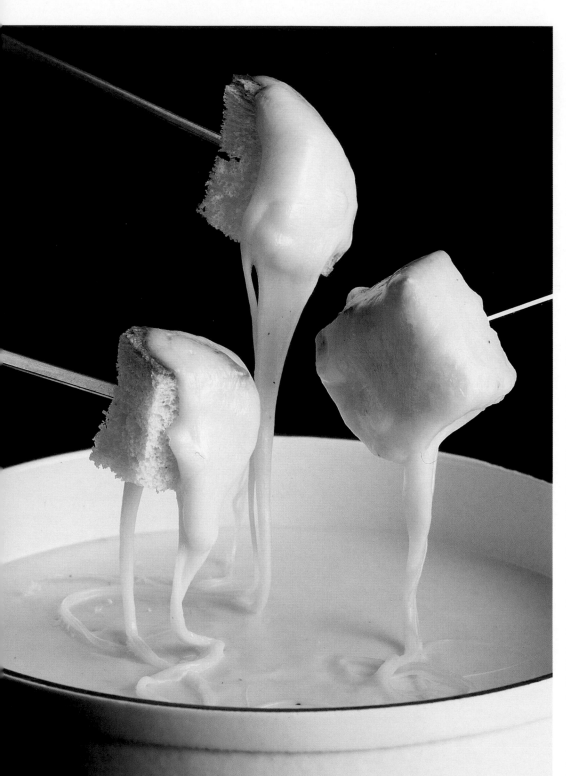

Cheese Fondue

Fondue Savoyarde, from the mountainous Savoie region of France, is properly made in a small earthenware pan, using two local cheeses. They are traditionally finely sliced, not grated, and then melted in the local dry white wine flavored with a shot of kirsch. Fondue is eaten by putting a cube of *pain de campagne*, or French country bread, on the end of a long-handled fork and swirling it in the molten mixture.

SERVES 4

8 ounces (250g) Emmental cheese
8 ounces (250g) Beaufort cheese
1 clove garlic, thickly sliced
1 cup (250ml) dry white wine, preferably from the Savoie
black pepper
2 tablespoons kirsch, or to taste

Finely slice the cheeses. Rub the inside of the fondue pan all over with the garlic slices, then discard them.

Bring the wine to a boil in the pan, and stir in the cheeses. Continue stirring (traditionally in a figure-of-eight motion) until the cheese melts. Set the pan over a table burner, and gently stir in black pepper and kirsch to taste. The burner should keep the fondue warm and liquid without it coming to a boil. Eat immediately.

Variation: Gruyère cheese can be used to make the fondue instead of Beaufort.

Serving Suggestions
Serve with cubes of *pain de campagne* or French bread, or with small, freshly boiled new potatoes and lightly blanched green vegetables such as broccoli florets.

Left: a table burner keeps Cheese Fondue warm and creamy while you enjoy it. Give the mixture a stir each time you dip in the bread.

Gnocchi-Topped Vegetable Casserole

Choose a really colorful combination of vegetables for this substantial winter dish. I think celery root is a must for its flavor and texture, plus a few Jerusalem artichokes, carrots, parsnips, and leeks—even a little cauliflower or broccoli, if desired. Don't worry about precise quantities for each vegetable, because it won't make any difference to the end result.

SERVES 6

FOR THE TOPPING:
2½ cups (600ml) milk
⅔ cup (85g) semolina
freshly grated nutmeg
salt and black pepper
1 extra large egg, beaten
1½ tablespoons (20g) unsalted butter, diced
½ cup (50g) freshly grated Parmesan cheese
¼ cup (25g) grated Gruyère or Emmental cheese
FOR THE CASSEROLE:
1 medium onion, minced
3 cloves garlic, minced
2 tablespoons olive oil
½ teaspoon ground coriander
¼ teaspoon ground cumin
1 14-ounce (400-g) can crushed tomatoes
8 ounces (250g) celery root, cut into thick strips
8 ounces (250g) mixed Jerusalem artichokes and carrots, chopped (about 2 cups)
4 ounces (125g) parsnips, diced (about 1 cup)
4 ounces (125g) leeks, cut into chunks (about 1 cup)
⅓ cup (75ml) vegetable stock
4 ounces (125g) broccoli or cauliflower florets (about 1 cup)
extra grated cheese, for sprinkling

To make the gnocchi topping, bring the milk to a boil in a large saucepan, stirring frequently. Stir in the semolina, nutmeg, and a little salt and pepper. Cook the mixture gently, stirring constantly, until it has thickened. Remove from the heat and beat in the egg, butter, and cheeses. Return the pan to the heat and cook gently, stirring constantly, for 2 to 3 minutes. Taste and adjust the seasoning as necessary, then let the mixture cool.

To make the casserole, gently cook the onion and garlic in the oil for 15 to 20 minutes or until very soft and slightly golden. Add the spices and cook, stirring, for 2 to 3 minutes. Stir in the tomatoes, celery root, artichokes, carrots, parsnips, and leeks. Add the stock and bring the mixture to a boil. Simmer gently for 10 minutes.

Preheat the oven to 400°F. Stir the broccoli or cauliflower florets into the vegetable mixture, then adjust the seasoning and remove from the heat. Transfer the mixture to a large, shallow, greased baking dish. Spread the gnocchi topping over the vegetables in an even layer. Sprinkle with extra cheese. Bake for 20 to 25 minutes or until the gnocchi topping is golden brown and the sauce is bubbling.

Boston Baked Beans

This old-fashioned recipe is traditionally flavored with a piece of salt pork, cooked overnight in a slow oven, and then often served with Boston brown bread, a moist steamed loaf made with molasses. There are many regional variations, made with locally grown beans (black-eyed peas, navy or pea beans), sweetened with maple syrup, brown sugar, or molasses, and containing smoked pork or ham.

SERVES 4

1½ cups (250g) dried white beans
1 onion, spiked with 1 clove
1 bouquet garni
FOR THE SAUCE:
2 tablespoons olive oil
1 small onion, minced
2 cloves garlic, minced (optional)
2 tablespoons tomato paste
2 tablespoons maple syrup
salt and black pepper

Soak the beans overnight in plenty of cold water. Next day, drain and rinse the beans, then put them into a large saucepan with enough fresh cold water to cover. Add the onion and bouquet garni; do not add salt to the beans at this stage because it will prevent them from softening as they cook. Bring to a boil, skimming frequently, and boil hard for 10 minutes, then lower the heat and let simmer for 45 to 50 minutes or until the beans are completely tender. Drain the beans, reserving the cooking liquid but discarding the flavorings.

Preheat the oven to 325°F. Heat the oil in an ovenproof Dutch oven and cook the onion gently for 20 minutes or until it is very soft and slightly golden. Stir in the garlic, tomato paste, and maple syrup and cook for 1 minute. Add the beans and stir well, adding enough of the bean cooking liquid (about 1¾ cups/400ml) to make a soupy sauce. Season lightly and bring it to a boil. Cover and cook in the oven for 45 minutes, stirring occasionally. If the mixture seems to be getting a bit too dry, stir in a little more of the cooking liquid.

Remove the pan from the oven and stir well. If the sauce is too runny, gently reduce it by simmering on top of the stove. Taste and adjust the seasonings as necessary before serving.

Variations: For a simpler dish, omit the onion and garlic. To add spice, you can stir ¼ teaspoon cayenne pepper into the onion with the garlic. For a fresh touch, before serving, stir in 2 tablespoons of minced herbs. For a more elaborate dish, fry 1 cup (150g) diced Canadian bacon or ham in the oil before adding the onion, and arrange 8 browned sausages on top of the beans before placing the pan in the oven.

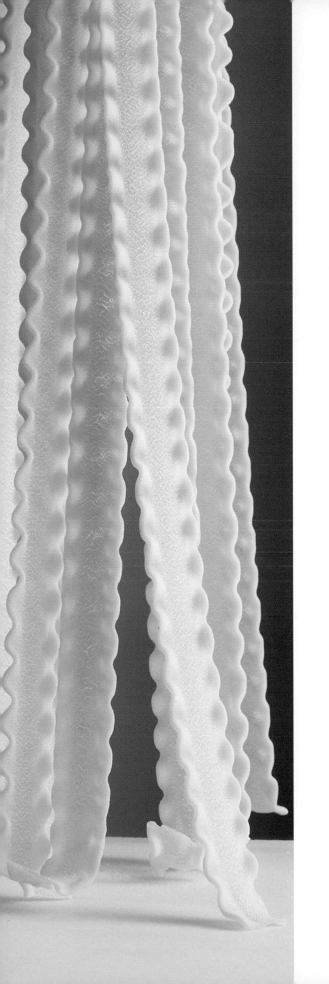

PASTA SAUCES

Pasta has lost its trattoria image and become the ultimate international fast food. It has also shed its stodgy reputation. Silky fine tagliatelle combined with luxurious olive oil and white truffle shavings, or quick-cooking Chinese egg noodles tossed with a few piquant flavorings, have a place on restaurant menus.

Sauces for pasta can be quick and simply prepared: crumbled goat cheese with a splash of lemon or a classic creamy carbonara. They can also be slowly cooked, richly flavored tomato or bolognese mixtures that taste even better when reheated the next day.

The advantage of these sauces is that there is a recipe for every occasion, every season, every appetite. There are cold spicy noodle salads for hot days and picnics, a hearty baked cannelloni for a warm, comforting meal, light low-fat vegetable sauces, and powerful pestos of every hue. Many need not be restricted to pasta and noodles, and work just as well as an accompaniment to polenta or rice.

Left (from top to bottom): Confetti Sauce, Pesto Genovese, Sweet Pepper and Tomato Sauce.

Fresh Tomato and Basil Sauce

SERVES 4 TO 6

5 plum tomatoes, about 1 pound (500g),
  peeled, seeded, and finely diced
1 small shallot, minced
1 clove garlic, minced
1 large bunch basil, torn into small pieces
⅔ cup (150ml) extra virgin olive oil
squeeze lemon juice, or to taste
salt and black pepper

Mix the tomatoes with the other ingredients in a bowl. Cover and set aside for at least 1 hour to let the flavors develop. If the sauce is to be kept any longer, refrigerate it, tightly covered, and use it within 24 hours.

Serving Suggestion
This is a versatile sauce for any pasta.

Confetti Sauce

SERVES 4

½ cup (125ml) olive oil
1 teaspoon minced garlic
1 teaspoon grated fresh ginger
1 teaspoon minced fresh mild green chili pepper
6 anchovy fillets, minced
2 red sweet peppers, cored and finely diced
2 yellow sweet peppers, cored and finely diced
½ cup (125ml) dry white wine or vegetable stock
2 tablespoons chopped flat-leaf parsley
salt and black pepper

Heat the oil in a small saucepan and gently fry the garlic, ginger, and chili pepper for 30 seconds, stirring constantly. Do not let the garlic burn or it will taste bitter.

Left: this uncooked Fresh Tomato and Basil Sauce for pasta features a generous bunch of basil leaves, torn roughly for a full, punchy flavor.

$\mathscr{T}$OMATO $\mathscr{S}$AUCE

Stir in the anchovy fillets and cook, stirring frequently, for about 2 minutes or until they dissolve into the oil. Add the peppers and stir over medium heat until they are soft.

Pour in the wine or stock and bring to a boil. Cover and let simmer for about 20 minutes or until the sauce is cooked and thickened. Add the parsley and salt and pepper to taste when you toss the sauce with the pasta.

Variation: For a more pungent sauce, add fresh hot chili pepper to taste.

Serving Suggestions
Farfalle pasta is best for this sauce, which can also be served with steamed couscous or slices of grilled polenta.

Celery and Tomato Sauce

This sauce has plenty of flavor even though it is low in fat. Use a food processor to make quick work of preparing the vegetables.

SERVES 4 TO 6

3 tablespoons olive oil
2 medium onions, minced
2 medium carrots, minced
4 large stalks celery, or 1 large celery heart, minced and any leaves reserved
3 cups (680g) canned crushed tomatoes
4 cloves garlic, or to taste, minced
1 tablespoon tomato paste or sun-dried tomato paste
salt and black pepper

Heat the oil in a large, heavy saucepan and stir in the onions, carrots, and celery. Cover and cook very gently for about 15 minutes or until soft and lightly golden. Stir in the tomatoes, garlic, tomato paste, and a little seasoning. Bring the mixture to a boil and stir well, then cover and simmer for 30 to

45 minutes or until the sauce is thick and well flavored. Taste and adjust the seasoning. Serve garnished with celery leaves.

The sauce can be cooled and then chilled overnight, or frozen for up to 1 month.

Serving Suggestions
This is suitable for pasta, rice, or couscous.

Sweet Pepper and Tomato Sauce

MAKES 3¼ CUPS (800ML)

3 tablespoons olive oil
1 medium onion, roughly chopped
2 large red sweet peppers, cored, seeded, and roughly chopped
4 large cloves garlic, roughly chopped
1½ pounds (750g) tomatoes, roughly chopped
1 large bouquet garni
salt and black pepper
2 to 3 drops hot red pepper sauce, or to taste
pinch sugar, or to taste
squeeze lemon juice, or to taste

Heat the oil in a large, heavy saucepan, add the onion, and stir well. Cover the pan with the lid or put a disk of dampened parchment paper on the onions. Cook very gently for about 20 minutes or until soft but not colored. Add the sweet peppers and garlic and stir well. Cook over medium heat for a couple of minutes, stirring frequently.

Add the chopped tomatoes to the pan along with the bouquet garni and a little seasoning. Stir well, then bring the mixture to a boil. Cover and simmer gently, stirring occasionally, for 35 minutes or until the vegetables are really tender. You should not have to add any extra liquid if the tomatoes are ripe and the pan is tightly covered.

Remove the bouquet garni, then transfer the sauce to a food processor or a blender and process it to make a thick purée.

Pour the sauce back into the rinsed-out pan and reheat. Season to taste with salt, pepper, a few drops of hot pepper sauce, and sugar or lemon juice, depending on the flavor—it may be a little acidic or too sweet.

Variations: To make a smoother sauce, pour the purée back into the pan through a coarse conical strainer, pushing down on the vegetables in the strainer with the back of a ladle so only the skin and seeds remain.

For a thin, glossy, elegant sauce, pour the purée back into the pan through a fine conical strainer, pushing down lightly with the back of a small ladle so that the sauce drains through, but all the skin, seeds, and thick pulpy flesh is left in the strainer. Reheat and season to taste. The sauce can be slightly thickened, made more glossy, and enriched by whisking in 3 tablespoons (45g) diced unsalted butter just before serving.

If you like, you can add more hot pepper sauce or cayenne pepper to make a hot spicy sauce; a few drops of Worcestershire sauce will add an extra kick.

For an herb sauce, add shredded basil or snipped chives just before serving; or you can add 2 teaspoons of dried oregano to the sauce when you add the tomatoes.

To make a heavier, richer sauce, add 1 tablespoon of sun-dried tomato paste when you add the red peppers.

You can add 2 tablespoons of roughly chopped black olives and/or 1 very finely shredded red sweet pepper to the sauce just before serving. Alternatively, stir 3 tablespoons of heavy cream or crème fraîche into the finished sauce.

Serving Suggestions
Serve with long pasta such as spaghetti and fettuccine. You can use the smooth, slightly thickened version of this sauce for lasagne, cannelloni, and similar pasta dishes. The thin, silky-smooth version mounted with butter can be served with roast cod or monkfish or with grilled chicken.

Pesto Genovese

This bright, pungent basil sauce comes from Genoa in Italy, where it is invariably matched with long, thin pasta. However, pesto has many more uses, and you will have great fun coming up with your own ideas. The cheeses that are traditionally used in making pesto are well-aged Parmesan or pecorino romano, both of which contribute a sharpening flavor to the sauce and give a texture that is more grainy than creamy.

MAKES 12 OUNCES (350G)

2 cups (100g) fresh basil leaves
1 cup (100g) freshly grated Parmesan or
pecorino romano cheese
½ cup (75g) pine nuts
5 cloves garlic, peeled
7 tablespoons (100ml) extra virgin olive oil
salt and black pepper

Put the basil, grated cheese, pine nuts, and garlic into a food processor and process just until the mixture becomes a rough paste, scraping down the side frequently. With the machine running, add the oil in a slow, steady stream until the mixture emulsifies and becomes a smooth purée. Season to taste with salt and pepper.

Store in a tightly covered jar in the refrigerator for no more than 1 week, making sure that a thin layer of oil covers the surface of the pesto (stir this in prior to use). If you want to freeze pesto, make it without garlic. Then, when the pesto has thawed, mince some garlic and stir it in.

Serving Suggestions
Use pesto in hot pasta dishes, cold pasta salads, or with grilled fish, lamb, or chicken. You can spread it on crostini and bruschetta, or use it as a topping for stuffed tomatoes, sweet peppers, or onions. Pesto is an excellent accompaniment to minestrone, or any tomato or sweet pepper soup, and makes a tasty topping for baked potatoes.

Cilantro and Almond Pesto

MAKES 12 OUNCES (350G)

2 cups (100g) cilantro leaves
1 cup (100g) freshly grated Parmesan or
pecorino romano cheese
½ cup (75g) roughly chopped blanched almonds
5 cloves garlic, peeled
7 tablespoons (100ml) extra virgin olive oil
salt and black pepper

Put the cilantro, grated cheese, chopped almonds, and garlic into a food processor and process just until the mixture becomes a rough paste, scraping down the sides frequently. With the machine running, add the oil in a slow, steady stream until the mixture emulsifies into a smooth purée. Taste and add salt and pepper as necessary. Store the sauce in a tightly covered jar in the refrigerator for no more than 1 week.

Serving Suggestions
This pesto goes particularly well with grilled or baked chicken and fresh seafood such as tuna, scallops, and mussels.

Sage Pesto

MAKES 8 OUNCES (250G)

1 cup (100g) freshly grated Parmesan or
pecorino romano cheese
3 tablespoons (25g) pine nuts
6 large sage leaves
3 cloves garlic, peeled
1 fresh hot red chili pepper, seeded and
chopped
⅓ cup (75ml) olive oil
salt and black pepper

Put the cheese, pine nuts, sage, garlic, and chili into a food processor and process just until the mixture becomes a rough paste,

Pesto Sauce

scraping down the side frequently. With the machine running, add the oil in a slow, steady stream until the mixture emulsifies into a smooth purée. Taste and add salt and pepper as necessary. Store the sauce in a tightly covered jar in the refrigerator for no more than 1 week.

Serving Suggestions

This is a good sauce for chicken, polenta, and tomatoes, as well as pasta.

Arugula and Goat Cheese Pesto

This sauce is mild and creamy, but has the peppery, slightly bitter taste of arugula.

MAKES 1 POUND (450G)

8 ounces (250g) soft fresh goat cheese
1 cup (100g) arugula leaves
½ cup (75g) pine nuts
5 cloves garlic, peeled
7 tablespoons (100ml) extra virgin olive oil
salt and black pepper

Put the goat cheese, arugula, pine nuts, and garlic into a food processor and process the mixture to a rough paste, scraping down the side frequently. With the machine running, add the oil in a slow, steady stream until the mixture emulsifies into a purée, then season to taste. Store in a tightly covered jar in the refrigerator for up to 1 week.

Serving Suggestions

A marvelous and unusual topping for baked potatoes, grilled lamb, or panfried filet mignon. You can also stir this pesto into warm white beans such as cannellini, or use it as a topping for grilled vegetables.

Left: fruity olive oil and sharp-flavored Italian cheese are blended with aromatic basil leaves to produce a traditional Pesto Genovese.

Red Pesto

MAKES 12 OUNCES (350G)

1 cup (100g) freshly grated Parmesan or
**   pecorino romano cheese**
½ cup (75g) pine nuts
½ cup (100g) sun-dried tomatoes packed
**   in oil, drained**
5 cloves garlic, peeled
7 tablespoons (100ml) extra virgin olive oil
salt and black pepper

Put the cheese, pine nuts, sun-dried tomatoes, and garlic into a food processor and process the mixture to a rough paste, scraping down the side frequently. With the machine running, add the oil in a slow, steady stream until the mixture emulsifies into a purée. Season to taste with salt and pepper. Store in a tightly covered jar in the refrigerator for no more than 1 week.

Serving Suggestions

Red pesto can be stirred into couscous as well as pasta. It is an excellent base for pizzas, bruschetta, and crostini, or can be layered with soft cheese and salad to make a flavor-packed sandwich filling.

Black Olive Pesto

MAKES 8 OUNCES (225G)

1⅓ cups (200g) pitted black olives
1 teaspoon thyme leaves
3 tablespoons extra virgin olive oil

Place the olives in a blender with the thyme leaves and process to a purée. Slowly blend in the olive oil until the mixture emulsifies.

Serving Suggestions

Use as the base of a pasta sauce, adding tomatoes or roasted sweet peppers for freshness. It can also be served as a dip or spread, or drizzled over pizzas.

Nut Sauce

Green Pepper and Pine Nut Sauce

SERVES 2 TO 4

3 tablespoons (25g) pine nuts
1 clove garlic, unpeeled
1 large green sweet pepper
grated zest of 1 lemon plus half its juice
1 heaping tablespoon cilantro leaves
½ teaspoon chopped fresh green chili pepper,
**   or to taste**
½ cup (125ml) extra virgin olive oil
salt and black pepper

Set the oven to 375°F. Toast the pine nuts in the heating oven for 7 minutes or until they turn light golden brown. At the same time, roast the unpeeled garlic clove for about 10 minutes or until soft. Let the pine nuts and garlic cool.

Char the sweet pepper under the broiler, turning frequently, until the skin is black all over. Cool, then peel it under cold running water. Quarter the pepper and discard its core and seeds. Peel the roasted garlic.

Place the lemon zest and juice in a food processor with the green sweet pepper, pine nuts, garlic, cilantro, and chili and process until smooth. With the machine running, slowly pour in the oil through the opening in the lid. Season to taste.

The sauce can be stored, tightly covered, in the refrigerator for up to 48 hours. Bring it to room temperature and stir before use.

Serving Suggestions

Serve with short pasta or steamed rice. This sauce also goes well with fish such as grilled halibut, swordfish, or tuna steaks, or alongside large shrimp that have been fried in garlic-flavored oil.

Above (left to right): Green Pepper and Pine Nut Sauce, Walnut and Gorgonzola Sauce, and Romesco Sauce all add a nutty taste to pasta.

Romesco Sauce

SERVES 4 TO 6

3 ripe plum tomatoes
2 red sweet peppers
4 cloves garlic, unpeeled
6 tablespoons (50g) pine nuts
1 large dried romesco chili pepper, or
**   1 to 2 dried ancho chili peppers**
1 to 2 tablespoons white wine vinegar
¼ cup (60ml) extra virgin olive oil
salt and black pepper

Set the oven to 425°F. Put the tomatoes, sweet peppers, and garlic into a nonstick roasting pan. Spread the pine nuts in a

Nut and Cheese Sauces

single layer in another baking pan. Place both pans in the oven. Remove the pine nuts when golden (after 5 minutes), the tomatoes and garlic when soft (about 10 minutes), and the peppers when dark brown (after about 35 minutes). Let them cool. Meanwhile, cover the dried chili pepper with hot water and let soak for 30 minutes.

Peel, quarter, and core the sweet peppers. Peel the tomatoes and garlic. Drain and chop the soaked chili pepper, discarding the seeds and stem. Blend them all together with the pine nuts and vinegar in a food processor. With the machine running, slowly pour in the oil through the opening in the lid. Season to taste, adding extra oil or vinegar as needed.

Store, covered, in the refrigerator for up to 48 hours and use at room temperature.

Variations: Add 2 minced anchovy fillets to the sauce. Replace the dried chili pepper with a fresh mild red chili pepper or a few drops of hot red pepper sauce.

Serving Suggestions
This is good with fish and shellfish as well as with all kinds of pasta.

Zucchini-Walnut Sauce

SERVES 4 TO 6

· ¼ cup (60ml) extra virgin olive oil
1 pound (500g) small zucchini, thinly sliced
1 large clove garlic, minced
3 heaping tablespoons minced parsley
3 extra large eggs, beaten
¾ cup (75g) walnut pieces
salt and black pepper
freshly grated Parmesan cheese, for sprinkling

While the pasta is cooking, heat the olive oil in a large, heavy-based skillet and cook the zucchini with the garlic until golden brown and soft, stirring frequently. Stir in the parsley.

Drain the cooked pasta, then return it to the hot, empty pasta pan. Immediately add the beaten eggs, and stir and toss the pasta quite vigorously to cook the eggs and mix them with the pasta. Add the walnuts and the contents of the frying pan to the pasta and mix well. Taste and add salt and pepper as necessary. Serve immediately with Parmesan cheese.

Variations: Omit the walnuts, if desired. For a stronger flavor, simply add more garlic, and vary the herbs as you like.

Serving Suggestions
Serve with pasta such as penne or fusilli.

Walnut and Gorgonzola Sauce

SERVES 4 TO 6

¾ cup (75g) finely chopped walnuts
1 to 2 cloves garlic, to taste, minced
⅔ cup (150ml) extra virgin olive oil
¾ cup (100g) crumbled Gorgonzola cheese
1 tablespoon minced flat-leaf parsley
salt and black pepper

Stir the walnuts and garlic into the oil. Mix thoroughly, then stir in the Gorgonzola. If using the sauce immediately, add the parsley; if not, add it just before serving. Season to taste, using salt only if necessary. Without the parsley, the sauce can be stored overnight in the refrigerator.

Serving Suggestions
Serve with long pasta such as fettuccine.

Instant Cheese Sauce

This recipe could not be quicker or simpler. The heat of the pan and the freshly cooked pasta melt the cheese to a smooth sauce that coats the pasta beautifully.

SERVES 4

5 to 6 ounces (150g) soft goat cheese
1 bunch chives, snipped
grated zest and juice of 1 small lemon
salt and black pepper

While the pasta is draining, crumble the cheese into the hot, empty pasta pan. Stir in the steaming pasta, then the chives and lemon zest and juice. Toss so the cheese melts to coat the pasta. Season and serve.

Serving suggestions
Serve with pasta such as farfalle or fusilli.

Sauce Miffi

SERVES 4 TO 6

2 tablespoons extra virgin olive oil
1 clove garlic, or to taste, minced
1 pound (500g) young spinach leaves
½ cup (115g) ricotta cheese
salt and black pepper
freshly grated nutmeg

While the pasta is cooking, heat the oil in a large, heavy saucepan, add the garlic, and cook gently for a few seconds. Add the spinach, raise the heat, and cook, stirring, until wilted. Put the spinach mixture into a food processor with the ricotta, and pulse to make a rough sauce.

Drain the pasta, then add the sauce to the hot, empty pasta pan. Add the hot pasta and toss until combined. Season with salt, pepper, and nutmeg to taste, and serve.

Variations: Add 1 cup (100g) shredded prosciutto or cooked crumbled bacon.

Serving Suggestions
Serve with pasta such as rigatoni.

FISH AND CHEESE SAUCES

Fettuccine with Smoked Salmon

Very quick and very elegant. For even faster preparation, buy a package of smoked salmon trimmings, which are already cut up.

SERVES 4

8 ounces (250g) dried fettuccine
FOR THE SAUCE:
2 cups (500ml) sour cream
6 ounces (175g) smoked salmon, cut in strips
black pepper
1 tablespoon chopped dill

Cook the pasta according to the package directions, then drain. Pour the cream into the hot, empty pasta pan and bring it just to a boil. Remove the pan from the heat and stir in the smoked salmon. Season with plenty of black pepper.

Tip the pasta into a warmed serving bowl and pour the hot sauce over. Sprinkle with the dill, then toss to combine thoroughly. Serve immediately.

Serving Suggestions
Accompany with a watercress salad. For a treat, garnish the pasta with salmon caviar.

Marco's Anchovy Sauce

SERVES 4 TO 6

3 tablespoons extra virgin olive oil
1 large tomato, peeled and thinly sliced
3 large cloves garlic, thinly sliced
4 anchovy fillets, roughly chopped
½ cup (115g) ricotta or cottage cheese
3 tablespoons black olive paste or tapenade
salt and black pepper
freshly grated Parmesan cheese, for sprinkling

While the pasta is cooking, heat the olive oil in a small pan, add the tomato and garlic,

and cook them very gently for 5 minutes, stirring frequently. Stir in the anchovies and continue cooking over the lowest possible heat for 15 minutes, stirring frequently.

Tip the contents of the pan into a food processor and add the cheese and black olive paste or tapenade. Process until the mixture is smooth; if you prefer a rough texture, just stir the ingredients together.

Drain the pasta. Pour the sauce into the hot, empty pasta pan, then add the steaming pasta and toss until thoroughly mixed. Season to taste and serve immediately, with grated Parmesan cheese.

Serving Suggestions
Serve with pasta such as penne.

Niçoise Sauce

A colorful, well-flavored sauce, this is made with canned tuna, anchovies, and olives (those marinated in herbs would be good).

SERVES 4

1 large onion, minced
3 large cloves garlic, or to taste, minced
3 tablespoons olive oil
1 14-ounce (400-g) can plum tomatoes
1 2-ounce (50-g) can anchovy fillets, drained
2 7-ounce (200-g) cans tuna in olive oil, drained
⅓ cup (50g) black olives
2 tablespoons chopped basil
salt and black pepper

Cook the onion and garlic very gently in the heated oil for 10 to 15 minutes or until really soft but not colored. Purée the tomatoes and their juice with the anchovies in a food processor or blender, add the mixture to the pan, and stir well. Let simmer gently for 10 minutes, stirring frequently.

Flake the tuna and stir it into the sauce. When it is thoroughly heated, stir in the olives and basil, and season to taste.

Variation: Omit the anchovies, olives, and basil. Add a 1¼-inch (3-cm) piece of fresh ginger, peeled and grated, with the onions and 1 minced fresh medium-hot chili pepper with the puréed tomatoes. Finish with 1 tablespoon of minced cilantro.

Serving Suggestions
Serve with rigatoni or penne or with polenta.

Fish and Four-Cheese Macaroni

SERVES 4

1½ pounds (750g) white fish fillet
12 ounces (350g) dried pasta, such as large elbow macaroni
FOR THE SAUCE:
3 tablespoons (45g) unsalted butter
¼ cup (35g) all-purpose flour
3 cups (750ml) milk
1 cup (100g) diced buffalo mozzarella cheese
1 cup (100g) grated Gruyère or Emmental cheese
¾ cup (100g) crumbled Gorgonzola cheese
salt and black pepper
½ cup (50g) freshly grated Parmesan cheese

Poach the fish, then let it cool. Flake the fish, removing the skin and bones.

Cook the pasta according to the directions on the package. Meanwhile, make the sauce. Melt the butter in a heavy-based saucepan and stir in the flour. Cook the roux over low heat, stirring constantly, for 1 minute, then whisk in the milk. Stir until smooth. Increase the heat to medium and stir constantly until the sauce boils and thickens. Simmer gently for 3 minutes, stirring frequently to prevent the sauce from sticking to the bottom of the pan.

Remove the pan from the heat and stir in the mozzarella, Gruyère, and Gorgonzola. When the cheeses have melted completely, add salt and pepper to taste.

Fish and Shellfish Sauces

Drain the cooked pasta and return it to the hot, empty pasta pan. Stir in the cheese sauce. Pour half the pasta mixture into a large buttered baking dish, cover it with the flaked fish, and add the remaining pasta. Sprinkle with the Parmesan cheese.

If serving immediately, put the dish under a hot broiler until the top is browned and bubbling. If you are making it in advance, cool the pasta mixture quickly, then cover and refrigerate for up to 24 hours. Reheat the dish in a preheated 375°F oven for 25 to 35 minutes or until bubbling, then finish it by browning it under the broiler.

Below: a curly pasta such as creste di galli or fusilli is best for Tuna and Artichoke Sauce. This recipe uses pantry ingredients, so you can rely on it when you have unexpected guests.

Tuna and Artichoke Sauce

This easy sauce has an unusual mixture of Italian and Chinese ingredients.

SERVES 4

1 14-ounce (400-g) can artichoke bottoms, drained and roughly chopped
¼ cup (60ml) olive oil
1 clove garlic, minced
1 7-ounce (200-g) can tuna in olive or sunflower oil
2 tablespoons sun-dried tomato paste
1 tablespoon sweet Chinese chili sauce
¼ cup (60ml) rice wine or dry white wine
2 tablespoons minced cilantro
black pepper

Lightly crush the artichoke bottoms with a mortar and pestle, or a fork, and set aside.

Heat the olive oil in a medium-size saucepan. Add the garlic and cook just until it turns golden—do not let it burn. Add the tuna, with the oil from the can, and break it into small pieces with a wooden spoon. Stir in the artichokes, tomato paste, and chili sauce and let simmer for 2 to 3 minutes. Add the wine and stir, then cover the pan and simmer for 15 minutes.

Just before serving, stir the cilantro into the sauce and season with black pepper.

Variation: Cook 1 teaspoon finely grated fresh ginger with the garlic.

Serving Suggestions
Toss with a curly pasta such as creste di galli or fusilli.

Sauce Vongole

SERVES 2

1 tablespoon olive oil
1 clove garlic, minced
8 plum tomatoes, chopped
1½ cups (200g) canned clams, drained
3 to 4 basil leaves
salt and black pepper

Gently heat the olive oil in a small saucepan or skillet. Add the garlic and cook for just 30 seconds, making sure it does not brown.

Add the tomatoes to the pan and let them cook over low heat for 10 to 15 minutes or until the mixture is thick and pulpy. Stir in the clams and heat for 2 to 3 minutes.

Tear the basil leaves into small strips and add them to the sauce. Season to taste with salt and pepper, then serve.

Serving Suggestions
Toss with long pasta, such as spaghetti, or serve with rice or polenta.

Beef and Mushroom Sauce

SERVES 4

½ ounce (15g) dried porcini mushrooms
1 pound (500g) ground beef round
1 medium onion, minced
2 tablespoons olive oil (optional)
1 clove garlic, minced
1 tablespoon tomato paste
salt and black pepper

Soak the mushrooms in 1 cup (250ml) of hot water for 20 minutes. Put the beef in a large skillet and cook, stirring frequently, until browned and crumbly. Add the onion to the skillet, with the oil if needed, and fry until soft but not browned.

Drain the mushrooms, saving the soaking liquid, then chop them roughly. Add to the meat with the garlic. Fry for 1 to 2 minutes, then add the strained mushroom liquid and tomato paste. Season lightly. Cover and simmer gently, stirring occasionally, for 20 minutes. Taste and adjust the seasoning.

The cooled sauce can be stored in the refrigerator for up to 4 days, or frozen for up to 1 month.

Serving Suggestions

Toss the sauce with pasta, or use it to make lasagne or fill crêpes. You can also use it to stuff vegetables, then bake them.

Cannelloni

For a lighter touch, I make cannelloni with a smooth, well-flavored tomato sauce instead of the usual rich and creamy béchamel.

SERVES 4 TO 6

8 ounces (250g) dried cannelloni tubes
Beef and Mushroom Sauce (see above)
¾ cup (75g) grated Parmesan cheese

FOR THE TOMATO SAUCE:
2 tablespoons olive oil
1 large onion, chopped
2 cloves garlic, minced
1 stalk celery, chopped
1 medium carrot, thinly sliced
1 28-ounce (800-g) can plum tomatoes in purée, chopped, or 4 cups (1kg) tomato purée
salt and black pepper

To make the tomato sauce, heat the oil in a heavy saucepan. Add the onion, cover, and

Above: a satisfying meal of Cannelloni. Tubes of pasta are stuffed with a hearty meat sauce, then baked with tomato sauce and grated cheese.

cook very gently for 15 minutes or until soft and golden. Stir in the garlic, celery, and carrot. Cover again and continue cooking for 5 minutes. Add the plum tomatoes or purée and seasoning, and cook gently for a further 20 minutes. Purée the mixture in a food processor, then taste and adjust the

Meat Sauce

seasoning. The cooled sauce can be stored in the refrigerator for up to 5 days.

To prepare the cannelloni, preheat the oven to 375°F. Cook the pasta tubes according to package directions, then drain. Stuff the tubes with the meat sauce.

Grease a large baking dish and put a layer of tomato sauce in the bottom. Arrange the filled cannelloni on top, in a single layer if possible. Spoon the rest of the tomato sauce over, then sprinkle with the Parmesan cheese. Bake for 25 minutes or until the pasta is tender and the sauce is bubbling.

Variations: Cannelloni can be filled with any ground meat. Beef is most common, but lamb, pork, chicken, turkey, and venison are also excellent.

Bolognese Sauce

There are more recipes for this sauce from Bologna than there are types of spaghetti, so I am giving my favorite. Bolognese should be made from a combination of meats, slowly simmered to taste really rich. I like it made with sweet Italian sausages.

SERVES 6

1 pound (500g) Italian sausage
1¼ pounds (600g) ground beef round
1 large onion, minced
1 stalk celery, finely diced
1 tablespoon tomato paste
1 28-ounce (800-g) can plum tomatoes in
**   tomato purée**
⅔ cup (150ml) dry red wine
3 cloves garlic, or to taste, minced
1 heaping tablespoon dried oregano
1 large bouquet garni
salt and black pepper

Slit the sausages lengthwise, peel off the skins, and put the meat into a large, heavy-based saucepan. Add the ground round.

Cook the meats until browned and crumbly, breaking them up with a spoon. Remove with a slotted spoon so the fat drains back into the pan. Lower the heat, and add the onion and celery to the pan. Cook gently, stirring frequently, until they are soft and golden. Stir in the tomato paste and cook for 1 minute. Add the tomatoes and roughly break them up with the spoon.

Return the sausage and beef to the pan along with the remaining ingredients. Add a little pepper (wait to add salt until the end of cooking). Bring the mixture to a boil, stirring well, then cover and simmer very gently for 2 hours, either on top of the stove or in a low oven. Stir occasionally.

The finished sauce should be thick and rich. Before serving, discard the bouquet garni, and taste and add salt and more pepper as needed. The sauce is best if quickly cooled, chilled overnight, and then reheated before serving. It can be frozen for up to 1 month.

Serving Suggestions
Serve with thick spaghetti and freshly grated Parmesan, or with polenta or brown rice.

Pasta alla Carbonara

This classic combination of bacon, eggs, and cheese should be seasoned with care.

SERVES 4

8 ounces (250g) dried linguine
FOR THE SAUCE:
1 tablespoon olive oil
2 cups (175g) pancetta or Canadian bacon,
**   cut in strips**
2 large cloves garlic, minced
2 extra large eggs (see caution about eggs
**   on page 11)**
¼ cup (30g) freshly grated Parmesan cheese
¼ cup (60ml) heavy cream
black pepper

Cook the pasta according to the directions on the package. Meanwhile, heat the oil in a skillet and cook the pancetta until crisp and golden. Add the garlic and cook for another minute, stirring.

In a medium bowl, beat the eggs with the cheese, cream, pepper.

Drain the pasta and return it to the hot, empty pan. Add the bacon and the egg mixture and toss gently together until thoroughly combined. Taste, season as necessary, and serve immediately.

Pasta with Mortadella, Cream, and Peas

SERVES 6

2 tablespoons (25g) butter
1 shallot, chopped
½ cup (125ml) dry white wine
½ cup (125ml) heavy cream
¾ cup (100g) frozen petite peas, thawed
1 pound (500g) dried pasta
8 ounces (250g) mortadella sausage, diced
½ cup (50g) freshly grated Parmesan cheese
grated zest of 1 lemon and half its juice
salt and black pepper

In a medium-size saucepan, melt the butter, then add the shallot and cook over low heat until softened. Add the white wine to the pan, raise the heat, and simmer the liquid until it has almost evaporated.

Add half the cream to the pan, lower the heat, and simmer gently for 5 minutes. Stir in the peas and continue cooking for about 5 minutes.

Cook the pasta according to the package directions. Drain the pasta well, then return it to the pan and place it over low heat. Toss the cream sauce into the pasta. Add the mortadella, Parmesan, lemon zest and juice, and the remaining cream. Toss again, season to taste, and serve.

𝒩OODLE 𝒟ISHES

Teriyaki Salmon and Japanese Noodles

The unusual ingredients for this recipe are generally available from Asian markets, in many health food shops, and even in some supermarkets nowadays. You'll need large, deep soup bowls to serve this.

SERVES 4

1 pound (500g) salmon fillet, skinned
8 ounces (250g) udon noodles
8 ounces (250g) soba noodles
1 quart (1 liter) Dashi broth (see page 10)
1 large bunch watercress, trimmed
FOR THE TERIYAKI MARINADE:
1½ tablespoons soy sauce
1½ tablespoons mirin
1½ tablespoons sake
FOR GARNISH:
4 green onions, sliced into long slivers
sliced pickled ginger, minced

Heat a cast-iron griddle or skillet until very hot. Mix the marinade ingredients in a small bowl and brush onto the salmon. Sear the fish for 1 to 2 minutes on each side, then remove the griddle from the heat, but leave the fish on it to cook through. When the salmon is pale pink and moist on the inside, break it into bite-size pieces.

Bring a large pot of water to a rolling boil. Add the udon noodles, then, after 3 minutes, add the soba noodles. When they are both cooked, drain them thoroughly.

Meanwhile, heat the dashi broth in a large saucepan until steam rises from the surface of the stock. For each serving, put a layer of mixed noodles in the center of a large soup bowl, cover it with a layer of watercress, then add a layer of salmon pieces. Finally, drench them with a generous ladle or two of the dashi broth.

Before serving, garnish each bowl with 1 tablespoon of slivered green onions and sprinkle with the minced pickled ginger.

Soba with Ginger and Soy Glaze

Soba noodles are made from buckwheat flour and can taste a little strong, but here they are enlivened with a sauce of fresh ginger juice and vegetables.

SERVES 2

3-inch (7.5-cm) piece fresh ginger, peeled
6 ounces (175g) soba noodles
2 tablespoons vegetable oil
1 small leek, halved and thinly sliced
1 red sweet pepper, seeded and finely diced
1 large carrot, halved and thinly sliced
1 cup (100g) fine green beans, cut in
    1-inch (2.5-cm) lengths
2 teaspoons soy sauce, plus extra to taste
½ cup (60g) roasted unsalted cashew nuts
4 ounces (125g) fresh tofu, diced
Asian sesame oil

Make the ginger juice by finely grating the ginger onto a board, then collecting all the pulp in your hand and squeezing it tightly so that the juice runs into a small bowl. Add any excess juice from the board to the bowl and set it aside.

Cook the soba noodles according to the package directions, then drain.

Meanwhile, heat the vegetable oil in a large saucepan and cook the leek and sweet pepper gently until they are softened but not colored. Add the carrot, beans, and soy sauce and stir-fry the vegetables over medium heat for 5 to 6 minutes.

Add the cashews, tofu, and cooked noodles to the pan. Toss carefully so that the vegetables and noodles are well mixed, but the tofu does not break up. Stir in the ginger juice and a few drops of sesame oil. Taste and add extra sesame oil and soy sauce as needed. The starch from the noodles will form a light glaze when combined with the ginger juice, sesame oil, and soy sauce.

Variation: If you cannot find roasted unsalted cashews, buy roasted salted cashews and rinse them before use.

Tahini Chicken Noodles

SERVES 6

1 pound (500g) dried Chinese egg noodles
1 teaspoon Asian sesame oil
4 skinless boneless chicken breast halves
¾-inch (2-cm) piece fresh ginger, thinly sliced
1 small onion, sliced
6 black peppercorns
FOR THE SAUCE:
¼ cup (85g) tahini
2 tablespoons soy sauce
1 tablespoon Asian sesame oil
3 cloves garlic, peeled
1 small fresh medium-hot red chili pepper, or
    to taste, seeded and quartered
1¼-inch (3-cm) piece fresh ginger, thinly sliced
1 teaspoon sugar
¾ teaspoon toasted ground Szechuan
    peppercorns
2 tablespoons minced cilantro
1 tablespoon toasted sesame seeds

Cook the noodles according to the package directions, then drain, rinse with cold water, and drain again thoroughly. Toss the noodles with the teaspoon of oil and set aside.

Put the chicken into a large pan with the ginger, onion, peppercorns, and water to cover. Bring to a boil, then cover and simmer for 20 minutes or until the chicken is cooked through. Let the chicken cool in the liquid, then drain and shred the flesh. Strain and reserve the poaching liquid.

To make the sauce, blend the tahini, soy sauce, sesame oil, garlic, chili, ginger, sugar, and Szechuan peppercorns in a food processor until smooth. Add enough of the poaching liquid to make a sauce with a creamy consistency. Taste and adjust the flavor with soy sauce, sugar, or tahini.

NOODLE SAUCE

Mix the noodles with the chicken and the sauce, then garnish the dish with cilantro and toasted sesame seeds. Cover and chill until ready to serve, for up to 12 hours.

Chili-Citrus Dressing

This sauce is the basis of my favorite Chinese noodle dish, a salad that I make for warm weather meals, indoors and out.

SERVES 4

1 lemon
1 orange
¼ cup (85g) tahini
¼ cup (60ml) vegetable oil
4 medium green onions, trimmed and sliced
2 tablespoons sweet Chinese chili sauce, or to taste
2 cloves garlic
2 tablespoons soy sauce
2 tablespoons sugar
1 tablespoon Asian sesame oil
½ teaspoon toasted ground Szechuan peppercorns
Chinese white rice vinegar, to taste (optional)

Grate the zest from the lemon and orange and squeeze out their juices. Place them in a food processor along with the remaining ingredients and process to a slightly textured sauce. Add more soy sauce, chili sauce, or white rice vinegar to taste—as noodles are bland, the sauce should be spicy and balanced between sweet, sour, and salty flavors. It can be stored, tightly covered, in the refrigerator for up to 3 days.

Serving Suggestions
Toss the dressing with hot egg noodles. Or make a salad by tossing it with cold noodles, then cover and chill for up to 12 hours: the longer you wait, the stronger the flavors and the drier the noodles. Serve alone or with Tahini Chicken Noodles, cold cuts, or fish.

Quick Curried Coconut Sauce

SERVES 4

1¼ cups (300ml) coconut cream
⅔ cup (175g) mild Malaysian curry paste
1 cup (150g) snow peas, halved crosswise
1½ cups (150g) baby carrots, halved crosswise
¼ cup (15g) minced cilantro

In a medium-size saucepan, stir together the coconut cream and curry paste over medium heat until smooth. Add the snow peas and carrots. Bring the mixture almost to a boil, then let simmer gently for about 5 minutes. Stir the minced cilantro into the sauce and serve hot.

Variation: If you cannot find coconut cream, you can use canned coconut milk instead. If Malaysian curry paste is not available, substitute a mild or moderately flavored Indian curry paste.

Serving Suggestions
Pour the sauce over cooked egg noodles and serve as a meal on its own or as part of a selection of Southeast-Asian dishes.

Below: lemon and orange add zest to Chinese egg noodles in Chili-Citrus Dressing, a spicy blend of sweet, sour, and salty flavors.

TANGY SAUCES

The heat in these hot, spicy, and aromatic sauces comes from adding a pungent, fiery ingredient. Chili peppers are the first to spring to mind, but other heat sources are garlic, fresh ginger, and mustard.

In this broad selection of recipes from all around the world, you will find the nutty satay of Indonesia, fragrant Thai curry pastes, harissa from Tunisia, and the most aromatic blends of Indian spices. There are creamy sauces from Kashmir, a black bean stir-fry from China, and a stunning chili jam from the fusion cooking style of the Pacific Rim area. Western or Asian, sweet and mild, fiery hot, fragrant, and appetizing, the range of sauces in this chapter will appeal to all palates.

Left (clockwise from top): Thai Red Curry Paste, Fresh Mango Salsa, Plum Sauce.

Fennel and Orange Salsa

This is best described as a sweet and sour salsa, with the sweetness of the orange enhanced by the aniseed flavor of the fennel and the bite of the chilies.

SERVES 4

½ bulb fennel, minced
1 fresh hot green chili pepper, such as jalapeño, minced
1 fresh hot red chili pepper, such as serrano, minced
grated zest and juice of 1 orange
sugar, to taste
salt and black pepper

Place the minced fennel and chilies in a bowl and add just enough orange juice to make a sauce. Stir in the grated orange zest, then add sugar to taste—the amount you need will depend on the sweetness of the orange. Season with salt and pepper. Chill for at least 1 hour before use.

Taste and adjust the seasoning as necessary before serving.

Serving Suggestions
This is an unusual salsa to serve with all kinds of seafood as well as chicken.

The Simplest Salsa

For the best texture, prepare the vegetables by hand rather than in a food processor.

SERVES 4

2 large ripe tomatoes
1 to 2 fresh green jalapeño peppers
½ teaspoon salt

Peel, seed, and roughly chop the tomatoes to make a lumpy purée. Seed and core the peppers, then mince them. Stir the peppers into the tomatoes with the salt. Chill the salsa until required.

Variations: For a deeper flavor, roast the jalapeño peppers until the skin is blackened;

Above: add a diced peach and some lemon juice to The Simplest Salsa for a lively, fresh fruit flavor, perfect with grilled fish steaks.

let them cool, then peel off the skins before mincing the flesh. If desired, you can add 2 tablespoons minced cilantro to the salsa when you add the salt, plus some canned corn kernels. Alternatively, add a large, finely diced yellow sweet pepper, a diced avocado, or a peeled and diced large, ripe peach with 2 teaspoons of freshly squeezed lemon juice.

Serving Suggestions
Serve your salsa ice-cold with tortilla chips, or grilled meat, chicken, or fish.

Tropical Salsa Picante

SERVES 6

⅓ cup (75g) minced honeydew melon
⅓ cup (75g) minced mango
⅓ cup (75g) minced pineapple
½ medium red sweet pepper, minced
1 small fresh hot red chili pepper, such as serrano, minced
3 tablespoons minced cilantro
2 to 3 tablespoons balsamic vinegar
¼ teaspoon salt

$\mathscr{S}$ALSA

Carefully stir all the ingredients together, adding any juice exuded from the fruit to the bowl and just enough balsamic vinegar to give a thick sauce. Refrigerate the salsa for 8 to 24 hours before use. Adjust the seasoning as necessary before serving.

Variations: Add some minced green onion or celery to the salsa, if desired.

Serving Suggestions
Serve with grilled fish, meats, and poultry.

Fresh Mango Salsa

For this fast, fresh-tasting salsa you need really ripe and juicy mangoes. Add chili pepper to suit your palate.

SERVES 4

2 large mangoes
juice of 1 lime, or to taste
¼ teaspoon sea salt
1 fresh green chili pepper (choose mild or hot), seeded and minced
¾-inch (2-cm) piece fresh ginger, peeled and grated

Dicing a mango: cut each half of the fruit into squares without cutting through the skin. Then bend it backwards and cut away the dice.

Halve the mango, cutting flesh away from the pit. Dice the flesh, then chop it fairly finely. Mix with the lime juice and sea salt. Stir in the chili and ginger. Taste the salsa and add more salt as needed. Cover and chill for up to 4 hours. Stir before serving.

Serving Suggestions
This is delicious with grilled chicken and fish.

Black Bean Salsa

There's no chili pepper in this salsa, but the green onions and cilantro still pack a punch.

SERVES 4

1¼ cups (200g) dried black beans
3 plum tomatoes, chopped
3 green onions, sliced
1 large bunch cilantro, minced
juice of 1 lime
1 tablespoon olive oil
salt and black pepper

Rinse the black beans, then put them in a bowl and cover with a generous quantity of cold water. Let the beans soak for 8 hours or overnight.

Drain the beans and put them in a medium-size saucepan with plenty of fresh cold water to cover. Cook the beans for 30 to 45 minutes or until tender, then drain. Refresh under cold running water, drain again thoroughly, and let the beans cool while you prepare the other ingredients.

In a medium-size bowl, gently stir the tomatoes, green onions, cilantro, lime juice, and olive oil with the beans. Taste and season with salt and pepper as necessary.

Serving Suggestions
The flavor of this salsa makes it an excellent match for hot-smoked salmon, or for grilled salmon. Accompany with Guacamole (see page 50), sour cream, and flour tortillas.

Avocado-Raisin Salsa

SERVES 4

⅓ cup (50g) golden raisins
grated zest and juice of 1 lime
1 avocado, minced
1 small red onion, minced
½ mango, minced
1 fresh hot green chili pepper, such as jalapeño, seeded and minced
3 tablespoons minced cilantro

In a medium-size bowl, combine the raisins with the lime zest and juice. Cover and chill for 8 hours or overnight.

To finish the salsa, stir in the remaining ingredients. Serve at room temperature.

Serving Suggestion
Chicken is best with this piquant salsa.

Sun-Dried Tomato Salsa

SERVES 4

7 ounces (200g) sun-dried tomatoes packed in olive oil
2 teaspoons garam masala
½ teaspoon cayenne pepper
1 small red onion, minced
¼ cup (60ml) red wine vinegar
salt and black pepper

Drain the oil from the sun-dried tomatoes into a small saucepan, and stir in the garam masala and cayenne. Heat the mixture gently for 5 minutes to let the flavors infuse. Remove from the heat and let cool.

Mince the sun-dried tomatoes, then stir them into the cooled spiced oil with the onion and vinegar. Season to taste with salt and black pepper.

Serving Suggestions
A versatile salsa, this can be served with grilled meats, firm white fish, or poultry.

Japanese Lemon Sauce

SERVES 4

2 tablespoons lemon juice
1 tablespoon soy sauce
1 tablespoon rice wine or dry sherry
2 teaspoons sugar
1 green onion, minced

In a small saucepan, gently heat the lemon juice, soy sauce, wine or sherry, and sugar until the sugar dissolves. When the mixture is quite hot but not boiling, stir in the minced green onion and remove the sauce from the heat. Serve warm or let cool.

Serving Suggestions
An excellent sauce to serve with vegetables such as grilled mushrooms and steamed broccoli. It can also be tossed with noodles.

Black Vinegar Sauce

Chinese black vinegar is available from Asian markets.

SERVES 4

1 tablespoon vegetable oil
3 to 4 drops Asian sesame oil
4 green onions, chopped
2 teaspoons finely grated fresh ginger
1¼ cups (300ml) fish stock
¼ cup (60ml) Chinese black vinegar
¼ cup (60ml) soy sauce
2 tablespoons firmly packed light brown sugar
1 tablespoon cornstarch
2 tablespoons cold water

Heat the oil in a medium-size saucepan and flavor it with the sesame oil. Add the green onions and ginger and cook gently for 1 to 2 minutes or until softened.

Stir in the fish stock, vinegar, soy sauce, and sugar. Bring the mixture to a boil and simmer for 10 minutes.

Teriyaki Sauce

The name of this simple sauce comes from the Japanese *teri* meaning glossy and *yaki* meaning grill. This recipe features naturally brewed Japanese soy sauce, sake (an alcohol made or brewed from fermented rice), and mirin (sweet rice wine), all of which are now often sold in supermarkets.

MAKES 6 TABLESPOONS

2 tablespoons soy sauce
2 tablespoons sake
2 tablespoons mirin
½ teaspoon sugar

Mix all the ingredients together in a small bowl or in a jar with a tight-fitting lid. The

Above: versatile Teriyaki Sauce from Japan makes an excellent marinade for tender cubes of meat which can then be placed on skewers and quickly grilled or broiled.

sauce can be kept, tightly covered, in the refrigerator for an indefinite period.

Variation: Add a minced clove of garlic and a ¾-inch (2-cm) piece of fresh ginger, peeled and grated, just before use.

Serving Suggestions
Marinate beef, chicken, or fish in the sauce, using the remainder to baste the ingredients halfway through cooking. It can also be used instead of plain soy sauce in stir-fries.

$\mathcal{S}$OY-BASED $\mathcal{S}$AUCE

In a small cup, blend the cornstarch with the water until smooth, then slowly stir it into the sauce. Cook for 1 to 2 minutes or until the sauce has a coating consistency.

Serving Suggestions
Serve with white fish, whole or in fillets, and vegetables steamed in the Chinese style.

Beef in Black Bean Sauce

The beans used in this sauce are soybeans that have been salted and fermented. They are sold in cans at Asian markets.

SERVES 2 TO 4

12 ounces (350g) beef flank steak
3 tablespoons vegetable or peanut oil
1 teaspoon Asian sesame oil
FOR THE MARINADE:
2 tablespoons soy sauce
2 teaspoons rice wine
2 teaspoons cornstarch
1 teaspoon Asian sesame oil
FOR THE BLACK BEAN SAUCE:
3 tablespoons fermented black beans
1 teaspoon sugar
2 tablespoons chicken or beef stock or water
1 tablespoon soy sauce
1 tablespoon rice wine
½ large red sweet pepper, sliced
4 medium green onions, sliced
2 cloves garlic, minced
1½-inch (4-cm) piece fresh ginger, finely grated

Chill the steak in the freezer for 5 minutes, then slice it into the thinnest possible strips. Mix all the marinade ingredients together in a large bowl and add the beef strips. Let marinate for 1 hour, if possible.

Sprinkle the rinsed and drained black beans with the sugar, then chop coarsely and set aside. Mix the stock, soy sauce, and rice wine together in a small bowl.

Heat the vegetable or peanut oil in a wok until smoking. Drain the meat, discarding any excess marinade, and stir-fry for 3 to 4 minutes or until evenly browned. Remove with a slotted spoon and drain in a colander.

Stir-fry the sweet pepper, onions, garlic, and ginger for 1 minute, then add the stock mixture and beans and bring to a boil. Stir in the beef and let it reheat. Remove from the heat, add the sesame oil, and serve.

Variations: Replace the beef with strips of chicken, lamb, or venison.

Serving Suggestions
Serve with rice, plus some leaves of bok choy that you have quickly stir-fried in another pan with a little sliced garlic.

Below: fermented soybeans add a rich flavor to the Chinese favorite, Beef in Black Bean Sauce.

Plum Sauce

SERVES 4 TO 6

1 pound (500g) damsons or other tart plums, pitted
½ cup (125ml) rice wine
¼ cup (50g) firmly packed light brown sugar
1 teaspoon sea salt
3 tablespoons vegetable oil
2-inch (5-cm) piece fresh ginger, grated
4 cloves garlic, minced
¼ to ½ teaspoon minced fresh hot green chili pepper

Put the plums and rice wine into a stainless steel pan. Cover and cook for 5 to 10 minutes or until soft. Purée in a blender or food processor, then return to the pan. Stir in the sugar and salt and cook until thick.

Heat the oil in a small, heavy pan. Add the ginger, garlic, and chili and stir-fry for 30 seconds. Stir this mixture into the fruit purée and cook for 1 minute or until the sauce is very thick and shiny.

Serving Suggestions
Serve with grilled or panfried pork chops.

Sweet and Sour Sauce

Fresh fruit juice makes this sauce better than that served in most Chinese restaurants.

SERVES 4

1 tablespoon vegetable oil
3 medium shallots, minced
2 tablespoons sugar
3 large tangerines
2 tablespoons white rice vinegar, or to taste
salt and black pepper
1 teaspoon cornstarch
l tablespoon cold water

Heat the oil in a medium-size saucepan and cook the shallots gently until soft. Sprinkle

with the sugar and cook over medium heat, stirring frequently, until the shallots are golden and slightly caramelized.

Meanwhile, peel the zest from one of the tangerines and cut the strips into needle-like shreds. Squeeze the juice from all the fruit and add it to the pan with the shredded zest and vinegar. Simmer gently for 5 minutes.

Taste and season with salt and pepper, then adjust the sweet-sour balance as necessary: you may need to add more vinegar. In a small bowl, mix the cornstarch with the water and stir into the sauce. Bring to a boil, stirring, to make a thick sauce.

Above: this Sweet and Sour Sauce takes its citrus flavor from fresh tangerines. Deep-fried pork and steamed rice turn it into a meal.

Serving Suggestions
Serve hot with large cubes of deep-fried lean meat such as chicken or pork: Marinate the meat for 30 minutes in a mixture of 1 beaten egg, 1 tablespoon cornstarch, 1 tablespoon soy sauce, 1 teaspoon Asian sesame oil, and some salt and black pepper. Toss the drained meat in cornstarch, then deep-fry until cooked and golden brown.

CHILI SAUCE

Chinese Chili Sauce

MAKES 1 CUP (250ML)

1 small sweet red pepper
½ cup (125ml) rice vinegar
¼ cup (50g) sugar
2 dried hot red chili peppers, seeded and chopped
2 cloves garlic, minced
1 teaspoon cornstarch

Put the sweet pepper, vinegar, sugar, chilies, garlic, and ¼ cup (60ml) water into a food processor. Process until smooth.

Transfer the sauce to a non-aluminum saucepan and set it over low heat. Cook for 10 minutes, skimming as necessary.

Meanwhile, in a small cup, blend the cornstarch with 1 tablespoon water. Slowly pour into the chili sauce, stirring constantly until the sauce thickens. Let cool, then pour into a clean bottle or jar. The sauce can be stored in the refrigerator for up to 2 weeks.

Variation: Add 1 teaspoon of chopped fresh ginger to the mixture in the food processor.

Serving Suggestions
Toss with cold cooked shrimp, noodles, and Napa cabbage to make a stylish salad, or serve it with deep-fried fish, shellfish, pork, or poultry. Can be used as a dipping sauce.

Harissa

MAKES 12 OUNCES (350G)

8 ounces (250g) fresh hot red chili peppers, seeded and chopped
1 head garlic, peeled
3 tablespoons minced cilantro
2 tablespoons olive oil
1 tablespoon ground coriander
1 tablespoon caraway seeds
1 tablespoon dried mint
1 tablespoon salt

Place all the ingredients in the bowl of a food processor or blender and process them to a smooth, thick paste. Add a little more oil if the mixture is too dry. Store the sauce, covered with a thin film of olive oil, in a jar in the refrigerator for up to 1 month.

Serving Suggestions
Serve in tiny quantities with grilled meats and poultry or Moroccan tagines.

Chili Jam

MAKES JUST UNDER 3 CUPS (700ML)

2 pounds (1kg) tomatoes
⅓ cup (75ml) olive oil
½ cup (125ml) cider vinegar
5 cloves garlic, peeled
2 tablespoons chopped fresh ginger
4 fresh hot red chili peppers, stems removed
1½ tablespoons (15g) cumin seeds
1½ tablespoons (15g) black mustard seeds
¾ cup (150g) firmly packed light brown sugar
2 tablespoons fish sauce
2 teaspoons turmeric
½ cup (25g) minced cilantro

Preheat the oven to 375°F. Place the tomatoes in a roasting pan and pour the oil over them. Roast the tomatoes for about 20 minutes or until soft but not browned.

In a food processor or blender, combine the vinegar, garlic, ginger, chilies, and cumin and mustard seeds, and process until smooth. Transfer to a large, heavy saucepan and add the tomatoes, sugar, fish sauce, and turmeric. Bring to a boil and simmer gently for 1½ to 2 hours or until very thick.

Lightly purée the mixture, then stir in the cilantro. Pour into a warm jar and seal. Store in the refrigerator for up to 1 month.

Serving Suggestions
Serve alongside panfried fish or pork, with Southeast Asian-style salads.

Salsa Chipotle

This cooked sauce from Mexico has a delicious smoky flavor provided by the dried chipotle chilies.

SERVES 4

6 dried chipotle chili peppers
½ cup (125ml) boiling water
4 cloves garlic, unpeeled
1 tablespoon olive oil
1 small onion, chopped
1¼ cups (200g) chopped tomatoes
1¼ cups (300ml) vegetable stock
salt and black pepper

Preheat the oven to 400°F. Place the dried chilies in a small bowl and pour the boiling water over them. Let them soak for at least 30 minutes.

Meanwhile, put the garlic cloves on a baking sheet and roast them in the oven for 10 to 15 minutes or until tender. Let cool, then peel and chop the cloves.

When the chilies have rehydrated, line a strainer with a piece of paper towel and strain the soaking water from the chilies into a bowl. Halve, core, and seed the chilies, chop the flesh roughly, and add it to the soaking water. Purée the chilies with a hand-held immersion blender until smooth.

Heat the oil in a small saucepan and add the onion. Cook over medium-low heat for 5 minutes or until the onion is softened but not browned. Stir in the chopped garlic and tomatoes and cook for 3 more minutes.

Pour the vegetable stock and the puréed chili liquid into the pan. Bring to a boil and simmer for 15 to 20 minutes or until the sauce is reduced to the consistency you desire. Taste and season as necessary with salt and black pepper. Serve hot.

Serving Suggestions
This salsa is delicious with grilled, broiled, or roasted beef, chicken, or lamb, or with meaty fish steaks.

S ATAY

Satay Sauce

MAKES 1¾ CUPS (400ML)

4 shallots, quartered
2 cloves garlic
½-inch (1-cm) cube shrimp paste
¼ teaspoon sea salt
1 teaspoon tamarind paste
1 tablespoon vegetable oil
1 tablespoon soy sauce
1 teaspoon dark brown sugar
½ teaspoon cayenne pepper
1¼ cups (300g) crunchy peanut butter
about 1¼ cups (300ml) water

If you have a spice grinder, process the shallots, garlic, shrimp paste, and salt until smooth; if not, mince them, then crush them in a mortar with a pestle.

Using a fork, mash the tamarind paste with 1 tablespoon water. Strain the mixture, reserving the liquid.

Heat the oil in a medium-size, heavy saucepan and fry the spice mixture for 20 seconds. Add the soy sauce, sugar, and cayenne and stir-fry for 30 seconds.

Add the peanut butter and water to the pan and bring to a boil. Simmer for about 10 minutes or until thick: if the sauce becomes too thick for dipping, add some more water. Stir in the tamarind liquid, then taste and adjust the flavoring, adding more salt or soy sauce as necessary.

This sauce can be stored in a jar, tightly covered, in the refrigerator for up to 5 days, then reheated before serving.

Serving Suggestions
Use to accompany marinated grilled meats or broiled or panfried chicken strips, lamb steaks, shrimp, or crudités.

Right: Gado-Gado is an Indonesian dish in which a variety of cold vegetables, cooked separately, are served with nutty Satay Sauce and garnished with crisply fried shallots.

Gado-Gado

SERVES 6

1 cup (100g) bean sprouts
1 cup (100g) green beans, trimmed
1 cup (100g) sliced carrots
1 cup (100g) cauliflower florets
⅔ cup (50g) shredded cabbage
1 large potato
¾ cup (100g) peeled and sliced English cucumber
¼ cup (60ml) vegetable oil
2 shallots, thinly sliced
Satay Sauce (see left), warmed

Steam the bean sprouts for 1 minute, or blanch them in boiling water. Drain, refresh them with cold water, drain again, and set aside. Steam or blanch the green beans for 3 minutes. Drain, refresh with cold water, drain again, and reserve. Steam or blanch the carrots and the cauliflower separately for 2 minutes each, and the cabbage for 1 minute. Drain, refresh with cold water, drain again, and reserve. Boil the potato in its skin until tender, then let cool, peel, and dice it. Arrange all the vegetables with the cucumber on a large platter.

To make the garnish, heat the oil in a skillet and cook the shallots until crisp. Drain them on paper towels. Spoon the warm sauce over the vegetables, then garnish with the fried shallots. Serve with rice or on its own as a first course.

*C*URRIED *D*ISHES AND *C*URRY *S*AUCE

Murgh Korma

Kormas should be aromatic rather than hot.

SERVES 4 TO 6

6 chicken pieces, skinned and halved
2 tablespoons (30ml) clarified butter, ghee, or vegetable oil
2 medium onions, chopped
1 cinnamon stick
1 small fresh medium-hot green chili pepper, sliced into thin rings and seeded
FOR THE MARINADE:
1 cup (250ml) plain whole-milk yogurt
4 large cloves garlic, minced
1¼-inch (3-cm) piece fresh ginger, grated
½ teaspoon sea salt
FOR THE DRY MIXTURE:
2 tablespoons shredded coconut
1 heaping tablespoon whole blanched almonds
½ teaspoon cardamom seeds
½ teaspoon cumin seeds
1 small dried hot chili pepper (optional)
½ teaspoon ground turmeric

Put the chicken into a non-metal dish. Mix the marinade ingredients and pour over the chicken. Cover and let marinate in the refrigerator for up to 12 hours.

Preheat the oven to 375°F. Put the coconut and almonds into a baking dish and toast them in the oven for about 10 minutes or until golden. Let cool.

Put the cardamom, cumin, and dried chili, if using, into a mortar and crush to a fine powder. Mix in the turmeric and the almond mixture and set aside.

Heat the butter, ghee, or oil in a large Dutch oven. Fry the onions, stirring frequently, until golden brown. Remove them from the pan with a slotted spoon.

Process the onions and dry spice mixture in a food processor or blender until smooth.

Reheat the fat in the pan. Add the chicken and marinade and cook, stirring gently, over medium-high heat for 2 to 3 minutes. Add the onion paste and the cinnamon stick and

stir until thoroughly combined. Bring the sauce to a boil, then cover the pan and simmer over very low heat, stirring frequently, for about 30 minutes or until the chicken is very tender. Taste and adjust the seasonings, and remove the cinnamon stick. Garnish with the sliced green chili and serve.

Variations: Replace the chicken with pieces of turkey or lamb.

Chicken Vindaloo

This Goan recipe is more authentic and much less fiery than most vindaloos.

SERVES 4

4 chicken pieces, skinned and trimmed
FOR THE SAUCE:
½ cup (125ml) cider vinegar
5 cloves garlic, minced
2-inch (5-cm) piece fresh ginger, grated
2 tablespoons cumin seeds
1 tablespoon black mustard seeds
seeds from 10 cardamom pods
1 teaspoon ground cinnamon
1 teaspoon sea salt
½ teaspoon cayenne pepper, or to taste
½ teaspoon black pepper
3 tablespoons vegetable oil

Put all the sauce ingredients, except the oil, in a food processor or blender and process until quite smooth.

In a large Dutch oven, heat the oil. Add the processed mixture and stir, off the heat, for a few seconds. Add the chicken and stir to coat it with the sauce. Bring the mixture to a boil, then cover and simmer for 40 minutes or until the chicken is tender, stirring frequently. Adjust the seasoning of the sauce to taste, adding salt, pepper, or vinegar as necessary, then serve.

Variation: Use lamb instead of chicken.

Green Chili and Apricot Sauce

SERVES 4

1 cup (100g) dried apricots
½ cup (125ml) cold water
2 medium onions, chopped
3 fresh medium-hot green chili peppers, seeded and chopped
3 cloves garlic, minced
¾-inch (2-cm) piece fresh ginger, sliced
seeds from 3 cardamom pods
3 tablespoons (45ml) clarified butter, ghee, or vegetable oil
1 cinnamon stick
4 chicken pieces, on the bone, trimmed
2 medium tomatoes, roughly chopped
salt and black pepper

Soak the apricots in the water for 2 hours; drain, reserving the liquid. Work the onions, chilies, garlic, ginger, and cardamom seeds together in a food processor or blender until finely chopped.

Heat the butter, ghee, or oil in a large Dutch oven, add the spice mixture and cinnamon stick, and stir over medium heat for 3 minutes or until lightly colored. Push the mixture to one side of the pan, then add the chicken and cook until lightly browned all over, adding a little more fat if necessary. Stir in the tomatoes, the soaking water from the apricots, and some salt and black pepper. Bring to a boil. Cover the pan, lower the heat, and simmer gently for 25 minutes, stirring occasionally.

Stir in the apricots and cook for 10 more minutes or until the chicken is thoroughly cooked. Taste and adjust the seasoning: the sauce should have a good balance of sweet, savory, and spicy, so add more salt and pepper or a squeeze of lemon juice. Remove the cinnamon stick before serving.

Variations: Replace the chicken with 1¾ pounds (800g) of diced turkey or lamb.

CURRIED DISHES AND CURRY SAUCE

Crab and Cilantro Sauce

A creamy, medium-hot curry sauce, this uses the white roots of cilantro as well as the stems and leaves.

SERVES 2 TO 4

1 heaping teaspoon tamarind paste
1 tablespoon hot water
1 small bunch cilantro, stems and leaves minced, white roots chopped and reserved separately
2 tablespoons vegetable oil
1¾ cups (400ml) canned coconut milk
2 cups (250g) flaked freshly cooked crab meat
1 to 2 tablespoons fish sauce
FOR THE SPICE PASTE:
1 red onion, chopped
3 large cloves garlic, minced
1 tablespoon vegetable oil
2-inch (5-cm) piece lemon grass, chopped
⅝-inch (1.5-cm) piece fresh ginger, sliced
½ to 1 fresh medium-hot chili pepper, seeded and chopped
1 teaspoon ground coriander
½ teaspoon turmeric
¼ teaspoon shrimp paste

Soak the tamarind paste in the hot water. Put the ingredients for the spice paste plus the white roots of the cilantro into the bowl of a food processor. Process, scraping down the side of the bowl every 20 seconds or so, until the mixture has formed a thick, smooth paste. This will take several minutes. If the paste is difficult to process, add 1 tablespoon of the coconut milk. (The spice paste can be made in advance and kept, tightly covered, in the refrigerator for up to 24 hours.)

Heat the oil in a large, heavy saucepan, add the spice paste, and fry over medium heat, stirring constantly, for about 5 minutes. Add the coconut milk and the strained tamarind water and stir until the mixture comes to a boil. Reduce the heat and simmer gently for 10 to 15 minutes or until the sauce thickens and lightly coats the back of a spoon. Stir in the crab meat and 1 tablespoon of fish sauce and cook gently for 5 minutes. Taste and add more fish sauce as needed. Stir in the cilantro leaves and stems, then serve.

Variations: Add 2 pounds (1kg) large raw shrimp, peeled, deveined, and gently flattened, or 1 pound (500g) large cubes of white fish such as halibut or monkfish, to the sauce along with the crab. Alternatively, cut 3 skinless boneless chicken breast halves into large cubes and add them to the sauce with the crab, then let the sauce simmer for 7 to 10 minutes or until the chicken is completely cooked.

Beef in Black Sauce

This is an Indonesian sauce, very thick, dark, and gently spiced. Choose beef or venison suitable for braising, for the best taste and texture—very lean meat will become too dry during the long cooking time.

SERVES 4

1 pound (500g) beef chuck steak or venison steak
2 heaping teaspoons tamarind paste
3 tablespoons hot water
2 medium red onions, chopped
4 cloves garlic, minced
¾-inch (2-cm) piece fresh ginger, sliced
3 tablespoons vegetable oil
1 cinnamon stick
2 whole cloves
¼ teaspoon coarsely ground black pepper
¼ teaspoon freshly grated nutmeg
¼ teaspoon ground cardamom
1 cup (250ml) unsalted beef or vegetable stock
3 tablespoons soy sauce
1 tablespoon palm sugar (jaggery) or dark brown sugar

Trim any excess fat from the meat, then cut it into large cubes. Soak the tamarind paste in the hot water for about 10 minutes. Meanwhile, put the onions, garlic, and ginger into the bowl of a food processor and process until finely chopped.

Heat the oil in a medium-size heavy saucepan or Dutch oven and fry the onion mixture over medium heat, stirring constantly, for about 3 minutes or until it starts to color. Push it to one side of the pan. Fry the cubes of beef or venison until browned on all sides, then stir in the onion mixture from the side of the pan. Add the whole, ground, and grated spices and cook, stirring constantly, for 1 minute. Stir in the stock, soy sauce, and sugar.

Mash the softened tamarind paste and liquid together, then strain the mixture. Add the tamarind-flavored water to the pan and stir. Bring the mixture to a boil. Cover and simmer very gently for 1½ to 2 hours or until the meat is very tender and the sauce very thick. If necessary, remove the lid and simmer the sauce until it thickens.

Taste and adjust the seasoning with more black pepper as necessary. Remove the whole spices before serving.

Thai Red Curry Paste

MAKES 8 OUNCES (225G)

1 tablespoon coriander seeds
1 tablespoon cumin seeds
1 tablespoon black peppercorns
¼ cup (60ml) vegetable oil
10 dried hot chili peppers, seeded and chopped
6 cloves garlic, minced
5 shallots, quartered
2 teaspoons salt
2 teaspoons chopped lemon grass
2 teaspoons freshly grated nutmeg
grated zest of 1 lime
¾-inch (2-cm) piece fresh ginger, minced
½ teaspoon shrimp paste

𝒞urried 𝒟ishes and 𝒞urry 𝒮auce

Grind the coriander and cumin seeds and peppercorns to a fine powder using a spice grinder or mortar and pestle. Put into a blender or food processor with all the other ingredients, and process to a smooth paste.

Store the curry paste in the refrigerator in a covered jar for up to 1 month.

Serving Suggestions
Combine with canned coconut milk to make chicken, seafood, and vegetable curries.

Green Curry Paste

The chili peppers to use are the tiny Thai chilies, which are extremely hot. It is a good idea to wear rubber gloves for protection when preparing chilies.

MAKES 8 OUNCES (250G)

½ cup (25g) roughly chopped cilantro,
    including the white roots
2 tablespoons vegetable oil
4 cloves garlic
4 fresh hot green chili peppers, chopped
3 shallots, roughly chopped
zest of 1 lime, roughly chopped
1¼-inch (3-cm) piece fresh galangal, peeled and
    roughly chopped
1 stem lemon grass, roughly chopped
2 teaspoons ground coriander
1 teaspoon ground cumin
1 teaspoon shrimp paste
1 teaspoon sea salt

Put all the ingredients into a food processor and process until smooth, scraping the mixture down the side from time to time. Store the curry paste, tightly covered, in the refrigerator for up to 1 week.

Serving Suggestions
This recipe is the basis of many Thai curry sauces, for chicken or turkey, firm fish, or vegetables such as potatoes and carrots.

Green Shrimp Curry

SERVES 2 TO 4

16 large raw shrimp
3 to 4 tablespoons Green Curry Paste (see left)
2 tablespoons vegetable oil
1¾ cups (400ml) canned coconut milk
4 kaffir lime leaves, central stem discarded,
    very finely shredded
1 small bunch Thai basil
2 teaspoons fish sauce, or to taste

Remove the shells from the shrimp, then slit them along the back and remove the black, thread-like intestinal vein. Open the shrimp out like a book and gently flatten them.

Above: once you have acquired the authentic Thai ingredients for this spicy, aromatic Green Shrimp Curry, it is very quick to prepare.

In a medium-size saucepan, cook the curry paste in the oil for 3 to 4 minutes. Add the coconut milk and lime leaves and simmer for 20 minutes, stirring frequently. Add a little water if the sauce becomes too thick.

Add the shrimp to the pan and cook gently for 3 minutes or until just firm to the touch. Pick the basil leaves from their stems and add the leaves to the curry with the fish sauce. Stir briefly to combine, then remove the pan from the heat and adjust the sauce seasonings as necessary. Serve the curry immediately, with steamed Thai rice.

DIPPING SAUCE AND CHUTNEY

Vietnamese Dipping Sauce

SERVES 6

1 fresh hot red chili pepper, such as serrano, chopped
1 clove garlic, minced
1 teaspoon sugar
3 tablespoons water
3 tablespoons fish sauce
1 tablespoon rice vinegar
2 teaspoons shredded carrot
2 teaspoons shredded daikon

Put the chili, garlic, and sugar in a mortar and pound them to a paste. Stir in the water, fish sauce, and vinegar, then the shredded carrot and daikon.

Variation: For a different type of acidity, replace the rice vinegar with lime juice.

Serving Suggestions
Serve with rice paper rolls and other Vietnamese appetizers and snacks.

Nutty Hoisin Sauce

SERVES 4 TO 6

1 teaspoon shredded carrot
1 teaspoon sugar
1 tablespoon rice vinegar
¼ cup (60ml) hoisin sauce
2 tablespoons water
1 tablespoon peanut butter
1 fresh hot red chili pepper, such as serrano, seeded and finely diced

Mix the carrot, sugar, and rice vinegar together in a small bowl and set aside to marinate for 15 minutes.

Meanwhile, in a small saucepan, bring the hoisin sauce and water to a boil. Simmer until you have a thick pouring sauce. Stir in the peanut butter, then remove from the heat and let the mixture cool.

Drain the shredded carrot, pressing hard on the carrot pulp to extract as much liquid as possible. Discard the liquid and add the carrot pulp to the cooled hoisin sauce mixture. Stir in the diced chili and serve.

Serving Suggestions
A thick, rich, slightly sweet sauce, this tastes best with unfried snacks. Try it in Chinese pancakes with cucumber and green onions.

Dark Soy Dipping Sauce

SERVES 8

¼ cup (60ml) soy sauce
2 tablespoons sugar
2 tablespoons minced green onions
1 tablespoon finely grated fresh ginger
1 teaspoon minced lemon grass
Asian sesame oil, to taste

Mix the soy sauce, sugar, green onions, ginger, and lemon grass together in a small bowl. Add the sesame oil a few drops at a time, tasting until you are happy with the balance of flavors.

Serving Suggestions
This dipping sauce is excellent with raw or cooked tuna and grilled shrimp. It can also be used as a salad dressing.

Date Sauce

SERVES 4

1 cup (150g) chopped fresh dates
juice of 1 lemon
1 cup (250ml) water
1 teaspoon ground cumin
½ teaspoon cayenne pepper
½ teaspoon salt

Put the dates in a small saucepan with the remaining ingredients. Bring to a boil, then lower the heat and simmer gently for 10 to 15 minutes or until the dates are soft.

Purée the mixture using a hand-held immersion blender or food processor, then rub it through a fine-mesh strainer to remove the tougher bits of date skin.

Serving Suggestions
An unusual sweet sauce for Indian poppadoms, onion bhajis, and pakoras.

Cilantro and Mint Chutney

SERVES 8

2 cups (100g) roughly chopped cilantro, including the stems
½ cup (25g) mint leaves
6 tablespoons plain yogurt
3 tablespoons water
2 tablespoons chopped green sweet pepper
2 cloves garlic
2 fresh hot green chili peppers, such as jalapeño, cored and seeded
1 tablespoon chopped onion
1 teaspoon grated fresh ginger
1 teaspoon sugar
1 teaspoon salt

Place all the ingredients in a food processor or blender and process to a smooth sauce, scraping down the side of the bowl occasionally. Taste and adjust the flavors to your liking, then chill before serving.

Variation: Omit the yogurt to give a fresh-tasting curry paste that will last for weeks in the refrigerator if covered with a little oil.

Serving Suggestions
Drizzle the chutney over fried Indian snacks such as bhajis, pakoras, and poppadoms.

CHUTNEY

Gujarati-Style Vegetable Pickle

This is an easy pickle, especially if you use a food processor to shred the vegetables.

SERVES 6 TO 8

3 tablespoons lemon juice
1 tablespoon vegetable oil
2 tablespoons ground mustard seeds
¾ teaspoon turmeric
1 to 1½ teaspoons cayenne pepper
1½ teaspoons salt
1 large carrot, coarsely shredded
1 small red or yellow sweet pepper, cored, seeded, and coarsely shredded
4 ounces (125g) fine green beans, sliced lengthwise

Place the lemon juice, oil, spices, and salt in a medium-size bowl and whisk until well mixed. Stir in the prepared vegetables. Chill for several hours. Bring to room temperature before serving.

Serving Suggestions
Offer this chutney as part of an Indian dip selection to serve with fried snacks or appetizers, or serve alongside curries.

Fresh Mint Raita

Raitas are a cooling accompaniment to spicy foods. Add a large pinch of sugar to the mint leaves as you chop them: this will help to release the herb oils.

SERVES 4

1 medium red onion, minced
1 medium carrot, finely grated
⅔ cup (150ml) plain yogurt
1 tablespoon minced mint leaves
¼ teaspoon sea salt
black pepper

In a small bowl, mix all the ingredients together, then taste and add more salt and pepper as necessary. Cover and chill for at least 30 minutes. Stir before serving.

Serving Suggestions
Serve alongside Indian curries and snacks.

Above: not hot itself, Fresh Mint Raita is a refreshing chilled mixture of yogurt, red onion, carrot, and mint to serve alongside spicy foods.

SIDE SAUCES

A tablespoon or two of these quirky condiments added at the table will bring a contrast of flavor to the main dish. Most of these recipes are traditional favorites. They include cooling, fruity jellies to go with sharp hard cheeses or cold cuts, juicy citrus-sharp cranberry sauce for roast turkey, creamy smooth bread sauce for game and chicken, and cold, piquant horseradish.

The fresh sauces can be quickly made and served hot or cold. The preserves—relishes, jellies, ketchup—are made when the ingredients are in season, then carefully put by, ready to bring out whenever appropriate.

Left (from left to right): Warm Mustard Sauce, Minted Apple Jelly, Applesauce.

Cranberry and Orange Sauce

SERVES 8 OR MORE

1 pound (500g) fresh or frozen cranberries
1 cup (200g) sugar, or to taste
finely grated zest and juice of 1 large orange

Pick over the cranberries (there is no need to thaw frozen fruit). Wash and thoroughly drain the fresh fruit, if using. Put it into a large non-aluminum pot with the sugar and orange zest and juice and cook over low heat until the sugar has dissolved.

Bring the mixture to a boil, then simmer it gently until the berries start to pop. Cover the pan, remove from the heat, and let stand for 15 minutes. Stir well, then let cool.

Store in a tightly covered jar in the refrigerator. Use the sauce within 1 week.

Serving Suggestions
A tangy sauce, traditionally served cold with the Thanksgiving turkey, but also good when served hot with game or duck, and at room temperature with cold cuts.

Above: England's Cumberland Sauce adds fruity sweetness to traditional roast turkey.

Cranberry and Port Sauce

SERVES 8

12 ounces (350g) fresh or frozen cranberries
¾ cup (175g) firmly packed light brown sugar
⅔ cup (150ml) port
grated zest and juice of 1 orange
¼ teaspoon ground apple-pie spice
black pepper

Put all of the ingredients into a large, non-aluminum saucepan and heat gently, stirring, until the sugar has dissolved. Bring the mixture to a boil, then reduce the heat and simmer, stirring frequently, for 25 minutes

or until the cranberries are really soft and the mixture is saucelike. The cooled sauce can be stored in a tightly covered jar in the refrigerator for up to 3 days.

Serving Suggestions
Cranberry and Port Sauce is best served hot with roast turkey or baked ham.

Cumberland Sauce

SERVES 6 TO 8

zest and juice of 1 lemon
zest and juice of 1 orange
¾ cup (250g) red-currant jelly
½ cup (125ml) port
1 tablespoon Grand Marnier

Cut the lemon and orange zests into very fine strips and put them into a small pan with cold water to cover. Bring to a boil, then remove the pan from the heat and drain the strips of zest.

Put the red-currant jelly into a medium-size, non-aluminum saucepan with the fruit juices. Heat gently, stirring to break up the jelly, until the mixture has melted to a smooth sauce. Add the port and simmer gently for 3 minutes. Remove the pan from the heat and stir in the blanched zest and the Grand Marnier. Let the sauce cool before serving. It can be kept, tightly covered, in the refrigerator for up to 1 week.

Fruit Sauce

Serving Suggestions
Spoon onto roast turkey or serve with cold roast meat and game (my grandmother liked this sauce with pressed tongue).

Applesauce

Use tart apples, such as Gravenstein or Greening, for this recipe.

SERVES 4 TO 6

12 ounces (350g) apples
3 tablespoons water
2 tablespoons (25g) butter, chilled and diced
sugar to taste

Wash the apples, then quarter and roughly chop them; there is no need to remove the peel and core. Put them into a medium-size, heavy-based, non-aluminum saucepan with the water. Cover and cook gently until the fruit is soft and pulpy. Cool the pulp slightly, then press it through a fine strainer.

Reheat the sauce, then beat in the butter. Add a little sugar only if necessary: the sauce should taste quite tart to counteract the rich meat it accompanies. Serve warm.

Serving Suggestions
This is the classic sauce for roast pork.

Gooseberry Sauce

Here the flavor of the fruit is enhanced with the aniseed taste of Florence fennel.

SERVES 4

8 ounces (250g) gooseberries
6 tablespoons water
1 tablespoon minced Florence fennel
¼ cup (50g) sugar, or to taste
2 tablespoons (25g) unsalted butter, chilled and diced

Rinse, then trim the gooseberries. Put them into a heavy-based, non-aluminum saucepan with the water and minced fennel. Cover and simmer gently until the fruit is very tender, stirring frequently.

Remove the pan from the heat and beat the mixture until smooth, or purée it in a processor or using a hand-held immersion blender. Stir in the sugar to taste, then whisk in the butter at the last minute.

To make this sauce in advance, prepare the recipe up to the point where the sugar is stirred in and keep it warm. Add the butter just before serving.

Serving Suggestions
Use this pale green sauce to accompany rich fish and roast pork.

Quince and Apricot Sauce

This pretty, utterly delicious sauce is simple to make, once you have the quince jelly.

SERVES 8 OR MORE

8 ounces (250g) dried apricots
1¼ cups (300ml) dry white wine
¼ cup (85g) Quince Jelly (see page 118)
3 tablespoons (45g) unsalted butter
salt and black pepper

Put the apricots in a bowl and pour the wine over them. Cover and let soak overnight.

Next day, transfer the apricots and wine to a small, non-aluminum saucepan. Cover and simmer the fruit gently until very soft.

Pour the contents of the pan into a food processor or blender. Add the quince jelly and butter and process the mixture until smooth, scraping down the side of the bowl from time to time. Taste and season the sauce as required with salt and pepper.

The cooled sauce can be kept, tightly covered, in the refrigerator for up to 4 days.

Serving Suggestions
Serve the sauce warm with lamb, either a roast or grilled chops, or serve it cold with cold roast meats such as duck, ham, and pork, or with bread and cheese.

Pumpkin Sauce

SERVES 6 TO 8

4 cups (480g) diced peeled pumpkin
1 tablespoon olive oil
2 medium onions, chopped
2½ cups (600ml) chicken stock
½ cup (125ml) dry white wine
1 small bunch thyme
1 tablespoon (15g) butter
salt and black pepper

Put the diced pumpkin in a large saucepan. Cover it with water, bring to a boil, and simmer for 15 to 20 minutes or until tender. Drain and refresh under cold running water, then let cool. Purée the pumpkin using a hand-held immersion blender or a food processor. Alternatively, mash it thoroughly and then push it through a strainer.

Heat the olive oil in a large saucepan and add the chopped onions. Cover and cook over low heat until softened but not browned, stirring occasionally. Raise the heat and add ½ cup (125ml) of the stock, the wine, and thyme. Bring to a boil and simmer until the liquid has almost all evaporated. Add the remaining stock, return to a boil, and simmer until the volume has reduced by a third, skimming as necessary.

Strain the liquid, discarding the solids. Stir in the puréed pumpkin, then the butter to make a gravylike consistency. Reheat if necessary, adding a little water if the sauce is too thick. Season to taste and serve.

Serving Suggestions
Roast turkey is the natural partner to this velvety pumpkin sauce.

Minted Apple Jelly

MAKES ABOUT 3 POUNDS (1.35KG)

2¼ pounds (1kg) apples, roughly chopped
juice of 1 large lemon
sugar (see recipe)
1 cup (40g) mint leaves

Put the apples into a non-aluminum preserving kettle with 5 cups (1.2 liters) of water and the lemon juice. Bring to a boil, stirring frequently, then lower the heat and simmer for 20 to 25 minutes or until the apples are soft. Stir frequently.

Suspend a jelly bag or conical strainer lined with cheesecloth over a large bowl. Transfer the apple mixture to the jelly bag or strainer and let it drip overnight or until all the liquid has strained through. Do not squeeze the bag or the jelly will be cloudy.

Measure the liquid, then put it into the cleaned kettle, adding 2½ cups (500g) of sugar to each 2 cups (500ml) of liquid. Heat the mixture gently, stirring frequently, until the sugar has dissolved. Bring to a boil, without stirring, and cook for 5 minutes.

Meanwhile, chop ¾ cup (30g) of the mint and tie it in a cheesecloth bag. Add the bag to the pan and stir gently. Continue cooking until jelly point is reached. To test for doneness, take the kettle off the heat and drop a spoonful of the jelly onto a chilled saucer to cool it quickly. Push a finger against the side of the jelly: if the surface wrinkles, the jelly will set; if not, continue boiling for 2 to 3 minutes and test again. Or use a jelly thermometer: jelly point is 220°F (104°C) at 1000 feet above sea level.

Remove the pan from the heat and let it stand for 5 minutes. Mince the rest of the mint, put it into a heatproof bowl, and pour boiling water over to cover. Let infuse for 2 minutes, then drain the mint in a fine-mesh strainer, squeezing out all the water. Remove the cheesecloth bag from the kettle, squeeze it between 2 small plates to extract all the juices, then discard. Stir the freshly minced mint into the jelly. Pour into hot sterilized jars, cover with lids, and place in a boiling-water bath. Process for 5 minutes.

Serving Suggestions
Serve with grilled or roast lamb.

Crab Apple and Cranberry Jelly

MAKES ABOUT 7 POUNDS (3KG)

5 pounds (2.25kg) crab apples, quartered
1 pound (500g) cranberries
sugar (see recipe)

Put the fruit into a non-aluminum preserving kettle with 3½ quarts (3.5 liters) of water. Bring the mixture to a boil and simmer for 30 minutes or until the fruit is soft and pulpy. Pour the mixture into a jelly bag, or conical strainer lined with cheesecloth, and set over a large bowl. Let drip overnight.

Measure the liquid from the bowl and put it into the cleaned preserving kettle, adding 2½ cups (500g) of sugar to each 2 cups (500ml) of liquid. Set the pan over low heat and cook, stirring frequently, until all the sugar has dissolved. Raise the heat and boil rapidly for 20 to 30 minutes or until jelly point is reached. Pour into jars, cover, and process (see Minted Apple Jelly, left).

Serving Suggestions
Serve with roast lamb, pork, or turkey.

Red-Currant Jelly

MAKES ABOUT 3½ POUNDS (1.6KG)

2¼ pounds (1kg) red currants, picked over
sugar (see recipe)

Put the fruit into a non-aluminum preserving kettle with 3 cups (750ml) of cold water. Bring to a boil, then simmer for 30 minutes or until the fruit is soft, squashing out the juice occasionally with a potato masher. Pour the mixture into a jelly bag, or conical strainer lined with cheesecloth, and set it over a clean bowl. Let drip overnight.

Measure the liquid, then put it into the cleaned kettle with 2½ cups (500g) of sugar to each 2 cups (500ml) of liquid. Stir over low heat until the sugar has dissolved, then raise the heat and boil rapidly until jelly point is reached. Skim, pour into jars, cover, and process (see Minted Apple Jelly, left).

Serving Suggestions
This is good with venison and lamb.

Quince Jelly

MAKES ABOUT 1 POUND (500G)

2¼ pounds (1kg) quinces, roughly chopped
finely grated zest and juice of 1 large lemon
sugar (see recipe)

Put the quinces into a non-aluminum preserving kettle with the lemon zest and enough cold water to cover the fruit. Bring to a boil, then cover and simmer for 1 hour, stirring occasionally, until the fruit is very soft. Pour the mixture into a jelly bag, or conical strainer lined with cheesecloth, and set it over a large bowl. Let drip overnight.

Measure the liquid and put it into the clean preserving kettle with 2½ cups (500g) of sugar to each 2 cups (500ml) of liquid. Add the lemon juice and stir over low heat until the sugar has completely dissolved. Raise the heat and boil rapidly for 10 to 15 minutes or until jelly point is reached. Skim, then pour into jars, cover, and process (see Minted Apple Jelly, left).

Serving Suggestions
Serve with roast lamb or game.

Bread Sauce

Old-Fashioned Bread Sauce

A creamy, richly flavored sauce, this should be light, smooth, and free from lumps.

SERVES 6

1¼ cups (300ml) whole milk or half-and-half
1 medium onion, peeled and spiked with
   3 whole cloves
6 black peppercorns
1 bay leaf
1 blade mace
½ cup (50g) fresh white bread crumbs

2 tablespoons (25g) unsalted butter, diced
salt and black pepper
1 tablespoon heavy cream

Place the milk in a small saucepan with the clove-spiked onion, peppercorns, bay leaf, and mace. Heat until scalding hot but not boiling. Remove from the heat, cover, and let infuse for 30 minutes.

Strain the milk into a clean saucepan, discarding the flavorings. Reheat, then stir in the bread crumbs. Cook, stirring constantly, for 2 to 3 minutes or until the sauce thickens. Remove the pan from the heat and stir in the butter. Season to taste (the sauce should not be bland), then stir in the cream and serve hot or warm. The sauce will thicken as it stands. Do not try to reheat bread sauce, as it will be ruined.

Serving Suggestions
This is a delicious partner for roast turkey as well as for roast chicken and game birds.

Below: rich milk is essential for a superior Bread Sauce, traditionally flavored with bay, mace, peppercorns, and a clove-spiked onion.

Crunchy Mustard

You will need to sterilize a small preserving jar for this pungent condiment.

MAKES JUST UNDER 12 OUNCES (325G)

⅔ cup (150ml) white wine vinegar
6 tablespoons (60g) white mustard seeds
6 tablespoons (60g) black mustard seeds
3 tablespoons honey
1 teaspoon sea salt
¼ teaspoon ground cinnamon

Put the vinegar and mustard seeds into a glass or china bowl, cover with plastic wrap, and leave for 36 hours.

Put the seed mixture into a blender with the honey, salt, and cinnamon and blend at maximum speed until the mixture is thick; if the paste is too dry, add a little more vinegar. Pack into a sterilized jar and seal tightly. Store the mustard in the refrigerator for up to 1 month. The mixture will rapidly dry out if not well sealed.

Serving Suggestions
Serve with cold cuts or use in vinaigrettes.

Piccalilli

The vegetables are brined to remove some of their water and to keep them crunchy.

MAKES 6½ POUNDS (3KG)

1½ pounds (750g) zucchini, diced
1 pound (450g) English cucumbers, diced
1¼ cups (375g) salt
2¼ quarts (2.25 liters) water
1 pound (450g) boiling onions or shallots, peeled
1 pound (450g) cauliflower florets (4½ cups)
1 pound (450g) green beans, cut into 1¼-inch (3-cm) pieces
3 cups (200g) shredded green cabbage
½ cup (50g) shredded red sweet pepper
½ cup (50g) shredded green sweet pepper

FOR THE MUSTARD SAUCE:
½-ounce (15-g) piece fresh ginger, bruised with a rolling pin
½ teaspoon black peppercorns
6 tablespoons (40g) turmeric
¼ cup (25g) English mustard powder
3 tablespoons all-purpose flour
3 tablespoons (20g) curry powder
5 cups (1.2 liters) distilled white vinegar
½ cup (115g) firmly packed light brown sugar

Layer the zucchini and cucumber in a large bowl, sprinkling the layers with ½ cup (150g) of the salt in total. Put the rest of the vegetables in a brine: dissolve the remaining salt in the water in a non-metal bowl; add the vegetables and cover with a plate so they remain below the surface. Cover both bowls and leave overnight.

To make the mustard sauce, tie the ginger and peppercorns in a piece of cheesecloth. In a small bowl, blend the turmeric, mustard powder, flour, and curry powder with a little of the vinegar. Put the rest of the vinegar into a large preserving kettle. Add the mustard paste and bag of spices. Stir over medium heat until boiling, then lower the heat and simmer for 15 minutes or until creamy. Stir in the sugar.

Brining the vegetables: set a plate on top of the vegetables to keep them weighted down so that they are fully immersed in the brine.

Drain all the vegetables very thoroughly and add them to the sauce. Simmer for 5 minutes. Remove the spice bag, then ladle into hot preserving jars, ensuring that the vegetables are covered with sauce. Cover the jars with lids. Place in a boiling-water bath and process for 10 minutes.

Serving Suggestions
This is good with cold pork and beef.

Warm Mustard Sauce

SERVES 6 TO 8

1½ tablespoons white wine vinegar
2 teaspoons black or brown mustard seeds, coarsely crushed
2 teaspoons white mustard seeds, coarsely crushed
1¼ cups (300ml) chicken stock
2½ tablespoons heavy cream
1 tablespoon lemon juice
1 tablespoon English mustard powder
1 tablespoon cold water
1 tablespoon cornstarch
2 tablespoons minced dill
salt and black pepper

In a small bowl, stir the vinegar with the mustard seeds. Let soak for 2 to 3 hours.

In a medium-size saucepan, combine the stock, cream, lemon juice, and mustard powder and slowly bring to a boil. Stir the water with the cornstarch until smooth, then slowly pour into the boiling sauce, stirring. Lower the heat and simmer for 3 minutes.

Remove from the heat. Stir the dill and vinegar and crushed mustard seeds into the sauce. Season to taste with salt and pepper. Serve hot or warm. The sauce will keep in the refrigerator for up to 3 days.

Serving Suggestions
Roast chicken, fish, or pork are best with this mild and creamy mustard sauce.

Horseradish Sauce and Relish

Left: Horseradish Sauce adds creamy piquancy to smoked trout and salad.

Drain the anchovy fillets and soak them in the milk for 10 minutes. Drain off the milk, then work the anchovies in a food processor or blender with the butter and seasonings until a smooth purée is formed. Store the paste in a covered container in the refrigerator for up to 3 weeks.

Serving Suggestions

This paste is good with baked potatoes and pasta, and spread on toast.

Red Onion Relish

Adjust the sharpness of this relish to taste: some onions are sweeter than others.

MAKES 1 POUND (500G)

1 pound (500g) red onions, thinly sliced in
   rounds
1¼ cups (300ml) water
½ cup (75g) large raisins
¼ cup (50g) firmly packed dark brown sugar
¼ cup (60ml) red wine vinegar
3 tablespoons olive oil
3 tablespoons sun-dried tomato paste
3 cloves garlic, minced
1 large bouquet garni
salt and black pepper

Place all the ingredients in a large non-aluminum pan. Bring the mixture to a boil, stirring frequently until the sugar completely dissolves. Let simmer gently, uncovered, for 45 minutes or until very soft and moist.

Taste and adjust the flavorings as needed. Remove the bouquet garni, then ladle the mixture into a hot jar and seal. Store in the refrigerator and use within 2 weeks.

Serving Suggestions

Serve with cold cuts and sharp cheeses.

Horseradish Sauce

SERVES 4

½ cup (125ml) heavy cream, chilled
1 tablespoon finely grated fresh horseradish, or
   to taste
juice of ½ lemon
pinch mustard powder
pinch sugar
salt and black pepper

Whip the cream until it forms soft peaks. Stir in the grated horseradish, lemon juice, mustard, and sugar, mixing well.

Taste the sauce, and add a little salt and pepper. Adjust the other flavorings as necessary. Cover and chill the sauce for up to 4 hours until ready to serve. Stir gently before serving.

Variation: Use sour cream instead of heavy cream. In this case you may only need a couple of drops of lemon juice.

Serving Suggestions

Horseradish sauce is most often served chilled with hot roast beef. It is also good with smoked fish, particularly trout.

Anchovy Paste

MAKES 8 OUNCES (250G)

3 2-ounce (50-g) cans anchovy fillets
6 tablespoons milk
10 tablespoons (140g) unsalted butter, softened
pinch cayenne pepper, or to taste
black pepper

121

Tomato Ketchup

This is only worth making if you have plenty of good, ripe, well-flavored tomatoes. Sun-ripened plum tomatoes usually have a more concentrated taste than watery greenhouse varieties.

MAKES 5 CUPS (1.2 LITERS)

2¼ pounds (1kg) ripe tomatoes, quartered
4 cups (450g) minced apples, with skin
1½ cups (250g) minced onions
5 cups (1.2 liters) distilled white vinegar
6 tablespoons (60g) coarse sea salt
2½ tablespoons (25g) mustard seeds, roughly crushed
1 dried hot chili pepper
1 cinnamon stick
3 blades mace
1 teaspoon black peppercorns
½ teaspoon grated nutmeg
1¼ cups (250g) sugar

Put the tomatoes, apples, and onions in a preserving ketttle with half the vinegar, the salt, crushed mustard seeds, chili pepper, cinnamon, mace, peppercorns, and nutmeg. Bring slowly to a boil, then simmer for 1 to 1½ hours or until reduced by a third. Stir frequently to prevent the mixture from sticking to the bottom of the pan.

Strain the hot mixture through a coarse-mesh conical strainer, discarding the solids. Put the pulp into the clean preserving kettle with the remaining vinegar and the sugar, and stir over low heat until the sugar has completely dissolved.

Bring to a boil and simmer for 30 to 45 minutes or until the ketchup is very thick. Pour the ketchup into hot, sterilized bottles or jars and seal. Place in a boiling-water bath and process for 5 minutes. Store in a very cool spot and use within 6 months. Once opened, store in the refrigerator.

Serving Suggestions
Serve with hot dogs and hamburgers.

Barbecue Ketchup

MAKES 3½ CUPS (850ML)

6 tablespoons (90g) unsalted butter
3 medium onions, minced
5 cloves garlic, minced
2 cups (500ml) tomato ketchup
3 tablespoons firmly packed dark brown sugar
3 tablespoons soy sauce
3 tablespoons cider vinegar
3 tablespoons Worcestershire sauce
2 to 3 drops hot red pepper sauce

Above: Oyster Ketchup (left) is flavored with mace and cayenne, while Barbecue Ketchup takes its heat from garlic and hot pepper sauce.

Heat the butter in a medium-size saucepan, add the onions and garlic, and stir well. Cover and cook gently, stirring occasionally, for about 20 minutes or until very soft but not browned. Add the rest of the ingredients and cook for 5 more minutes. Taste and adjust the flavorings to suit your palate.

ℋETCHUP

The cooled ketchup can be kept, tightly covered, in the refrigerator for up to 1 week or frozen for up to 1 month.

Serving Suggestions

Serve the ketchup at room temperature or hot with plainly grilled meats and sausages. When cold, this sauce can also be used as a baste to brush over ribs, chops, or chicken pieces toward the end of cooking.

Oyster Ketchup

This is an old English recipe. You can use either dry or sweet cream sherry.

MAKES ABOUT 3 CUPS (750ML)

8 fresh oysters
2½ cups (600ml) sherry
1 tablespoon salt
4 blades mace
pinch cayenne pepper or paprika
1 tablespoon brandy

Shuck each oyster by holding the rounded side down on a board and inserting an oyster knife into the hinged end to pry it open. Cut out the oyster, being careful to reserve the liquor, and put it into a mortar. Pour the liquor into a bowl and set aside.

Pound the oysters with a pestle to a smooth paste: this is vital, as otherwise the sauce will be lumpy. Place the pounded oysters in a saucepan with the reserved liquor and the sherry and bring to a boil.

Add the salt, mace, and cayenne pepper or paprika, and boil for 1 more minute. Skim the mixture, then strain it through a fine-mesh strainer and let cool. Stir in the brandy. Pour into bottles or jars and cover. It can be stored in the refrigerator for up to 6 weeks.

Serving Suggestions

An unusual ketchup for steak. Add a few drops to casseroles and pasta sauces, too.

Tamarind Sauce

This is spicy and aromatic rather than hot. Buy tamarind paste in blocks from Asian and Indian markets or other specialist food stores. You will need to soak it well and remove the pits before use.

MAKES 2 CUPS (500ML)

8 ounces (250g) tamarind paste
1¼ cups (300ml) hot water
⅔ cup (100g) raisins
2 tablespoons (20g) black mustard seeds
1½ tablespoons (20g) chopped fresh ginger
6 cloves garlic
3 medium-size dried hot red chili peppers
1½ cups (350ml) brown malt vinegar
1¾ cups (350g) firmly packed dark brown sugar
1 tablespoon coarse sea salt

In a non-metal bowl, combine the tamarind and two-thirds of the hot water (just over ¾ cup). Put the raisins in another bowl and cover with the remaining hot water. Let both soak overnight.

Next day, drain the raisins and put them into the bowl of a food processor with the mustard seeds, ginger, garlic, and chilies. Add 4 tablespoons of the vinegar and process to make a smooth paste.

In a large, non-aluminum saucepan, mix the rest of the vinegar with the sugar and salt. Heat gently until the sugar dissolves.

Meanwhile, using your fingers, squeeze and break up the pieces of tamarind in the soaking liquid to give a thick, pulpy slurry. Remove the pits and any fibrous pieces of tamarind, then add the tamarind mixture and the spice paste to the pan of vinegar. Bring to a boil, then lower the heat and simmer for 15 to 20 minutes or until the sauce is very thick and dark. Push the sauce through a coarse strainer, then pour into hot, sterilized bottles or jars and seal. Place in a boiling-water bath and process for 15 minutes. Keep the sauce for 1 month before using. Once opened, store in the refrigerator.

Serving Suggestions

This richly spiced, dark, thick sauce can be used as a ketchup with hot or cold cooked meats and poultry. It can also be used as a marinade or baste. You can add a little to mayonnaise to make a quick sauce for a chicken salad, or add it to gravies, stews, and casseroles for extra flavor.

Roasted Garlic Sauce

MAKES 2 CUPS (500ML)

8 ounces (250g) garlic cloves, unpeeled
¾ cup (150g) chopped fresh ginger
⅓ cup (50g) black mustard seeds
2 fresh medium-hot red chili peppers, cored, seeded, and chopped
1¾ cups (400ml) cider vinegar
1½ cups (300g) firmly packed light brown sugar
2 teaspoons coarse sea salt

Preheat the oven to 375°F. Put the garlic into a baking dish and roast it in the hot oven for 10 minutes or until aromatic, golden, and soft. Let it cool, then squeeze the cloves out of the skins.

Put the garlic cloves into a food processor with the ginger, mustard seeds, and chilies. Process until smooth, adding a little of the vinegar if necessary.

In a non-aluminum saucepan, slowly heat the rest of the vinegar with the sugar, without boiling, until the sugar has dissolved. Raise the heat, add the garlic purée, and stir as the mixture comes to a boil. Simmer very gently, stirring frequently, for 20 minutes or until the sauce is very thick. Add the salt.

Pour the sauce into hot, sterilized jars and seal. Place in a boiling-water bath and process for 15 minutes. Store for 1 month before use. Once opened, keep refrigerated.

Serving Suggestions

Serve as a ketchup with hot or cold cooked meats, or use as a marinade and baste.

123

DESSERT SAUCES

For those with a sweet tooth, a meal is incomplete without dessert. This chapter offers ways to turn simple ice cream into a midweek treat, or to make weekend brunch pancakes extra special. For grand occasions, there are fruit sauces that can be spectacularly flamed at the table and classic dinner party favorites like crêpes suzette, zabaglione, and cream puffs. Old-fashioned creamy custards and even a pudding baked in its own sauce are perfect for Sunday lunch and family get-togethers.

All your favorite flavors are here: autumnal berries, tropical and citrus fruits, chocolate of all descriptions, coffee, toffee, brandy and rum, coconut and pecans. There's plenty of butter, eggs, and sugar, too, but also a variety of low-fat recipes so that everyone can enjoy a sweet treat.

Left (from left to right): Chocolate Cream Sauce, Passion Fruit Syrup, Red Fruit Slump.

Melba Sauce

This attractive and easy sauce was created by Escoffier, the famous chef of London's Savoy Hotel. He named it in honor of the soprano Dame Nellie Melba, who was a regular guest when she sang at Covent Garden. Escoffier spooned the sauce over peaches and vanilla ice cream.

SERVES 6 TO 8

1 pound (500g) fresh raspberries, or thawed frozen raspberries
confectioners' sugar, to taste

Purée the raspberries in a food processor. Add confectioners' sugar to taste: the amount you will need depends on the tartness of the fruit (frozen raspberries usually require more than fresh) and on how the sauce is to be used. Process again for 1 minute to thicken the mixture.

Press the sauce through a nylon strainer into a bowl. Taste and adjust the flavor if necessary: if the sauce is too sweet, add a few drops of fresh lemon juice; if it is too tart, add a little more sifted confectioners' sugar, beating well to avoid lumps.

Cover the sauce tightly and chill until required. The sauce can be stored in the refrigerator for up to 2 days. If fresh fruit is used, the sauce can be frozen for up to 1 month; do not freeze a sauce made from thawed frozen raspberries.

Variation: Add 1 to 2 tablespoons kirsch or framboise (raspberry eau-de-vie).

Serving Suggestions
Use as a sauce for fresh fruit, ice cream, or rich desserts such as chocolate mousse cake and cream puffs. An effective presentation is to drizzle a little Crème Anglaise (see page 24) on the plate, then some Melba Sauce, place the cake or pastry on top, and dust with confectioners' sugar or unsweetened cocoa powder.

Hunza Apricot Purée

When cooked, dried whole Hunza apricots (sold in health food stores) have a rich, slightly caramelized flavor.

SERVES 4

5 ounces (150g) dried Hunza apricots
confectioners' sugar, to taste (optional)

Place the dried apricots in a bowl and cover with water. Let soak overnight.

Drain the apricots, put them in a small saucepan, and cover with fresh water. Bring to a boil and simmer until tender. At the end of cooking the water should only just cover the apricots, so boil to reduce if necessary.

Squeeze the pits from the apricots and return the flesh to the cooking liquid. Purée the apricots with the liquid using a hand-held immersion blender or food processor. Sweeten to taste, if desired. Reheat if necessary, or let cool.

Below: one of the simplest sweet sauces, Melba Sauce provides a red silky finish to this dish of poached fresh peaches and vanilla ice cream.

Fruit Sauce

Variation: Use 1½ cups (150g) dried apricot halves, which may not need soaking if they are plump and juicy.

Serving Suggestions

Serve as a sauce for thick plain yogurt or ice cream, particularly apricot, caramel, or vanilla. It also works well with desserts made from phyllo pastry.

Kiwi-Coconut Sauce

SERVES 4

2 kiwi fruit, halved
⅔ cup (150ml) canned coconut milk
2 tablespoons sugar, or to taste

Using a teaspoon, scoop the flesh from the kiwi fruit and place it in the bowl of a food processor or blender. Pour in the coconut milk and process until smooth.

Stir in the sugar, then taste and add a little more if necessary—this will depend on the sweetness of the fruit and coconut milk. Serve at room temperature or chilled.

Serving Suggestions

A spoonful of this sauce on top of a tropical fruit salad is delicious. Alternatively, use it to fill warm rolled crêpes and top with some lightly toasted shredded coconut.

Rhubarb and Fig Jam

MAKES ABOUT 4 POUNDS (1.8KG)

3 pounds (1.3kg) rhubarb
1 pound (500g) plump dried figs
3 pounds (1.3kg) sugar (6½ cups)
juice of 2 large lemons

Wash the rhubarb and chop it into pieces about ¾ inch (2cm) long. Chop the figs as coarsely or finely as you wish. Put both

fruits into a large china or glass bowl with the sugar and stir well. Cover and leave for 24 hours—the sugar should have almost completely dissolved.

Transfer the mixture to a preserving kettle and add the lemon juice. Slowly bring to a boil, stirring frequently. Raise the heat a little, then simmer until the jam has thickened and will set. Pour into hot sterilized jars, cover with lids, and place in a boiling-water bath. Process for 5 minutes.

Variation: *Rhubarb and Orange Jam*
Replace the figs and lemon juice with the chopped flesh of 1 large orange, 2 pieces of preserved ginger in syrup, minced, and 2 teaspoons of ground ginger. Since this mixture contains no dried fruit, it can be put into the preserving kettle without soaking.

Serving Suggestions

Warm this richly flavored jam until bubbling, then thin it with a little water to make a pourable sauce for hot puddings or crêpes. Or it can be served cold with scones.

Lemon Curd

MAKES ABOUT 1 POUND (500G)

1¼ cups (250g) sugar
½ cup (125g) unsalted butter, diced
grated zest and juice of 3 large lemons
3 extra large eggs, beaten

Put the sugar, butter, and lemon zest and juice in a double boiler or in a non-metal bowl set over a pan of simmering water. Stir until the sugar has dissolved and the butter has melted.

Strain the beaten eggs into the pan and cook, stirring constantly, over low heat until the mixture thickens—do not boil or the mixture will scramble. Pour into hot jars and cover. When cold, store the curd in the refrigerator and use within 1 month.

Serving Suggestions

Make a quick sauce by folding the lemon curd into whipped cream. Alternatively, use it to fill little tartlet shells, or spread it on buttered toast or scones.

Oranges in Red Wine

This is an excellent recipe for summer parties, as most of the preparation can be done the day before.

SERVES 6

2 cups (500ml) light red wine
⅔ cup (150ml) water
⅓ cup (80g) sugar
1 vanilla bean
1 cinnamon stick
2 whole cloves
6 thin-skinned sweet oranges
1½ cups (250g) sliced strawberries

Put the wine, water, sugar, vanilla bean, cinnamon, and cloves into a large non-aluminum saucepan. Heat gently, stirring, until the sugar completely dissolves, then bring the mixture to a boil. Simmer until the liquid has reduced to a syrup measuring about 1¼ cups (300ml).

Meanwhile, holding the oranges over a large heatproof bowl to catch the juice, peel them with a sharp knife; remove the skin and all the white pith. Slice the oranges thinly, removing any seeds. Arrange the slices in the heatproof bowl. When it is ready, strain the hot wine sauce over the oranges. Leave them until cooled, then stir well, cover, and let macerate in the refrigerator overnight.

An hour before serving, gently stir the strawberries into the orange and wine mixture. Return to the refrigerator to continue macerating until ready to serve.

Serving Suggestions

Serve alone or with vanilla ice cream.

Crêpes Suzette

This dish of delicate crêpes in an orange liqueur sauce used to be a *coup de théâtre* in grand French restaurants where the *maitre d'* would finish the dish at the table by flaming the alcohol to applause from the diners. Crêpes Suzette is thought to have been created by accident at the Café de Paris, in Monte Carlo, when the Prince of Wales, later King Edward VII, dined there with friends. The nervous chef ignited the sauce and the spectacular result was named in honor of the youngest member of the party. In my version, the sauce is less sweet and more refreshingly fruity than the classic. There is no need to set fire to the final dish as it really does nothing for the taste of the orange sauce.

SERVES 4

FOR THE CRÊPES:

¾ cup (110g) all-purpose flour

1 large pinch salt

1 extra large egg plus 1 extra large egg yolk

1¼ cups (300ml) milk

1½ tablespoons (20g) unsalted butter, melted

1 teaspoon Grand Marnier or other orange liqueur

extra melted butter or oil for frying

FOR THE FILLING:

10 sugar cubes

2 large oranges

1 tablespoon Grand Marnier or other orange liqueur

½ cup (125g) unsalted butter, softened

FOR THE SAUCE:

juice of the 2 oranges above

3 tablespoons Grand Marnier or other orange liqueur

Make the crêpe batter by sifting the flour and salt into a large bowl and making a well in the center. Place the whole egg, yolk, and milk in the well and gradually stir in the flour. Whisk in the melted butter and liqueur, then cover and let stand for 30 minutes.

Heat a 6-inch (15-cm) crêpe pan and grease it lightly using a paper towel dipped in melted butter or oil. Put a large spoonful of the batter in the pan and swirl it around until the bottom of the pan is covered with a thin layer. Cook over medium heat until golden brown, then use a metal spatula to loosen the edges of the crêpe and flip it over to brown the other side. Tip out the cooked crêpe and keep it warm while cooking the rest of the batch: you will need 16 crêpes. When necessary, grease the pan as before. If you want to cook the crêpes in advance, stack them on a plate, interleaved with wax paper, then cover tightly with foil.

To make the filling, rub the sugar cubes over the oranges until they absorb all the oil from the skin. Put the sugar cubes into a small bowl, add the liqueur, and stir until dissolved. Beat the butter until creamy, then gradually beat in the sugar and liqueur mixture. Reserve a tablespoon of the flavored butter to fry the crêpes later.

Above: fresh orange juice and orange liqueur combine in a buttery sauce for Crêpes Suzette, here garnished with a little zest from the fruit.

Spread a teaspoon of flavored butter on each crêpe, then fold them in quarters. The filled crêpes can be covered and chilled for up to 6 hours before finishing.

When ready to serve, heat a large, heavy, and preferably nonstick, skillet. Add the reserved flavored butter. Quickly fry the folded crêpes, in batches, for 2 minutes on each side or until they are thoroughly heated and lightly browned. Keep the crêpes warm on a serving dish while frying the remainder.

When all the crêpes have been fried, add the orange juice to the skillet and bring it to a boil, stirring over medium heat to dissolve the sugary pan juices. Cook until reduced to a thin, syrupy sauce. Remove the pan from the heat and stir in the liqueur. Spoon a little sauce over the crêpes and pour the rest into a warmed sauce boat. Serve immediately.

Variation: Fill the crêpes with Pastry Cream (see page 130) and heat through gently before serving with the sauce.

Cherries Jubilee

For this quickly made fruit sauce you can use fresh, canned, bottled, or frozen black cherries. Make sure they are drained thoroughly before use. Any excess juice can be used later for a red fruit salad.

SERVES 4

1 tablespoon (15g) unsalted butter
2 cups (300g) pitted black cherries
¼ cup (50g) sugar
grated zest and juice of 1 orange
¼ cup (60ml) brandy, cherry brandy, kirsch, or
    orange liqueur

Heat the butter in a heavy, non-aluminum skillet or sauté pan. When it begins to foam, add the cherries, shaking the pan so they are well coated with butter. Sprinkle the sugar over the fruit. Cook over medium-high heat for 2 to 3 minutes or until the sugar just begins to caramelize.

Carefully add the orange zest and juice to the hot mixture in the pan, then lower the heat and stir gently until the mixture boils and makes a syrupy sauce. Add the brandy or liqueur. Ignite with a match so that the sauce flames. Shake the pan until the flames die down, then serve immediately.

Variations: White peaches, fresh or bottled, can be used instead of cherries. You can then replace the brandy with peach liqueur.

Serving Suggestions
Cherries Jubilee is delicious with vanilla ice cream and crisp cookies. It also makes an unusual sauce for sweet batter puddings and adds a luxurious richness to chocolate cakes and puddings.

Hot Blackberry Sauce

SERVES 4 TO 6

2 cups (250g) fresh or frozen blackberries
⅓ cup (60g) firmly packed light brown sugar,
    or to taste
2 tablespoons water
squeeze of lemon juice (optional)

Put the fruit (there is no need to thaw frozen fruit) and sugar into a medium-sized non-aluminum saucepan. Add the water and simmer the fruit for 5 minutes or until soft.

Press the fruit mixture through a fine nylon or stainless steel strainer into a clean pan. Taste the sauce and adjust the sweetness, if necessary. If it is not tart enough, add a squeeze of lemon juice. Reheat and serve.

Serving Suggestions
This sauce can be served with sorbets and hot puddings as well as ice cream.

Hot Strawberry and Orange Sauce

This is a good recipe for using strawberries that are slightly past their best.

SERVES 4

3 cups (450g) strawberries, hulled and halved
½ cup (100g) sugar
¼ cup (60ml) freshly squeezed orange juice
2 to 3 tablespoons orange liqueur

Sprinkle the fruit with half the sugar. Put the remaining sugar into a heavy, non-aluminum sauté pan or skillet and heat carefully until it has melted and is starting to caramelize. Remove the pan from the heat and stir in the orange juice, then return it to the heat and simmer until the sauce is syrupy.

Add about ⅓ cup (50g) of the prepared strawberries to the sauce, stirring and mashing using a wooden spoon, until the

fruit has become a pulp. Add the rest of the fruit and the liqueur to the sauce. Reheat gently, stirring constantly, then serve.

Variation: Add some chopped rhubarb to the pan and cook it gently for 10 minutes before adding the strawberries.

Serving Suggestions
Crêpes and pancakes are delicious with this sauce. Serve them with a dollop of whipped cream or thick plain yogurt, too, if desired.

Red Fruit Slump

For this hot sauce the fruit can be fresh or frozen. The name refers to the way the soft berries break down during cooking.

SERVES 4 TO 6

1 pound (500g) fresh or frozen red fruits, such
    as pitted cherries, red and black currants,
    loganberries, blackberries, raspberries,
    and/or strawberries
3 to 4 tablespoons sugar, to taste
2 tablespoons water or crème de cassis
    (black-currant liqueur)

Put the firmer fruit (such as cherries and red and black currants) into a non-aluminum sauté pan. Heat gently for about 2 minutes or until the juices start to run from the fruit.

Stir in the softer fruit, the sugar, and water or crème de cassis. Simmer the mixture over low heat for 5 minutes or until the fruit starts to soften, then cover the pan and continue simmering for 4 to 5 minutes or until the fruit is tender. Serve the sauce hot.

Serving Suggestions
Sweet dumplings flavored with a pinch of ground cinnamon can be poached in the simmering fruit sauce after it has been cooking for 5 minutes. Serve with spoonfuls of plain yogurt or vanilla ice cream.

Egg and Cream Sauces

Pastry Cream

MAKES 1½ CUPS (350ML)

1¼ cups (300ml) rich creamy milk or half-and-half
1 vanilla bean, split, or 1 tablespoon vanilla
    extract
4 large egg yolks
5 tablespoons (60g) sugar or vanilla-flavored
    sugar
2 tablespoons all-purpose flour

Put the milk and vanilla bean (but not the extract, if using) into a heavy saucepan and heat slowly until scalding hot. Remove from the heat, cover, and let infuse for 20 minutes.

In a medium-size bowl, whisk the egg yolks and sugar until light and thick, then whisk in the flour. Remove the vanilla from the pan and whisk the milk into the eggs.

Return the mixture to the pan and bring it to a boil, whisking constantly. Lower the heat and cook the mixture gently, whisking, for 2 to 3 minutes or until the flour no longer tastes raw. Remove from the heat and stir in the extract, if using. Sprinkle with sugar to prevent a skin from forming, then let cool.

The pastry cream can be stored, covered, in the refrigerator for up to 2 days.

Variations: Flavor with brandy or liqueur to taste; with 4 ounces (125g) of melted chocolate; or with 1½ tablespoons of instant coffee powder dissolved in the milk.

Serving Suggestions
Pastry Cream is the traditional filling for French pastries and tarts.

Crème Chantilly

MAKES ABOUT 1¾ CUPS (400ML)

1 cup (250ml) heavy cream, well chilled
½ teaspoon vanilla extract, or 1 tablespoon
    sweet cream sherry
1½ tablespoons sugar

Chill a whisk and mixing bowl for 1 hour in the refrigerator or freezer. Use them to whip the chilled cream until just thickened, then add the vanilla or sherry and whip again until the cream almost forms stiff peaks. Beware: The cream may separate later if you overwhip it at this stage.

Serving Suggestions
Use this whipped, sweetened cream to fill and decorate meringue and layer cakes, as well as pastries such as napoleons, cream puffs, and éclairs.

Honey Yogurt Cream

SERVES 6 TO 8

½ cup (125ml) heavy cream
1 tablespoon honey
½ cup (125ml) strained yogurt

In a large bowl, whip the cream until it forms soft peaks. Stir the honey into the yogurt, then use a large metal spoon to fold the yogurt into the whipped cream. Cover and let chill before serving.

Serving Suggestions
Serve this cream on top of juicy fruit salads flavored with a dash of fruit liqueur or eau-de-vie. Alternatively, you can dollop it onto waffles and pancakes spread with jam. It also goes well with granola.

Cinnamon and Mascarpone Cream

SERVES 8

½ cup (125ml) heavy cream
1 cup (250g) mascarpone cheese
1 tablespoon confectioners' sugar
½ teaspoon ground cinnamon

In a large bowl, whip the cream until it forms soft peaks. In a separate bowl, beat the mascarpone cheese with the confectioners' sugar and cinnamon until soft and creamy.

Fold the mascarpone mixture into the whipped cream and chill until ready to serve.

Variation: Add 1 tablespoon of brandy, Marsala, or Madeira wine to the mascarpone before you beat it.

Serving Suggestions
This is best served in small quantities, alongside pastry and fruit desserts or with baked fruit or caramel puddings. For an attractive presentation, shape into ovals.

Orange Custard Sauce

SERVES 4

2 tablespoons (25g) unsalted butter, softened
¼ cup (50g) sugar
grated zest and juice of 1 orange
2 teaspoons all-purpose flour
1 egg

In a small saucepan, off the heat, beat the butter until it is creamy. Gradually stir in the sugar, orange zest, flour, and egg until you have a thick paste. Measure the orange juice and add enough cold water to the juice to yield ⅔ cup (150ml).

Gradually stir the diluted orange juice into the paste. When it is thoroughly combined, place the pan over low heat. Cook the sauce, stirring constantly, until it thickens and the raw taste of the flour has disappeared. Add a little extra water if necessary to keep the sauce at a pourable consistency. Serve warm.

Serving Suggestions
Use as you would stirred egg custard, with puddings and pastry desserts, especially those made with fruit.

ℰGG AND ℂREAM ℐAUCES

Fruit Bavarian Cream

A bavarian cream is a Crème Anglaise lightened with whipped cream and then set with gelatin. It has a smooth, creamy texture, different from the fluffy lightness of a mousse. The custard used for a bavarian cream is prepared in the same way as a stirred custard; however, the proportions of the ingredients need to be a little different in order to make a superior dessert: simply adding whipped cream and gelatin to a stirred custard would give the bavarian cream a heavy texture. To make this dessert, you will need a 1½-quart (1.5-liter) loaf-shaped mold, oiled and lined with parchment paper or plastic wrap.

SERVES 8

2 envelopes unflavored gelatin
3 tablespoons cold water
1 cup (250ml) heavy cream
1½ cups (175g) raspberries, loganberries, or
  boysenberries
1¼ cups (175g) strawberries or blackberries
2 small (or 1 large) peaches or nectarines
FOR THE CRÈME ANGLAISE:
1¼ cups (300ml) creamy milk or half-and-half
3 extra large egg yolks
7 tablespoons (85g) sugar
grated zest of ½ orange
1 to 2 tablespoons orange liqueur, to taste

Make the Crème Anglaise with the milk, egg yolks, and sugar, but omitting the vanilla (see directions on page 24). Stir in the orange zest and liqueur, then let cool.

In a small heatproof bowl, sprinkle the gelatin over the cold water and let it soften for 5 minutes. Set the bowl in a pan of simmering water and dissolve the gelatin, stirring gently. Cool it slightly, then stir the gelatin into the cooled custard.

Whip the cream until it forms soft peaks. Using a large metal spoon, fold it into the custard. Chill the mixture until it has almost set, but is still smooth and soft.

Meanwhile, pick over the berries, carefully wash them, and gently pat them dry with paper towels.

Pour some boiling water over the peaches and scald them for 30 seconds, then drain and peel off the skins. Cut the peaches in half, remove the pits, and finely dice or slice the flesh.

Spread a third of the custard mixture in the bottom of the prepared loaf-shaped mold. Cover tightly and chill for 30 minutes or until the custard is set.

Cover the set custard with half the fruit: You can layer the fruits separately or mix them together. Spoon half the remaining custard mixture over the fruit, smooth the surface, and chill again until set.

Top this layer with the remaining fruit and smooth on the final layer of custard. Cover

the mold tightly with plastic wrap and chill the bavarian cream for 4 hours or until it has completely set.

Unmold the bavarian cream and serve it in slices, accompanied by Melba Sauce (see page 126). The dessert can be made up to 1 day ahead, but cannot be frozen.

Below: fresh red berries and peach slices are set in an orange-flavored custard to make a stunning and delicious Fruit Bavarian Cream.

Wine Sauce and Flavored Butter

Brandy Sauce

SERVES 4 TO 6

1 tablespoon cornstarch
1¼ cups (300ml) milk
2 tablespoons brandy
1 tablespoon sugar

In a small bowl, blend the cornstarch to a smooth paste with a little of the milk. Put the remaining milk into a small saucepan and heat, watching carefully, until it comes to a boil. Remove the pan from the heat and slowly pour in the cornstarch paste, stirring constantly until it is completely mixed.

Return the pan to the heat, add the brandy and sugar, and cook, stirring frequently, for 2 to 3 minutes or until thick and smooth.

Serving Suggestion
This sauce is a reasonably light alternative to stirred custard, and can be served with traditional steamed plum pudding.

Red Wine Sauce

Wine sauces are often thickened with cornstarch, but this relies on reduction.

SERVES 4

1½ cups (350ml) dry red wine
½ cup (100g) sugar
1 cinnamon stick

In a small saucepan, stir the red wine and sugar together. Add the cinnamon stick and bring to a boil, stirring occasionally. Lower the heat and simmer until the liquid has reduced by half and the mixture is syrupy.

Discard the cinnamon stick and serve the sauce hot, warm, or at room temperature.

Serving Suggestions
This adds a rich, adults-only flavor to ice cream, baked custards, and lemon tart.

Rum Butter

Hard butter sauces are too often over-rich and cloyingly sweet, thus overwhelming the steamed pudding they accompany. I've added some lemon zest and juice as well as some honey to the recipe to lighten this traditional favorite.

SERVES 6

7 tablespoons (100g) unsalted butter, at room temperature
⅓ cup (80g) firmly packed light brown sugar
1 tablespoon honey
grated zest and juice of ½ lemon
3 tablespoons rum

Beat the butter until it is very light and creamy, then beat in the sugar a tablespoon at a time until the mixture is fluffy. Beat in the honey and lemon zest, then add the lemon juice and rum a teaspoon at a time, beating well after each addition—this will prevent the mixture from curdling.

Spoon the sauce into a dish, then cover and chill until firm. You can store it, tightly covered, in the refrigerator for up to 1 week, or freeze it for up to 1 month.

Beating the butter until light and fluffy: start with the butter at room temperature and dice it so that it breaks down quickly. Beat vigorously until the butter is like thick whipped cream.

Variations: Replace the rum with brandy. For a richer hard sauce, replace the light brown sugar with dark brown sugar.

Serving Suggestions
Serve, well chilled, with mince pie or plum pudding. This sauce is also good with baked apples, crêpes, and even breakfast (or brunch) pancakes.

Syllabub

This is an old-fashioned dessert and dipping sauce that is well worth trying.

SERVES 4

¾ cup (175ml) sweet cream sherry
½ cup (115g) sugar
3 tablespoons brandy
zest and juice of ½ lemon
2 cups (500ml) heavy cream, well chilled
freshly grated nutmeg

Put the sherry, sugar, brandy, and lemon zest and juice into a measuring cup. Let the mixture infuse for about 20 minutes. Remove and discard the lemon zest.

Pour the cream into a large, well-chilled bowl. Start whipping, then gradually pour in the sherry mixture, whipping well as you go. Continue whipping until it is very thick and light. Spoon the syllabub into chilled glasses and decorate with a light dusting of freshly grated nutmeg. Serve immediately, or cover and chill for up to 4 hours.

Variation: Stir in some toasted slivered almonds and pomegranate seeds.

Serving Suggestions
Syllabub can be served on its own, with ladyfingers for dipping. Or use it to make a trifle, with layers of thick stirred custard, and sponge cake moistened with sweet cream sherry and spread with jam or preserves.

𝒲ine 𝒮auce

Zabaglione

SERVES 2 TO 4

4 egg yolks
6 tablespoons Marsala wine
¼ cup (50g) sugar
2 tablespoons water

Combine all the ingredients in a heatproof bowl set over a pan of just simmering—but not boiling—water. Whisk the mixture for about 5 minutes or until it turns light in color and becomes very thick; it should leave a ribbon-like trail on its surface when the whisk is lifted from the bowl.

Remove the bowl from the heat and continue whisking the mixture until it is cool. Serve the zabaglione warm or at room temperature, within 1 hour.

Variations: Replace the Marsala wine with ¼ cup (60ml) of kirsch, or with ½ cup (125ml) of dry white wine or champagne. Alternatively, let the mixture cool, then fold in ½ cup (125ml) of lightly whipped cream.

Serving Suggestions

Zabaglione is a marvelous sauce for light sponge cakes, fresh fruit, fruit desserts, trifles, and parfaits. You can also serve it in tall glasses accompanied by Italian cookies such as savoiardi or biscotti, which are dipped into the sauce before eating.

Left: a tempting plate of luscious mixed berries, currants, and crunchy Italian cookies is topped with generous spoonfuls of creamy Zabaglione to make a luxurious but simple dessert.

CHOCOLATE SAUCE

Chocolate Sauce

For the best flavor, use chocolate with a high proportion of cocoa butter (over 35 percent, if possible), which is available in specialty food stores.

SERVES 4 TO 6

4 ounces (125g) bittersweet or semisweet chocolate, chopped
7 tablespoons (100ml) water
¼ cup (60g) unsalted butter, diced

Put the chopped chocolate, water, and butter in a heatproof bowl and set it over a pan of steaming water. Stir the mixture frequently until the chocolate has melted and the sauce is very smooth. Remove the bowl from the heat and stir well until the sauce is glossy and slightly thickened. As the sauce cools it will thicken further. Serve warm.

Variations: For a creamier sauce, replace the water with an equal quantity of light cream; for a flavored sauce, replace 1 to 2 tablespoons water with brandy or rum.

Cream Puffs

SERVES 6

FOR THE CHOUX PASTRY:
¾ cup (115g) all-purpose flour
¾ cup (185ml) cold water
6 tablespoons (80g) unsalted butter, diced
large pinch salt
large pinch sugar
3 large eggs, beaten
extra beaten egg for brushing
FOR THE FILLING:
Crème Chantilly or Pastry Cream (see page 130)
TO SERVE:
Chocolate Sauce (see above), Toffee Sauce (see page 137), Creamy Caramel Sauce (see page 27), or Melba Sauce (see page 126)

To make the choux pastry, sift the flour onto a piece of paper. Put the water, butter, salt, and sugar into a medium-size saucepan and heat gently until the butter has completely melted. Rapidly bring the mixture to a boil, then immediately remove the saucepan from the heat and tip in all the flour. Beat the mixture vigorously with a wooden spoon until it comes together to make a smooth, heavy clump of dough.

Return the pan to the heat and beat the dough over low heat for 30 seconds to dry it slightly. It should come away from the sides of the pan to form a smooth ball. Transfer the dough to a large mixing bowl and let it cool until tepid.

Using an electric mixer (you can use a wooden spoon instead, but it is hard work), gradually add the beaten eggs to the dough, beating well after each addition, to make a smooth and shiny paste-like dough that falls from the spoon when lightly shaken. Keep the dough covered until ready to use.

Preheat the oven to 375°F, and grease and dampen two baking sheets. Put the choux pastry into a pastry bag fitted with a ½-inch (1.5-cm) plain nozzle. Pipe rounded mounds, about 1 inch (2.5cm) wide and ½ inch (1.5cm) high, spacing them well apart on the baking sheets. Lightly brush the puffs with beaten egg, making sure it does not drip down and glue the pastry to the sheet.

Below: luscious dark Chocolate Sauce oozes temptingly over a pile of Cream Puffs, to make a special occasion dessert.

Chocolate Sauce

Bake for about 20 minutes or until crisp and golden. Wash and dry the pastry bag.

Remove the puffs from the oven and, using a skewer or toothpick, make a small hole in the side of each puff to let out the steam. Return them to the oven and bake for 3 to 4 more minutes. Transfer to a wire rack to cool.

To fill the puffs, spoon the Crème Chantilly or Pastry Cream into the dry, clean pastry bag fitted with the plain nozzle. Pipe the filling into the puffs through the steam hole, enlarging it if necessary. Filled puffs can be kept, in a cool spot, for up to 30 minutes before serving. When ready to serve, pile the filled cream puffs in a dish, pour some of your choice of sauce over, and pass the remaining sauce separately.

Cream puffs without filling can be kept in an airtight container for 2 days or frozen for up to 1 month. Frozen cream puffs may need to be crisped for 5 minutes or so in a hot oven before use.

Variation: If you do not have a pastry bag, use a teaspoon (heaping) to make the small mounds of dough on the baking sheets. To fill the puffs, split them in two and use a teaspoon to spoon in the filling. With this method, you can use slightly softened ice cream to fill the puffs instead of Crème Chantilly or Pastry Cream.

Chocolate Cream Sauce

This is a really quick, rich sauce.

SERVES 4

½ cup (125ml) heavy cream
3 ounces (85g) bittersweet or semisweet chocolate, finely chopped
½ teaspoon vanilla extract

Gently heat the cream in a small, heavy-based saucepan, stirring frequently. When the cream comes to a boil, remove the pan from the heat and add the chopped chocolate. Stir the sauce gently until it is smooth, then stir in the vanilla at the last moment and serve immediately.

Variations: Just before serving, the sauce can be flavored with rum, brandy, or coffee liqueur to taste. For a thinner sauce, mix the heavy cream with a little milk or coffee.

Serving Suggestions
This sauce is best served with ice cream and cream puffs. Garnish it with grated chocolate, if desired.

Chocolate Self-Saucing Pudding

This simple pudding comes with its own hot sauce, hidden underneath a sponge studded with chocolate pieces and pecans.

SERVES 4

½ cup (125g) unsalted butter, softened
½ cup plus 2 tablespoons (125g) sugar
4 extra large eggs, beaten
½ cup plus 1 tablespoon (125g) self-rising flour, or use all-purpose flour with 2 teaspoons baking powder
½ teaspoon vanilla extract
⅓ cup (30g) unsweetened cocoa powder, sifted
¼ cup (30g) pecan pieces
1½ ounces (45g) semisweet chocolate, chopped
1 tablespoon milk
FOR THE SAUCE:
⅓ cup (30g) unsweetened cocoa powder, sifted
½ cup plus 2 tablespoons (125g) firmly packed light brown sugar
1¼ cups (300ml) very hot water

Preheat the oven to 350°F, and grease a 2-quart (2-liter) baking dish.

Beat the butter until creamy using an electric mixer. Add the sugar and beat until light and fluffy. Gradually beat in the eggs. Add a little flour with the last egg (this mixture will look curdled).

Stir in the vanilla followed by the rest of the flour and the cocoa powder. When the mixture is thoroughly combined, fold in the nuts and chopped chocolate, then the milk. Spoon the batter into the buttered dish.

To make the sauce, mix the cocoa powder and sugar in a medium-size bowl. Stir in the very hot water until smooth. Gently pour the sauce over the pudding. Bake for 30 to 35 minutes or until the sponge is cooked in the center and the sauce beneath is thick and bubbling. Serve immediately.

Serving Suggestion
This pudding needs no accompaniment, but you could serve it with cream, if desired.

Mint Chocolate Sauce

Here the delicious and popular combination of mint and chocolate is used in a rich but easy-to-make sauce.

SERVES 6

4 ounces (125g) semisweet chocolate, chopped
¼ cup (60ml) light cream
1 tablespoon minced mint
2 to 3 drops peppermint extract

Place all the ingredients in the top of a double boiler or in a heatproof bowl set over a pan of steaming water. Do not let the water come into contact with the chocolate or the mixture could seize. Stir constantly until the chocolate melts and forms a silky sauce. Serve the sauce hot.

Serving Suggestions
Serve spooned over chocolate, coffee, or vanilla ice cream, with meringue-based desserts, or with fruits such as sliced bananas or poached pear halves.

CHOCOLATE SAUCE

Above: a light, delicate pool of White Chocolate Sauce makes a dramatic complement to this rich dark chocolate roulade filled with whipped cream.

White Chocolate Sauce

The flavor of this simple sauce depends on the quality of the white chocolate, so choose the best that is available.

SERVES 6 TO 8

7 ounces (200g) white chocolate
1 cup (250ml) heavy cream
⅓ cup (80ml) milk

Break the white chocolate into small pieces and melt it very gently in a heatproof bowl set over a saucepan of steaming water. Remove the bowl from the heat and stir the chocolate until smooth.

In a small saucepan, heat the cream with the milk just to boiling point, then remove the pan from the heat and whisk the mixture into the melted white chocolate.

When the sauce is smooth, pour it into a warmed pitcher and serve immediately. Or let the sauce cool, then refrigerate it for up to 48 hours. Stir well before serving.

Serving Suggestions
Serve the sauce hot with ice cream. When chilled, it is an excellent accompaniment to fresh red berries or cherries, as well as dark chocolate desserts.

Chocolate Fudge Sauce

The richer the chocolate you choose for this recipe, the deeper the flavor of the sauce. Even if your taste is for milk chocolate, use dark chocolate, because once combined with the cream the sauce will taste milky.

SERVES 4 TO 6

1 cup (200g) sugar
¾ cup (175ml) heavy cream
3 tablespoons golden syrup or light corn syrup
pinch salt
3 ounces (90g) bittersweet or semisweet chocolate
2 tablespoons (25g) unsalted butter, diced
½ teaspoon vanilla extract, or to taste (optional)

Put the sugar, cream, golden or corn syrup, and salt into a small saucepan and heat, stirring, until the sugar dissolves completely and the mixture is very smooth.

Meanwhile, chop the chocolate. When the cream mixture is smooth, add the chocolate. Bring to a boil, then lower the heat and simmer gently for 20 minutes, stirring frequently, until the sauce is very thick.

Remove the pan from the heat and gradually whisk in the pieces of butter. Stir in the vanilla extract, if using. This sauce can

Chocolate and Caramel Sauces

be kept for up to 2 days in the refrigerator, where it will set to a thick paste. Gently reheat it before serving.

Serving Suggestion
The coldness of ice cream will make this hot sauce set to a chewy fudge.

Mocha Fudge Sauce

If you want to boost the coffee flavor of this sauce with instant coffee, choose powder and not granules, as the powder will dissolve much more easily.

SERVES 4

⅓ cup (75ml) freshly brewed strong coffee
6 tablespoons (75g) firmly packed dark
 brown sugar
1¼ cups (115g) unsweetened cocoa powder
pinch salt
2 tablespoons (25g) unsalted butter, diced
¼ cup (60ml) heavy cream
1 teaspoon instant espresso coffee powder
 (optional)

Put the hot coffee and the sugar into a small saucepan over medium heat and stir until the sugar has completely dissolved. Use a whisk to blend the cocoa powder into the mixture, then add the salt and continue whisking until the sauce is smooth.

Lower the heat under the pan. Gradually whisk in the diced butter, then the cream, and finally the instant coffee powder, if using. Keep whisking until the coffee powder has completely dissolved.

Serve immediately, or let cool and store in the refrigerator for up to 2 weeks.

Serving Suggestions
This makes a rich treat poured over vanilla ice cream. Alternatively, you can serve it with desserts of meringue and cream and, perhaps, some flavorsome strawberries.

Butterscotch Fudge Sauce

SERVES 6

1 cup (200g) firmly packed dark brown sugar
6 tablespoons (90g) unsalted butter
2 tablespoons golden syrup or light corn syrup
⅓ cup (75ml) heavy cream

Combine the sugar, butter, and golden or corn syrup in a small saucepan and stir with a wooden spoon over low heat until the sugar dissolves completely—this may take as long as 10 minutes.

When the mixture is velvety smooth, stir in the cream and heat the sauce until it is piping hot. Pour the sauce into a sauce boat and serve immediately.

The sauce can be poured into a heatproof bowl and cooled until quite firm, then covered tightly and stored in the refrigerator for up to 1 week. It will need to be reheated to a pourable consistency before serving.

Serving Suggestions
A rich, chewy, caramelized sauce, this is particularly good with ice cream and in sundaes, especially banana splits.

Toffee Sauce

SERVES 6

1 cup (200g) firmly packed dark or light
 brown sugar
7 tablespoons (100g) unsalted butter
6 tablespoons (90ml) heavy cream
½ teaspoon vanilla extract

Crush the sugar with a wooden spoon to remove any lumps, then put it into a heavy saucepan with the butter and cream. Stir over low heat until the butter has melted.

Bring the mixture to a boil and simmer gently for 2 to 3 minutes or until toffee-

colored. Remove the pan from the heat, stir in the vanilla extract, and serve immediately.

The cooled sauce can be kept, covered, in the refrigerator for up to 1 week. Warm it through gently before serving.

Serving Suggestions
Serve with ice cream, crêpes, baked puddings, or cream puffs. This is also delicious spooned over pound cake.

Caramel-Cream Sauce

This rich, creamy caramel sauce is similar to the South American treat, *dulce de leche,* for which a can of sweetened condensed milk is boiled until thick and caramelized.

SERVES 8

5 tablespoons (75g) unsalted butter
¼ cup (50g) firmly packed brown sugar
1 cup (250ml) canned sweetened
 condensed milk
2 to 4 tablespoons light cream

In a small saucepan, melt the butter, then stir in the sugar. Slowly bring the mixture to a boil, stirring constantly until the sugar dissolves. Simmer for 1 minute.

Remove the pan from the heat and stir in the condensed milk and 2 tablespoons of the cream, mixing thoroughly to give a smooth sauce. Return the pan to the heat and bring the sauce to a boil. Lower the heat and simmer, stirring, for 2 minutes or until rich and thick. If you would like a thinner sauce, stir in the remaining cream.

Serve warm or at room temperature.

Serving Suggestions
Made without the second addition of cream, this sauce can be used to fill pie shells: top with sliced bananas and whipped cream. Use the thinner version in ice cream sundaes or serve it with baked apples and apple pie.

Mint Syrup

MAKES 3 CUPS (750ML)

1¼ cups (250g) sugar
2 cups (500ml) water
juice of 1 lemon
⅓ cup (15g) mint

Put the sugar and water into a small non-aluminum saucepan and slowly bring to a boil, stirring frequently. Simmer until the sugar has completely dissolved and the liquid is clear, then stir in the lemon juice (there is no need to strain it). Remove the pan from the heat.

Roughly chop the mint leaves. Place them in a heatproof bowl. Pour the hot syrup onto the leaves. Set the syrup aside to infuse.

When the syrup has cooled to room temperature, strain it through a fine-mesh strainer and discard the mint leaves. Store the syrup in a tightly covered bottle or jar in the refrigerator for no more than 1 week.

Variation: *Vanilla and Basil Syrup*
Replace the lemon juice and mint with 3 split vanilla beans and a bunch of chopped basil.

Serving Suggestions
Use the syrup to flavor fruit salads or to moisten chocolate cake layers.

Lemon Syrup Sauce

SERVES 6

2 teaspoons arrowroot
⅔ cup (150ml) water
¼ cup (60ml) golden syrup or light corn syrup
2 tablespoons lemon juice

In a small saucepan, blend the arrowroot with the water, then stir in the golden or corn syrup and lemon juice until the mixture is smooth. Slowly bring the sauce to a boil over low heat, stirring constantly. Simmer

for 1 to 2 minutes or until the sauce is thick enough to coat the back of a spoon. Serve hot or warm.

Serving Suggestions
This is an excellent sauce to serve with puddings and cakes fresh from the oven. Let the sauce cool slightly if you want to serve it with ice cream and sundaes, or with pancakes and waffles.

Passion Fruit Syrup

A recipe from Brazil, this is a pretty, well-textured, and intensely flavored cold fruit sauce. Make sure you choose ripe passion fruit, which look very wrinkled.

SERVES 6 TO 8

10 passion fruit, halved
⅓ cup (75ml) water
¼ cup (50g) sugar

Scoop the flesh and seeds from the passion fruit and set aside. Put the water and sugar into a small saucepan and heat gently, stirring frequently, until the sugar has

Removing the pulp from a passion fruit: use a teaspoon to scoop out all the edible seeds, pith, and juices from each half of the fruit.

dissolved. Bring to a boil and simmer for about 2 minutes to make a thin syrup.

Remove the saucepan from the heat and let the syrup cool for a minute, then stir in the passion fruit flesh and seeds. Beat the sauce well for about 1 minute to break down the fleshy fibers of the fruit. Let the sauce cool, then cover and chill before serving.

The sauce can be kept, covered, in the refrigerator for up to 24 hours.

Serving Suggestions
Serve with orange-flavored cakes (the Mediterranean cake that is made from fresh oranges and ground almonds is particularly good), as well as with ice cream and chocolate desserts.

Pineapple Syrup

SERVES 4

2 cups (250g) diced fresh pineapple
½ cup (125ml) water
¼ cup (50g) sugar
¼ cup (60ml) pineapple juice
2 to 3 teaspoons rum, or to taste
squeeze lemon juice

Purée ¾ cup (90g) of the pineapple in a blender or food processor. Strain the purée, pressing through the strainer, then set aside. Mince the remaining pineapple.

Put the water and sugar into a medium-size saucepan and bring to a boil. Simmer until the sugar has dissolved. Add the minced pineapple and cook gently for 2 to 3 minutes. Stir in the pineapple juice and reserved purée and remove the pan from the heat. Let cool, then stir in the rum and lemon juice to taste. Chill before serving.

Serving Suggestions
Pour over white or yellow cakes, dark chocolate cakes, coconut ice cream, or rice pudding made with coconut milk.

Raisin and Honey Syrup

SERVES 4

¾ cup (125g) raisins
6 tablespoons brandy
1 cup (250ml) orange juice
6 tablespoons honey

Place the raisins and brandy in a small bowl and let marinate for 3 hours.

When the raisins have plumped up, put them into a small saucepan with the soaking liquid and add the orange juice and honey. Bring the mixture to a boil, stirring occasionally, then let it simmer for 8 to 10 minutes or until the syrup has a light coating consistency. Serve warm or chilled.

Serving Suggestions
Spoon over vanilla ice cream or serve as an accompaniment to apple pie or rice pudding.

Maple-Pecan Sauce

SERVES 4 TO 6

2 small apples, quartered and cored
⅔ cup (150ml) maple syrup
½ cup (50g) pecan halves

Peel the quartered apples only if the skin is very thick and tasteless. Cut the fruit into medium dice. Gently warm the maple syrup in a small saucepan, then mix in the apple dice and pecan halves. Serve immediately.

Serving Suggestions
Serve with pancakes, crêpes, ice cream, or steamed sponge puddings.

Below: three simple ingredients—crunchy pecans, maple syrup, and sweet apples—are gently heated to give a speedy Maple-Pecan Sauce. For the best results, use very fresh pecans.

$\mathscr{I}$NDEX BY $\mathscr{A}$CCOMPANIMENT

beef: aromatic braised steak 74; au vin 81; barbecue ketchup 122; beef and mushroom sauce 96; in black bean sauce 105; black sauce 110; boeuf en daube provençale 75; bolognese sauce 97; brandied ginger steak 30; brown sauce 69; cannelloni 96; carbonnade 74; chili-citrus dressing 99; country red wine casserole 79; crab sauce 66; crunchy mustard 120; Cumberland sauce 116; deviled steak 30; five-spice marinade 39; flavored gravy 34; four-pepper butter 36; ginger and lemon grass butter 36; herb marinade 41; horseradish butter 37; horseradish sauce 121; oyster ketchup 122; pepper steaks with cream and mushrooms 30; piccalilli 120; rib-eye steak 30; roasted garlic and cilantro 33; salsa chipotle 107; salsa verde 51; sauce béarnaise 64; sauce bordelaise 69; sauce chasseur 68; sauce choron 64; sauce paloise 64; sauce ravigote 64; steak chasseur 68; teriyaki sauce 104; Texan meat pie 60; whole-grain mustard butter 36; in wine and port 74

bread: anchovy paste 121; black olive pesto 91; cottage cheese and walnut dip 55; goat cheese dip 55; hummus 55; lemon curd 128; pesto genovese 90; quince and apricot sauce 117; red pesto 91; rhubarb and fig jam 127; rhubarb and orange jam 127; roasted eggplant and yogurt dip 52; white bean and rosemary/basil dip 54

cakes: cherries/peaches jubilee 129; crème anglaise 24–25; crème chantilly 130; lemon syrup sauce 138; Melba sauce (raspberry coulis) 126; mint syrup 138; passion fruit syrup 138; pineapple syrup 138; vanilla and basil syrup 138; zabaglione 133

cheese: jelly 118; piccalilli 120; quince and apricot sauce 117; red onion relish 121; sauce vierge 47

chicken: apricot marinade with yogurt sauce 38; avocado-raisin salsa 103; barbecue ketchup 122; black bean salsa 103; blue cheese dressing 53; bread sauce 119; brown sauce 69; buttermilk dressing 53; Caesar salad 47; cannelloni 96; chanterelles sauce 80; chestnut cream 33; chili-citrus dressing 99; Chinese chili sauce 107; cilantro and almond pesto 90; cilantro and lime dressing 51; coq au vin 81; coronation chicken 51; country red wine casserole 79; crab and cilantro sauce 110; cranberry and orange sauce 116; cream sauce 21; curry cream sauce 67; fennel and orange salsa 102; five-spice marinade 39; flavored gravy 34; fresh mango salsa 103; gazpacho dressing 50; goat cheese dip 55; green chili and apricot sauce 109; green peppercorn sauce 33; korma 109; leek and chive sauce 67; lemon and rosemary sauce 81; lime marinade 40; lime and walnut dressing 45; in oats with mild mustard sauce 32; paprika sauce 81; pesto genovese 90; quick white wine sauce 71; red spicy marinade 38; roasted eggplant and yogurt dressing 52; sage pesto 90; salsa chipotle 107; salsa verde 51; sauce allemande 60; sauce bigarade 70; sauce diable 70; sauce suprême 60; sauce vierge 47; sauce vin blanc 64; shallot and Sauternes sauce 67; simplest salsa 102; spicy lemon marinade 40; sweet pepper and tomato sauce 89; sweet and sour sauce 106; tahini chicken noodles 98; tarragon and sherry sauce 70; teriyaki sauce 104; Thai red curry paste 110; tikka 38; tomato and onion baste 39; vindaloo 109; warm mustard sauce 120; whisky cream sauce 67

crêpes and pancakes: beef and mushroom sauce 96; brandy butter 132; caramel sauces 27–28; crème anglaise 24–25; hot rhubarb, strawberry, and orange sauce 129; kiwi-coconut sauce 127; maple-pecan sauce 139; pastry cream 129; rum butter 132; Suzette 128; toffee sauce 137

duck: cranberry and orange sauce 116; crispy duck salad 46; quince and apricot sauce 117; sauce bigarade 70

eggs: aïoli 48; béchamel sauces 20–21, 58–59; cheese sauce 58; curry cream sauce 67; hollandaise sauces 22–23; leek and chive sauce 67; sauce meurette 71; tomato sauce 59

fish and seafood: aïoli 48; anchovy butter 36; aromatic oil 37; béchamel sauces 20–21, 58–59; beurre blancs 64–65; black bean salsa 103; black vinegar sauce 104; buttermilk dressing 53; Caesar salad 47; chantilly mayonnaise 48; cheese sauce 58; chili-citrus dressing 99; chili jam 107; Chinese chili sauce 107; cilantro and almond pesto 90; cilantro and lime dressing 51; cod in oats with mild mustard sauce 32; cod with roasted garlic and cilantro 33; crab and cilantro sauce 110; crab sauce 66; cream sauce 21; curry cream sauce 67; dark soy dipping sauce 112; fennel and orange salsa 102; fettuccine with smoked salmon 94; fish and four-cheese macaroni 94; four-pepper butter 36; fresh mango salsa 103; gazpacho dressing 50; ginger and lemon grass butter 36; gooseberry sauce 117; green goddess dressing 48; green pepper and pine nut sauce 92; green shrimp curry 111; halibut with roasted garlic and cilantro 33; hollandaise sauces 2–2-3, 62–63; horseradish butter 37; horseradish sauce 121; leek and chive sauce 67; lemon, anchovy, and cilantro dressing 47; lemon and chili dressing 46; lemon and cumin dressing 45; lime-chili oil 37; lime marinade 40; lime and walnut dressing 45; maître d'hôtel butter 36; mango, chili, and yogurt dressing 52; mussels with cilantro, chili, and lemon grass 82; mustard-dill dressing 50; niçoise sauce 94; parsley butter 36; parsley sauce 58; pesto genovese 90; pistachio butter 36; quick white wine sauce 71; romesco sauce 92–93; rosemary marinade 41; rouille 50; saffron casserole 82; saffron hollandaise 63; saffron marinade 40; saffron sauce 60; salmon with champagne beurre blanc 64; salmon with roasted garlic and cilantro 33; salsa chipotle 107; sauce beurre rouge 64; sauce maltaise 63; sauce meurette 71; sauce vierge 47; sauce vin blanc 64; sauce vongole 95; seafood stew 82; shallot and Sauternes sauce 67; simple soy baste 38; simplest salsa 102; smoked salmon butter 36; sole meunière 32; sorrel hollandaise 63; sorrel sauce 59; sun-dried tomato salsa 103; sweet pepper and tomato sauce 89; tartar sauce 49; teriyaki salmon and Japanese noodles 98; teriyaki sauce 104; Thai red curry paste 110; tropical salsa picante 102; tuna and artichoke sauce 95; warm mustard sauce 120; watercress mayonnaise 48; whisky cream sauce 67; whole-grain mustard butter 36, 37; yogurt salad dressing 52

fruit: bavarian cream 131; brandy butter 132; brandy sauce 132; butterscotch fudge sauce 137; caramel-cream sauce 137; caramel sauces 26–27; chocolate mint sauce 135; cinnamon and mascarpone cream 130; crème anglaise 24–25; crème chantilly 130; honey yogurt cream 130; kiwi-coconut sauce 127; Melba sauce (raspberry coulis) 126; mint syrup 138; mocha cream sauce 135; mocha fudge sauce 137; orange custard sauce 130; rum butter 132; syllabub 132; vanilla and basil syrup 138; white chocolate sauce 136; zabaglione 133

game: aromatic braised 74; bread sauce 119; country red wine casserole 79;

*I*NDEX BY *A*CCOMPANIMENT

crab apple and cranberry jelly 118; cranberry and orange sauce 116; Cumberland sauce 116; quince jelly 118; red-currant jelly 118; traditional gravy 34

ham and bacon: Boston baked beans 85; cranberry and port sauce 116; old-fashioned liver and bacon 35; pasta alla carbonara 97; quince and apricot sauce 117; salsa verde 51; sauce meurette 71; sauce vierge 47

ice cream: butterscotch fudge sauce 137; caramel-cream sauce 137; caramel sauce 26–27; cherries/peaches jubilee 129; chocolate cream sauce 135; chocolate fudge sauce 136; chocolate mint sauce 135; crème anglaise 24–25; hot blackberry sauce 129; Hunza apricot purée 126; lemon syrup sauce 138; maple-pecan sauce 139; Melba sauce (raspberry coulis) 126; mocha fudge sauce 137; oranges in red wine 127; passion fruit syrup 138; pineapple syrup 138; raisin and honey syrup 139; red wine sauce 132; toffee sauce 137; white chocolate sauce 136

lamb: almond and herb sauce 63; apricot marinade with yogurt sauce 38; black bean sauce 105; crab apple and cranberry jelly 118; and fava bean tagine 76; gigot brayaude 76; green chili and apricot sauce 109; Irish stew 76; korma 109; leg with flageolet beans 77; Marsala, tomato, and olive sauce 31; minted apple jelly 118; pesto genovese 90; quince and apricot sauce 117; quince jelly 118; roasted garlic and cilantro 33; rosemary gravy 34; salsa chipotle 107; spicy lemon marinade 40; tikka 38; tomato and onion baste 39; vindaloo 109; whisky cream sauce 67

liver: and bacon 35; onion gravy 34; parsley butter 36; sauce Robert 69; sweet pepper and tomato sauce 89

meringue desserts: caramel sauce 27–28; crème anglaise 24–25; crème chantilly 130; orange custard sauce 130

pasta and noodles: *see Pasta Sauces chapter plus* anchovy butter 36; anchovy paste 121; béchamel sauces 20–21, 58–59; blue cheese dressing 53; chanterelles sauce 80; Chinese chili sauce 107; crab sauce 66; fava bean and pancetta sauce 59; four-pepper butter 36; ginger and lemon grass butter 36; Japanese lemon sauce 104; lemon-chili dressing 46; pistachio butter 36; salsa verde 51; smoked salmon butter 36; tomato sauce 18

pastries: caramel sauce 27–28; chocolate cream sauce 135; chocolate sauce 134; cinnamon and mascarpone cream 130; cream puffs 134; crème anglaise 24–25; crème chantilly 130; éclairs 134; Hunza apricot purée 126; lemon curd 128; lemon syrup sauce 138; maple-pecan sauce 139; Melba sauce (raspberry coulis) 126; orange custard sauce 130; pastry cream 130; raisin and honey syrup 139; red wine sauce 132; toffee sauce 137

pork and sausages: applesauce 117; apricot marinade with yogurt sauce 38; au vin 81; Boston baked beans 85; braised chops with dried fruits 78; chili jam 107; Chinese chili sauce 107; chorizo with onions and sherry vinegar 33; country red wine casserole 79; crab apple and cranberry jelly 118; filet de porc normande 79; gooseberry sauce 117; onion sauce 58; piccalilli 120; quince and apricot sauce 117; red-currant jelly 118; red onion relish 121; red spicy marinade 38; roasted garlic sauce 123; sauce bigarade 70; sauce Robert 69; simple soy baste 38; simplest salsa 102; sun-dried tomato salsa 103; sweet and sour sauce 106; tamarind sauce 123; tenderloin with cognac 31; tomato and onion baste 39; warm mustard sauce 120

potatoes: anchovy butter 36; anchovy paste 121; green mayonnaise 48; herb beurre blanc 65; lemon, anchovy, and cilantro dressing 47; mango, chili, and yogurt dressing 52; pesto genovese 90;

pistachio butter 36; smoked salmon butter 36; yogurt salad dressing 52

poultry: *see also entries under chicken, duck, game, and turkey plus* guacamole 50; harissa 107; lime pickle dressing 45; sauce aurore 60; sauce chasseur 68; sun-dried tomato salsa 103; tamarind sauce 123; tomato sauce 59; traditional gravy 34; tropical salsa picante 102; velouté sauce 60

puddings: blackberry sauce, hot 129; brandy butter 132; brandy sauce 132; cherries jubilee 129; chocolate cream sauce 135; chocolate self-saucing pudding 135; cinnamon and mascarpone cream 130; crème anglaise 24–25; kiwi-coconut sauce 127; lemon syrup sauce 138; maple-pecan sauce 139; orange custard sauce 130; peaches jubilee 129; pineapple syrup 138; raisin and honey syrup 139; rhubarb and fig jam 127; rhubarb and orange jam 127; rum butter 132; toffee sauce 137; white chocolate sauce 136

rice: *see Tangy Sauces chapter plus* bolognese sauce 97; curry cream sauce 67; four-pepper butter 36; ginger and lemon grass butter 36; green pepper and pine nut sauce 92; pesto genovese 90; sauce vongole 95

salads: *see Summer Sauces chapter plus* Chinese chili dressing 107; soy dipping sauce 112; noodles with chili-citrus dressing 99; tahini chicken noodles 98

soups: aïoli 48; pesto genovese 90; rouille 50

turkey: bread sauce 119; cannelloni 96; chestnut cream 33; crab apple and cranberry jelly 118; cranberry and orange sauce 116; cranberry and port sauce 116; Cumberland sauce 116; flavored gravy 34; green chili and apricot sauce 109; korma 109; pumpkin sauce 117; sauce diable 70; Texan meat pie 60; tikka 38

veal: piccata 30; old-fashioned liver and bacon 35

vegetables: aïoli 48; aromatic oil 37; béchamel sauces 20–21, 58–59; beef and mushroom sauce 96; beurre blancs 64–65; black olive pesto 91; black vinegar sauce 104; blue cheese dressing 53; Boston baked beans 85; chantilly mayonnaise 48; cheese sauce 58; cream sauce 21; fava bean and pancetta sauce 59; four-pepper butter 36; gado-gado 108; gazpacho dressing 50; ginger and lemon grass butter 36; gnocchi-topped casserole 85; goat cheese dip 55; green goddess dressing 48; guacamole 50; hollandaise sauces 22-3, 62-63; hummus 55; Japanese lemon sauce 104; leek and chive sauce 67; lemon, anchovy, and cilantro dressing 47; lemon-chili dressing 46; lime pickle dressing 45; maître d'hôtel butter 36; mango, chili, and yogurt dressing 52; mayonnaise 19; onion sauce 58; orange and sesame dressing 45; parsley butter 36; parsley sauce 58; pesto genovese 90; poppyseed dressing 45; sauce allemande 60; sauce aurore 60; sauce beurre rouge 64; sauce maltaise 63; sauce vin blanc 64; simple soy baste 38; sorrel sauce 59; spinach tarts with hollandaise 62; Thai red curry paste 110; tomato sauce 59; velouté sauce 60; watercress mayonnaise 48; white bean and rosemary/basil dip 54

venison: black bean sauce 105; black sauce 110; carbonnade 74; country red wine casserole 79; Cumberland sauce 116; red-currant jelly 118; Texan meat pie 60; whisky cream sauce 67; in wine and port 74

waffles: caramel sauce 27–28; honey yogurt cream 130; lemon syrup sauce 138; maple-pecan sauce 139; raisin and honey syrup 139

yogurt: hot blackberry sauce 129; hot rhubarb, strawberry, and orange sauce 129; Hunza apricot purée 126; Melba sauce 126; passion fruit syrup 138.

GENERAL INDEX

Page numbers in italics indicate that the recipe is illustrated

aïoli 48
almond and herb sauce 63
anchovy: butter 36; paste 121
applesauce 117
apricot: custard 25; Hunza purée 126; marinade with yogurt sauce 38
aromatic oil *37*
arrowroot 14
arugula and goat cheese pesto 91
Asian chicken stock 10
avocado: avocado-raisin salsa 103; papaya and watercress salad 44

barbecue ketchup *122*
baste: 7, 36–38; simple soy 38; tomato and onion 39
bavarian cream, fruit *131*
béarnaise sauce 7, 64
béchamel sauce 7, *20–21*; cheese 58; fava bean and pancetta *59*; medium-thickness 20; mushroom 58; onion 58; parsley 58; sorrel 59; thick 21; thin 21; tomato 59
beef: aromatic braised steak 74; in black bean sauce *105*; brandied ginger steak 30; cannelloni *96*; carbonnade 74; en daube provençale *75*; deviled steak 30; and mushroom sauce 96; pepper steaks with cream and mushrooms 30; rib-eye steak 30; with roasted garlic and cilantro 33; steak chasseur 68; Texan meat pie 60; in wine and port 74
beurre blanc 7; à la crème 64; champagne 64; with herbs *65*
beurre manié *14*
black bean salsa 103
black olive pesto 91
black pepper 11
black sauce 105
black vinegar sauce 104
blackberry sauce, hot 129
blenders 12–13
blue cheese dressing *53*

bolognese sauce 97
Boston baked beans 85
brandy: butter 132; sauce 132
bread sauce *119*
brown sauce: 68, 68–69; sauce bigarade 70; sauce bordelaise 69; sauce chasseur *68*; sauce diable 70; sauce Robert 69
butter 11, 14; anchovy 36; brandy 132; four-pepper *36*; ginger and lemon grass 36; horseradish 37; maître d'hôtel 36; parsley 36; pistachio *36*; rum 132; smoked salmon *36*; whole-grain mustard *36*, 37
buttermilk dressing 53
butterscotch fudge sauce 137

Caesar salad 47
caramel sauce: *26–27*; caramel-cream 137; coffee 27; creamy 27
carbonara sauce 97
cardamom custard 25
celery and tomato sauce 89
cheese: blue cheese dressing *53*; cottage, and walnut dip 55; fish and four-cheese macaroni 94; fondue *84*; goat cheese dip 55; instant cheese sauce 93; sauce miffi 93; walnut and gorgonzola sauce *92*, 93
cherries jubilee 129
chicken: with chanterelles sauce *80*; coq au vin 81; coronation *51*; with green peppercorn sauce 33; korma 109; tahini chicken noodles 98; tikka 38; vindaloo 109
chili: chili-citrus dressing *99*; Chinese chili sauce 107; harissa 107; jam 107; salsa chipotle 107
Chinese chili sauce 107
chocolate: 11; cream sauce 135; custard 25; fudge sauce 136; mint sauce 135; mocha fudge sauce 137; pudding, self-saucing 135; sauce *134*; sauce, white *136*
chorizo with onions and sherry vinegar 33
Christmas plum pudding: brandy/rum butter 132

chutney: cilantro and mint 112; Gujarati-style vegetable pickle 113
cilantro: and almond pesto 90; and crab sauce 110; and lime dressing 51; and mint chutney 112
cinnamon and mascarpone cream 130
Classic Sauces 56–71
coconut sauce: kiwi 127; quick curried 99
coffee caramel sauce 27
colanders 12-13
confetti sauce 88
consistency 17
Cooking Sauces 72–85
cornstarch 14
cottage cheese and walnut dip 55
coulis 7; raspberry (Melba sauce) *126*
crab apple and cranberry jelly 118
crab sauce *66*
cranberry: and orange sauce 116; and port sauce 116
cream: 11, 15; chantilly 130; cinnamon and mascarpone 130; honey yogurt 130; leek and chive 67; pasta with mortadella, peas, and 97; pastry 130; sauces 21, 66–7, 128; shallot and Sauternes sauce 66; whisky sauce 67
cream puffs *134*
creamy caramel sauce 27
crème anglaise *24-5*
crêpes Suzette 128
crunchy mustard 120
Cumberland sauce *116*
curried dishes: beef in black sauce 110; chicken with crab and cilantro sauce 110; chicken with green chili and apricot sauce 109; chicken vindaloo 109; fish with crab and cilantro sauce 110; green shrimp *111*; lamb with green chili and apricot sauce 109; lamb vindaloo 109; murgh korma 109; Thai red curry paste 110; turkey with green chili and apricot sauce 109
custard sauce 24–25, 130, 131; apricot 25; bavarian cream *131*; cardamom 25; chocolate 25; crème anglaise *24–25*; espresso 25; orange 130; peach 25

dark soy dipping sauce 112
dashi 10; broth 10
date sauce 112
deglazing 30
Dessert Sauces 124–139
dips: black olive pesto 91; cheese and smoked trout 55; Chinese chili sauce 107; cottage cheese and walnut 55; dark soy dipping sauce 112; date sauce 112; fresh mint raita *113*; goat cheese 55; guacamole 50; Gujarati-style vegetable pickle 113; hummus 55; nutty hoisin sauce 112; plum dipping sauce 106; ricotta and walnut 55; roasted eggplant and yogurt 52; Vietnamese dipping sauce 112; white bean and rosemary/basil 54
dressings: aromatic oil *37*; blue cheese 53; buttermilk 53; chili-citrus 99; cilantro and lime 51; gazpacho 50; hummus 55; lemon, anchovy, and cilantro 47; lemon-chili 46; lemon and cumin 45; lime and walnut 45; lime pickle 45; mayonnaise 48–50; mustard-dill 50; orange and sesame 45; poppyseed 45; salsa verde 51; sauce vierge 47; vinaigrette 44; yogurt *52*
duck: à l'orange 70; crispy duck salad *46*
dumplings: red fruit slump 129

egg emulsions 7; almond and herb sauce 63; béarnaise sauce 64; beurre blanc 64; beurre blanc with herbs *65*; champagne beurre blanc 64; hollandaise sauce *22–23*; mayonnaises *19*, 48–50; saffron hollandaise 63; sauce beurre rouge 64; sauce choron 64; sauce maltaise 63; sauce mousseline 23; sauce moutarde 23; sauce paloise 64; sauce ravigote 64; sauce vin blanc 64; sorrel hollandaise 63; tomato and basil sauce 63
eggplant, roasted, and yogurt dressing 52
eggs 11; yolks 15
equipment 12-13
espresso custard 25

General Index

fava bean and pancetta sauce *59*
fennel and orange salsa 102
fish and shellfish: cod in oats with mild
  mustard sauce 32; fettuccine with
  smoked salmon 94; fish and four-
  cheese macaroni 94; Marco's anchovy
  sauce 94; mussels with cilantro, chili,
  and lemon grass *82*; niçoise sauce 94;
  saffron fish casserole 82; salmon with
  champagne beurre blanc 64; sauce
  vongole 95; seafood stew 82; sole
  meunière 32; teriyaki salmon and
  Japanese noodles 98; tuna and
  artichoke sauce *95*
five-spice marinade *39*
flour 11
fondue, cheese *84*
food processors 12
fresh mint raita *113*
fruit bavarian cream *131*
fruit sauces: apple 117; cherries jubilee
  129; cranberry and orange 116;
  cranberry and port 116; Cumberland
  116; gooseberry 117; hot blackberry
  129; hot rhubarb, strawberry, and
  orange 129; hot strawberry and orange
  129; Hunza apricot purée 126; kiwi-
  coconut 127; lemon curd 128; lemon
  syrup 138; Melba *126*; orange custard
  128; oranges in red wine 127; passion
  fruit 138; peaches jubilee 129;
  pineapple 138; pumpkin 117; quince
  and apricot 117; raisin and honey
  syrup 139; red fruit slump 129; rhubarb
  and fig jam 127; rhubarb and orange
  jam 127
fudge sauce: butterscotch 137;
  chocolate 136; mocha 137

gado-gado *108*
game: aromatic braised 74
garlic: roasted, with salmon and cilantro
  33; roasted, sauce 123
gnocchi-topped vegetable casserole 85
goat cheese dip 55
gooseberry sauce 117
gravy: 7; flavored 34; onion 34, *35*;
  rosemary 34; traditional 34;
  unthickened 34
green chili and apricot sauce 109
green curry paste 111

green goddess dressing 48
green pepper and pine nut sauce 92
green shrimp curry *111*
guacamole 50
Gujarati-style vegetable pickle 113

harissa 107
herbs: 11; marinade 41
hollandaise sauce 7, *22–23*; saffron 63;
  sorrel 63; spinach tarts with *62*; with
  tomato and basil 63
honey yogurt cream 130
horseradish: butter 37; sauce *121*
hot blackberry sauce 129
hot rhubarb, strawberry, and orange
  sauce 129
hot strawberry and orange sauce 129
hummus 55
Hunza apricot purée 126

ice cream: in cream puffs *135*; made with
  crème anglaise 24; with peaches and
  Melba sauce *126*
ingredients 11
Irish stew 76

Japanese lemon sauce 104
Japanese noodles and teriyaki salmon 98
jam: rhubarb and fig 127; rhubarb and
  orange 127
jelly: crab apple and cranberry 118;
  minted apple 118; quince 118;
  red-currant 118

ketchup 7; barbecue *122*; oyster *123*;
  roasted garlic 123; tamarind 123;
  tomato 122
kitchen bouillon 9
kiwi-coconut sauce 127

ladles *12–13*
lamb: and fava bean tagine 76; gigot
  brayaude 76; Irish stew 76; leg with
  flageolet beans *77*; with Marsala,
  tomato, and olive sauce 31
leek and chive sauce 67
lemon 11; anchovy and cilantro
  dressing 47; and cumin dressing 45;
  curd 128; Japanese sauce 104; lemon-
  chili dressing 46; spicy marinade *40*;
  syrup sauce 138; vinaigrette 44

lime: lime-chili oil 37; marinade 40; pickle
  dressing 45; vinaigrette *44*; and walnut
  dressing 45
liver: old-fashioned liver and bacon 35

maître d'hôtel butter 36
mango: chili and yogurt dressing 52;
  salsa, fresh 103
maple-pecan sauce *139*
Marco's anchovy sauce 94
marinade 7; five-spice *39*; herb 41;
  lime 40; red spicy 38; rosemary *41*;
  saffron 40; spicy lemon *40*; tikka 38
mayonnaise 7, *19*; aïoli 48; chantilly 48;
  coronation chicken *49*; creamy salad
  dressing 48; green 48; green goddess
  dressing 48; mustard-dill dressing 50;
  rouille 50; tartar sauce 49; thousand
  island dressing 48; watercress 48
measuring cups/spoons *12–13*
Melba sauce *126*
miffi sauce 94
mint: chocolate sauce 135; syrup 138
minted apple jelly 118
mocha fudge sauce 137
mortar and pestle 12
mousseline 7, 23
murgh korma 109
mushroom sauce 58
mustard 11; butter, whole-grain 37;
  crunchy 120; mild sauce 32; piccalilli
  120; warm sauce *120*

niçoise sauce 94
noodles: soba with ginger and soy glaze
  98; tahini chicken 98; teriyaki salmon
  with Japanese *10*, 98
nuts 11; green pepper and pine nut
  sauce 92; maple-pecan sauce *139*;
  walnut and cottage cheese dip 55;
  walnut and gorgonzola sauce 93;
  zucchini-walnut sauce 93

oils 11; aromatic *37*; lime-chili 37
old-fashioned bread sauce *119*
old-fashioned liver and bacon 35
onion gravy 34, *35*
orange: custard sauce 130; and sesame
  dressing 45
oranges in red wine 127
oyster ketchup *122*, 123

pans *12–13*
pan sauces 30–35; brandied ginger steak
  30; chestnut cream chicken 33; chicken
  with green peppercorn sauce 33;
  chorizo with onions and sherry vinegar
  33; cod in oats with mild mustard sauce
  32; deviled steak 30; flavored gravies
  34; lamb with Marsala, tomato, and
  olive sauce 31; old-fashioned liver and
  bacon 35; onion gravy 34, *35*; pepper
  steaks with cream and mushrooms 30;
  pork tenderloin with cognac *31*; rib-eye
  steak 30; rosemary gravy 34; salmon
  with roasted garlic and cilantro 33; sole
  meunière *32*; traditional gravy 34;
  unthickened gravy 34; veal piccata 30
parsley: butter 36; sauce 58
passion fruit syrup 138
pasta: alla carbonara 97; with mortadella,
  cream, and peas 97
Pasta Sauces 86–99
pastry cream 130
peach custard 25
pesto sauce: black olive 91; cilantro and
  almond 90; genovese *90*; red 91;
  arugula and goat cheese 91; sage 90
piccalilli 120
pineapple syrup 138
pistachio butter 36
poppyseed dressing 45
pork: chops braised with dried fruits *78*;
  country red wine casserole 79; filet de
  porc normande 79; tenderloin with
  cognac *31*
potato flour 14-15
pumpkin sauce 117
puréeing 15
purées: 7, 15; cilantro and lime
  dressing 51; gazpacho dressing 50;
  guacamole 50; Hunza apricot 126;
  salsa verde *51*; tomato sauce *18*

Quick and Simple Sauces 28–41
quick white wine sauce 71
quince and apricot sauce 117
quince jelly 118

raisin and honey syrup 139
raita 7; fresh mint *113*
red-currant jelly 118
red fruit slump 129

143

GENERAL INDEX

red onion relish 121
red pesto 91
red spicy marinade 38
red wine sauce 132
reduction 15
relish: red onion 121
rhubarb: and fig jam 127; and orange jam 127; strawberry and orange sauce, hot 129
roasted eggplant and yogurt dressing 52
roasted garlic sauce 123
romesco sauce *92*
rosemary: gravy *34*; marinade *41*
rouille 50
roux-based sauces 7, 16; allemande 60; aurore 60; béchamel *20–21*; cheese 58; cream 21; fava bean and pancetta 59; onion 58; mushroom 58; parsley 58; poulette 60; saffron 60; shrimp 59; simple white 21; sorrel 59; suprême 60; tomato 59; velouté 60
roux bases 16
rum butter 132

sabayon 7
saffron: hollandaise 63; marinade 40; sauce 60
sage pesto 90
salad: avocado, mango/papaya, and watercress *45*; Caesar 47; crispy duck *46*; potato *52*
salsa: 7; avocado-raisin 103; black bean 103; chipotle 107; fennel and orange 102; fresh mango 103; simplest *102*; sun-dried tomato 103; tropical picante 102; verde *51*
salt 11
satay sauce *108*
sauce: allemande 60; aurore 60; béarnaise 7, 64; beurre rouge 64; bigarade 70; bordelaise 69; chasseur *69*; choron 64; diable 70; maltaise 63; meurette 71; miffi 93; mousseline 7, 23; moutarde 23; paloise 64; poulette 60; ravigote 64; Robert 69; suprême 60; vierge 47; vin blanc 64; vongole 95
seafood stew *73*, 83
shallot and Sauternes sauce 67
Side Sauces 114–23
smoked salmon butter *36*
soba with ginger and soy glaze 98

sorrel: sauce 59; hollandaise 63
soups: onion 35
soy: sauce 11; simple soy baste 38
soy-based sauces: black bean *105*; black vinegar 104; dark soy dipping 112; Japanese lemon 104; teriyaki *98*, 104
spatulas 12
spicy lemon marinade *40*
spinach tarts with hollandaise *62*
spoons 12–13
stock 8–10; Asian chicken 10; basic beef *8*; basic chicken *8*; brown beef 8; brown chicken 8; dashi 10; fish 9; game 9; kitchen bouillon 9; lamb 9; vegetable 9
stock pots 12
strainers 12–13
strawberry and orange sauce, hot 129
Summer Sauces 42–55
sweet and sour sauces 106
sweet pepper and tomato sauce 89
syllabub 132
syrup 7; caramel sauce *26*; lemon 138; maple-pecan sauce *139*; mint 138; passion fruit 138; pineapple 138; raisin and honey 139; vanilla and basil 138

tahini chicken noodles 98
tamarind ketchup 123
Tangy Sauces 100–113
tarragon and sherry sauce 70
tartar sauce 49
techniques 14–27
teriyaki sauce *98*, 104
Texan meat pie *60*
Thai red curry paste 110
thickening 14–17
thousand island dressing 48
tikka marinade 38
toffee sauce 137
tomato 11; ketchup 122; and onion baste 39; soup 18
tomato sauce: *18*, 59, 96; aurore 60; and basil sauce, fresh *88*; and celery sauce 89; confetti sauce 88; and sweet pepper sauce 89; sun-dried tomato salsa 103
traditional gravy 34
tropical salsa picante 102

unthickened gravy 34

vanilla and basil syrup 138
veal piccata 30
velouté sauce 7, 60; Texan meat pie *60*; saffron sauce 60; sauce allemande 60; sauce aurore 60; sauce poulette 60; sauce suprême 60
Vietnamese dipping sauce 112
vinaigrette 7, 44–45; basic 44; herb 44; lemon 44; lemon and cumin dressing 45; lime *44*; lime and walnut dressing 45; lime pickle dressing 45; orange and sesame dressing 45; poppyseed dressing 45
vinegars 11

walnut: and gorgonzola sauce *93*; zucchini-walnut sauce 93
warm mustard sauce 120
water-bath 12
whisks 12
whisky cream sauce 67
white bean and rosemary/basil dip 54
white sauce, simple 21
white wine sauce, quick 71
whole-grain mustard butter *36*, 37

yogurt: honey cream 130; and mango chili dressing 52; and roasted eggplant dressing 52; salad dressing *52*

zabaglione 7, *133*
zucchini-walnut sauce 93

ACKNOWLEDGMENTS

The author and publisher would like to thank the following for their help: Alan Hertz, Annette Hertz, Yvonne Jenkins, Sharon Turner, Barbara Levy, Norma MacMillan, Jenni Muir, Sue Storey, Meg Jansz, Patrice de Villiers, Helen Ridge, Tanya Robinson, Victoria Richards, Alison Bolus, Simon Le Fevre.